D1171280

THE GREAT RECESSION

With a Postscript on Stagflation

DATA RESOURCES SERIES

Volume 3

OTTO ECKSTEIN

NORTH-HOLLAND PUBLISHING COMPANY
AMSTERDAM • NEW YORK • OXFORD

THE GREAT RECESSION
With a Postscript on Stagflation

OTTO ECKSTEIN

NORTH-HOLLAND PUBLISHING COMPANY
AMSTERDAM • NEW YORK • OXFORD

The Data Resources Series

This series contains econometric studies developed for the Data Resources National Economic Information System. These include econometric models of national economies and of specific industries, various policy analyses, as well as methodological studies for the development of such systems.

ISBN North-Holland for this series 0 7204 9400 3
ISBN North-Holland for this volume 0 444 85204 2

1st edition 1978
reprinted 1979

Publishers

NORTH-HOLLAND PUBLISHING COMPANY
AMSTERDAM • NEW YORK • OXFORD

Distributors for the U.S.A. and Canada

ELSEVIER NORTH-HOLLAND INC.
52 VANDERBILT AVENUE
NEW YORK, N.Y. 10017

Library of Congress Cataloging in Publication Data

Main entry under title:
The great recession, with a postscript on stagflation.
(Data resources series: v. 3)
"An earlier version of this book was presented as the Royer lectures at the University of California at Berkeley, in May 1975."
Includes index.
1. United States—Economic conditions—1971. 2. Inflation (Finance)—United States. 3. Depressions—1973. I. Title.

HC106.7.E28 330.9'73'0924 78-58880
ISBN 0-444-85204-2

PRINTED IN THE U.S.A.

CONTENTS

PREFACE

In the years 1973-76, the world economy passed through its most dangerous adventure since the 1930's. There is no way to tell whether those years were just bad luck, or a turning point. But exciting times do offer fertile material for the historian. Calm times teach few lessons. The true characteristics of economic and social systems can only be discovered in periods of stress.

The Great Recession—a name chosen to assert that it was an episode and not a turning point—was produced by a combination of causes. The traditional methods of verbal diagnosis, arithmetic comparison, and abstract theorizing are needed to get the analysis started, but only a coherent, quantified representation of the economy can sort out how the various forces actually worked themselves through. This book uses the Data Resources (DRI) Econometric Model of the U.S. Economy to try to reconstruct just how the Great Recession came about.

Historical model analysis is easier work than forecasting the future. Looking backwards, there are fewer surprises in the economy's structure or in individual behavior. It is possible to construct the model so it tracks the past very well. No such assurance exists in forecasting. The data are more seasoned, and the older historical record is less likely to be rewritten by the government statistical agencies. Policies, for better or worse, are known.

The DRI model was tailor-made for this historical analysis. It adds three key ingredients to traditional macroeconomic models: the flows-of-funds of businesses and households to model credit crunches and their impact on the economy; the effects of inflation and unemployment on consumer confidence and hence on consumer spending; and the impact of energy, agricultural and other materials prices on inflation.

An earlier version of this book was presented as the Royer Lectures at the University of California at Berkeley, in May 1975. I am grateful to the Department of Economics for inviting me to give these lectures. The invitation arrived at a moment when I wished to undertake this study. The book would probably not have been written without this catalyst.

The book would never have been produced without the professional collaboration of several members of the Data Resources National Forecasting Group. I am particularly indebted to Sara Johnson, who developed the model simulations of the study, carried out much of the research, and reviewed the entire manuscript. Eunice Shields got the project off to a good start. Edward Green and Allen Sinai have been my principal collaborators in the building of the DRI model. Lyn Hadden produced the manuscript and saw it through the printers.

Otto Eckstein
Lexington, Massachusetts
December 27, 1976

CHAPTER 1

INTRODUCTION

The last twelve years have seen increasing instability in the American economy, climaxing in the 1973-75 recession. Double-digit inflation was followed by unemployment of 9% of the labor force (figure 1.1). Its worldwide character and the associated bankruptcies and financial disturbances made this episode the long-awaited postwar economic crisis.

Comparison with the normal pattern of economic development reveals the severity of the situation. By the trough of the recession in the spring of 1975, real GNP had fallen 14.5% below the full employment growth path (figure

Figure 1.1
The unemployment rate, 1954-1976:3
(percent of civilian labor force)

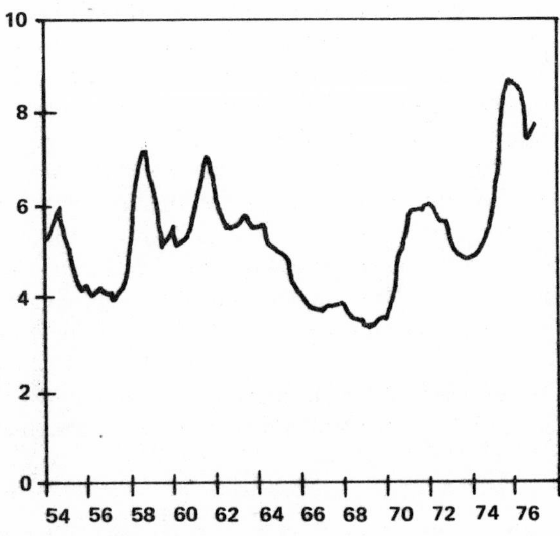

Source: Bureau of Labor Statistics, U.S. Department of Labor

Figure 1.2
Actual versus real gross national product, 1965-75
(billions of 1958 dollars)

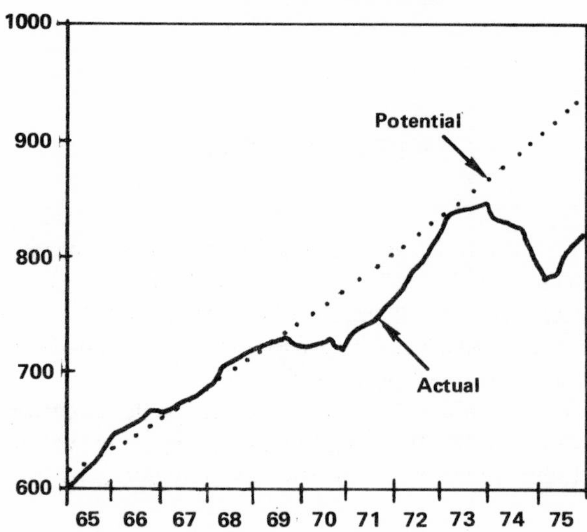

Sources: Bureau of Economic Analysis and "Business Conditions Digest," Bureau of the Census, U.S. Department of Commerce

1.2).[1] The process of capital formation, which had already been inadequate in the preceding ten years, was disrupted once more. The rate of real business investment fell at least 25% below the normal path, and declined 13% in a single year. The housing stock, which normally grows by a million and a half units annually, grew by only 700,000 units in 1975; relative to the growing population, it will not return to equilibrium for some time.

The consumer was the first to experience the severity of the recession (figure 1.3). For the first time since World War II, the real volume of consumption fell; and the real spendable earnings of a typical American worker retreated to a level no higher than ten years earlier. The recent history of key economic parameters of the U.S. economy is summarized in Table 1.1.

The immediate causes for the economic crisis are well known. The Vietnam War set loose an inflationary spiral that persisted stubbornly through the

[1]Full employment is based on President Kennedy's 4% interim target of 1961, with demographic and other changes upping the measure by 1%.

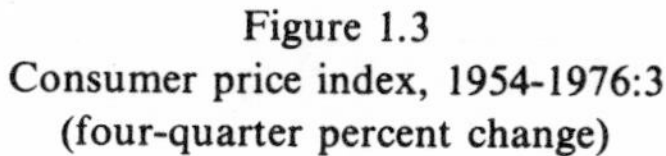
Figure 1.3
Consumer price index, 1954-1976:3
(four-quarter percent change)

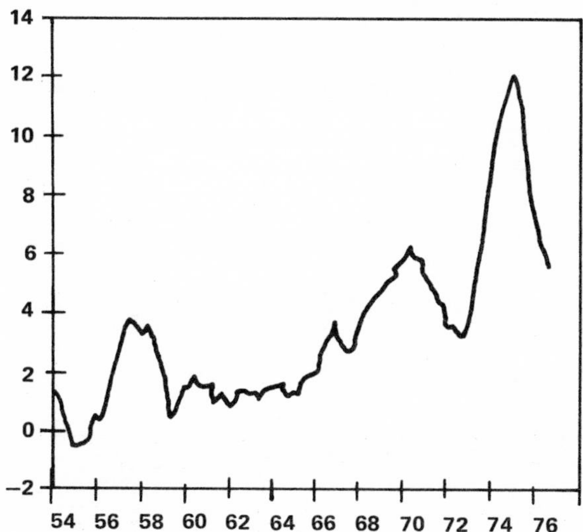

Source: Bureau of Labor Statistics, U.S. Department of Labor

early 1970's. Monetary and fiscal policies of the previous ten years were needlessly volatile, creating a series of shocks on the private economy which repeatedly disrupted the normal growth process. The episode of economic controls led to uncertainties and distortions in the price-cost structure. The devaluation, while coming ten years too late and a great boon to the American economy, was a shock to industry and agriculture, particularly when combined with the domestic price control program. The worldwide business cycle, with all the Western industrial economies closely synchronized, caused the world to run out of basic resources. When the world supply of agricultural commodities declined through a series of natural disasters and policy errors in 1972-74, food prices exploded. Finally, the oil embargo of November 1973, and the subsequent tripling of the world price of oil, interacted with the other factors to ignite an inflation that was unparalleled in peacetime.

These experiences were so frightening to consumers, businesses and government policymakers that their combined actions led the economy into a severe recession. Consumer spending fell sharply in the final months of 1973 as inflation reached the explosive stage. Businesses, particularly in the more basic sectors, kept their courage longer. But by the fall of 1974, confronted by

Table 1.1
Summary of the U.S. economy, 1964-75.

	Years											
	1964	1965	1966	1967	1968	1969	1970	1971	1972	1973	1974	1975
GNP and its components—billions of dollars												
Gross national product	632.4	684.9	749.8	793.9	864.2	930.3	977.1	1054.9	1158.0	1294.9	1397.4	1477.5
Real GNP (1958 dollars)	581.0	617.8	658.1	675.2	706.7	725.6	722.5	746.3	792.5	839.2	821.2	797.7
Inventory investment	5.9	9.7	14.8	8.2	7.1	7.8	4.5	6.3	8.6	15.4	14.2	-14.8
Net exports	8.5	6.9	5.3	5.2	2.5	1.9	3.6	-0.1	-6.0	3.9	2.2	12.9
Prices and wages—annual rates of change												
Implicit price deflator	1.6	1.8	2.8	3.2	4.0	4.8	5.5	4.5	3.4	5.6	10.3	8.8
Consumer price index	1.3	1.6	3.0	2.8	4.2	5.4	5.9	4.3	3.3	6.2	11.0	9.1
Wholesale price index	0.2	2.0	3.3	0.2	2.5	3.9	3.6	3.2	4.5	13.1	18.8	9.2
Average hourly earnings index	2.7	3.7	4.1	4.9	6.2	6.6	6.7	7.1	6.5	6.4	8.2	8.8
Key economic measures												
Unemployment Rate (percent)	5.2	4.5	3.8	3.8	3.6	3.5	5.0	6.0	5.6	4.9	5.6	8.5
Industrial production (67=1)	0.816	0.890	0.977	0.998	1.055	1.105	1.067	1.067	1.151	1.254	1.243	1.134
Annual rate of change	6.9	9.1	9.8	2.1	5.8	4.7	-3.5	0.0	7.9	9.0	-0.9	-8.7
Housing starts (millions)	1.54	1.47	1.17	1.28	1.50	1.49	1.43	2.04	2.36	2.05	1.34	1.17
Unit car sales (millions)	8.1	9.4	9.1	8.3	9.6	9.6	8.5	10.3	10.9	11.5	9.0	8.7
Federal budget surplus (NIA)	-3.0	1.2	-0.2	-12.4	-6.5	8.1	-11.9	-21.9	-17.5	-5.6	-8.1	-72.9
Money and interest rates												
Money supply (M1)	160.2	167.1	174.7	181.6	194.3	206.5	215.7	230.7	245.6	263.8	278.7	290.5
Annual rate of change	4.0	4.3	4.5	3.9	7.0	6.3	4.5	7.0	6.4	7.4	5.7	4.2
New high-grade corp. bond rate (percent)	4.40	4.54	5.44	5.77	6.48	7.67	8.50	7.36	7.16	7.65	8.96	9.01
Federal funds rate (percent)	3.50	4.07	5.11	4.22	5.66	8.21	7.18	4.66	4.43	8.73	10.50	5.82
Prime rate (percent)	4.50	4.54	5.63	5.63	6.28	7.95	7.91	5.70	5.25	8.02	10.80	7.86
Incomes—billions of dollars												
Personal income	497.5	538.9	587.2	629.3	688.9	750.9	808.3	864.1	944.9	1055.0	1150.5	1239.7
Real disposable income	408.1	434.8	458.9	477.6	499.0	513.5	534.7	555.4	580.5	619.5	602.9	610.4
Annual rate of change	7.0	6.5	5.5	4.1	4.5	2.9	4.1	3.9	4.5	6.7	-2.7	1.3
Saving rate (percent)	6.0	6.0	6.3	7.4	6.7	6.0	8.1	8.1	6.5	8.2	7.9	8.6
Profits after tax (percent change)	16.3	20.8	7.5	-6.6	2.4	-6.2	-12.5	17.5	25.1	26.5	16.6	-9.9
Details of real GNP—annual rates of change												
Gross national product	5.4	6.3	6.5	2.6	4.7	2.7	-0.4	3.3	6.2	5.9	-2.1	-2.9
Total consumption	5.8	6.4	5.1	2.9	5.3	3.6	1.8	4.0	6.2	4.7	-2.3	0.7
Business fixed investment	11.3	14.8	11.7	-1.1	3.3	5.9	-3.6	-0.6	9.1	12.8	-0.4	-13.2
Equipment	13.7	13.8	13.7	0.9	3.3	6.9	-4.1	-0.0	11.8	15.3	-1.7	-15.3
Nonresidential construction	6.7	16.8	7.6	-5.7	3.3	3.9	-2.4	-2.0	2.7	6.4	3.4	-7.8
Residential construction	-2.4	-1.3	-10.6	-4.5	13.9	2.0	-6.1	30.6	18.1	-4.1	-26.9	-21.4
Federal government	-2.4	-0.3	12.9	14.1	4.6	-5.9	-12.4	-5.4	0.2	-6.1	-1.4	3.5
State and local governments	6.0	6.9	7.6	7.3	6.2	4.0	3.5	4.6	4.7	6.0	2.8	1.8

an unfavorable market situation and a deteriorated liquidity position, businesses slashed investment plans, unloaded inventories, and laid off 2½ million employees in just five months. Government policymakers were so terrified by the double-digit inflation that fiscal stimulus was not seriously considered until unemployment had surpassed 7%.

These events have raised deep questions about the future of our economy:

(1) Have we entered an era of evermore frequent and violent shocks with the potential to create such uncertainty that the capitalist system could no longer function acceptably?

(2) Has the strength and quality of political leadership deteriorated to the point where it is unable to manage economic policy in a tolerable fashion?

(3) Has the globe become so integrated as an economic system and so polycentric as a political system that the two are intolerably inconsistent?

(4) In other words, has the time come when it is only common prudence for every household and business to plan its future as if the economic order were soon to change?

1. A Method of Analysis

One cannot come to secure answers to these questions. But it is possible to do more than to recite the troubles and to stab for answers based on nothing but the observer's psychological propensities or his particular brand of economic philosophy. This book presents a formal analysis of these problems using the econometric modeling technique.

This study is an exercise in contemporary cliometrics. A large-scale econometric model has been simulated over the last ten years assuming that the peculiar events had not occurred. What would the economy look like today if there had been no Vietnam War? No food crisis? No oil embargo? What if monetary and fiscal policies had been less ambitious in the pursuit of economic and political goals? By removing the "shocks" one at a time, some of the underlying changes in the economy are revealed. The technique also provides estimates of the relative importance of these different factors. Where did the fault lie: in oil, food prices, money, fiscal policy, or the outside world? These are legitimate questions and they require answers if we are to have a serious prospect of doing better.

The model employed for these simulations is the Data Resources Quarterly Model of the U.S. Economy.[2] This 900-equation model follows the income-expenditure approach of previous models in many regards, and introduces

[2]An account of this model can be found in the volume, *The Data Resources Model of the U.S. Economy*, North-Holland, forthcoming, and in this book's Appendix.

the modeling of some processes that are now essential to an analysis of our economy. The circular flow of income and expenditures, as measured in the national income accounts, relates the spending and income variables. The investment equations, following the neoclassical approach of Dale Jorgenson, incorporate a rental price of capital and rational sales expectations, modified for pollution control requirements and business balance sheet conditions. The consumption equations link expenditures to disposable income, relative prices, demographic factors, the stock of durables and housing, as well as household financial assets and the consumer debt repayment burden. The model explicitly relates housing activity to financial and mortgage flows on the supply side, and income and population structure on the demand side, using a flexible accelerator stock adjustment process. There is a wholly endogenous, behavioral modeling of the state and local government sector, relating revenues and expenditures to macroeconomic conditions, demographic factors and to the financial conditions of the sector's operating budget. The financial behavior of households and businesses, the wage-price mechanism, and industry production, investment and capacity are simultaneous with the expenditure block of the model. The wage equation is based on a near-accelerationist view of the Phillips curve.

The 1975 version of the DRI model, built with the benefit of the experience of the recent record, represents in its structure many of the phenomena that underlie our current difficulties. The model contains a fuller representation of the inflationary process: a stage-of-processing sector begins with the behavior of such crude prices as oil, agricultural commodities, chemicals, metals, lumber, and rubber, and traces these material cost effects through the later stages of production to the retail level. Shortages of industrial capacity are modeled and have a strong impact upon the behavior of particular prices. Worldwide demands and the U.S. exchange rate, which also affect production and price behavior, are explicitly represented in a 100-equation block of U.S. international trade flows.

Finally, and most importantly, the financial system, as represented by the Federal Reserve Board's flow-of-funds data for households and businesses, is built into the macro model, so that changing liquidity positions are felt in the decisions to invest in plant and equipment, to hold inventories, to employ workers, to finance housing and to buy durable consumer goods. Thus, the national income-expenditure approach which underlies all large-scale models has been integrated with the flow-of-funds approach which fully recognizes the financial situation of businesses and households.

As forecasters, the managers of the DRI model did not foresee the full violence of the recent decline, although a sharp slowdown was evident to us by April 1973. With the benefit of hindsight, we have elaborated the structure of the forecasting model to reflect the newer developments. If we had possessed the current model three years ago, and if we had foreseen the actual pattern of the fiscal and monetary policies, the actual world price of oil, and the disasters in agriculture, the model would have forecast the full extent of the current economic decline. Figure 1.4 contrasts full historical simulations using the old model of conventional design with the 1975 model results. In historical simulations, the new model tracks actual experience closely through this difficult decade. Because it is a reasonable *ex-post* representation of the dynamic interactions of the economy in the period under study, it can be applied as a historical analytical device to test the impacts of different

Figure 1.4
Simulation performance of
Successive generations of econometric models

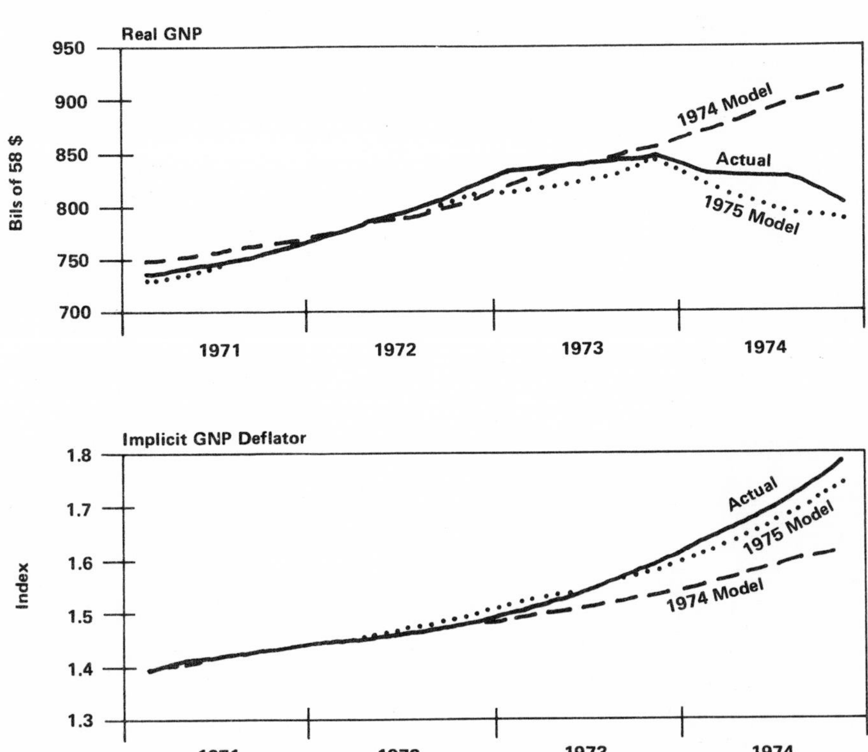

Source: Data Resources, Inc.

assumptions relating to policies, food and energy prices, international developments and the Vietnam War.

Since individual behavioral equations in the model include an error term, a full dynamic simulation will not reproduce history exactly. For this reason, the observed error terms of each stochastic equation were added to estimates of the dependent variable. This procedure generates a tracking simulation which accurately reproduces history.[3] Alternative historical scenarios can be tested by exogenously changing variables in the tracking solution, solving the model, and comparing the results. A summary of the tracking solution, which serves as the base for alternative simulations reported in this book, is presented in table 1.2.

[3]A fuller discussion of the treatment of error terms is presented in the Appendix to Chapter 2.

Table 1.2
Historical tracking solution, 1964-75

	1964	1965	1966	1967	1968	1969	1970	1971	1972	1973	1974	1975
	Years											
GNP and its components—billions of dollars												
Gross national product	632.2	684.1	748.9	792.4	863.1	930.1	976.5	1056.0	1160.2	1298.2	1397.7	1472.0
Real GNP (1958 dollars)	580.7	617.1	657.4	674.7	707.0	727.0	723.1	747.8	794.1	841.0	820.5	794.5
Inventory investment	5.8	9.5	14.8	8.1	7.1	8.3	5.0	6.6	8.9	15.6	14.0	-15.4
Net exports	8.5	7.0	5.2	5.4	2.5	1.8	3.6	-0.2	-6.3	3.5	2.0	11.4
Prices and wages—annual rates of change												
Implicit price deflator	1.6	1.8	2.7	3.1	3.9	4.8	5.6	4.6	3.5	5.7	10.4	8.7
Consumer price index	1.3	1.6	3.0	2.7	4.1	5.4	5.9	4.3	3.4	6.3	11.1	9.1
Wholesale price index	0.4	1.8	3.1	0.2	2.4	3.7	3.7	3.3	4.6	13.2	18.8	9.2
Average hourly earnings index	2.7	3.7	4.0	4.9	6.2	6.6	6.7	7.1	6.5	6.4	8.3	8.9
Key economic measures												
Unemployment rate (percent)	5.2	4.5	3.8	3.9	3.6	3.4	5.0	5.9	5.5	4.8	5.6	8.7
Industrial production (67=1)	0.814	0.888	0.975	0.995	1.056	1.111	1.070	1.071	1.156	1.260	1.241	1.128
Annual rate of change	6.7	9.0	9.9	2.0	6.1	5.2	-3.7	0.1	7.9	9.0	-1.5	-9.1
Housing starts (millions)	1.53	1.48	1.19	1.26	1.50	1.49	1.43	2.04	2.36	2.05	1.32	1.18
Unit car sales (millions)	8.5	9.7	8.8	8.2	9.6	9.6	8.4	10.3	10.9	11.5	8.9	8.6
Federal budget surplus (NIA)	-3.1	1.1	-0.4	-12.8	-6.4	8.7	-11.8	-21.3	-16.5	-4.7	-8.4	-75.0
Money and interest rates												
Money supply (M1)	160.2	167.1	174.7	181.3	194.2	206.5	215.6	230.9	245.8	264.2	278.8	290.3
Annual rate of change	4.0	4.3	4.6	3.8	7.1	6.3	4.4	7.1	6.5	7.5	5.5	4.1
New high-grade corp. bond rate (percent)	4.40	4.55	5.42	5.74	6.42	7.61	8.50	7.38	7.20	7.71	9.00	8.97
Federal funds rate (percent)	3.49	3.94	4.92	4.20	5.58	8.18	7.25	4.62	4.52	8.96	10.58	5.72
Prime rate (percent)	4.51	4.43	5.46	5.63	6.21	7.90	7.97	5.67	5.32	8.14	10.89	7.83
Incomes—billions of dollars												
Personal income	497.4	538.4	585.9	627.8	687.8	750.5	808.0	865.2	947.8	1059.4	1153.1	1236.3
Real disposable income	408.0	434.3	457.8	476.8	498.9	514.1	535.2	556.7	582.4	622.0	603.6	608.1
Annual rate of change	7.0	6.4	5.4	4.1	4.6	3.0	4.1	4.0	4.6	6.8	-3.0	0.7
Saving rate (percent)	6.0	6.0	6.3	7.3	6.7	6.0	8.2	8.2	6.7	8.4	8.0	8.5
Profits after tax (percent change)	16.1	20.3	7.7	-6.7	2.9	-5.5	-12.9	18.0	25.1	26.5	15.1	-10.7
Details of real GNP—annual rates of change												
Gross national product	5.4	6.3	6.5	2.6	4.8	2.8	-0.5	3.4	6.2	5.9	-2.4	-3.2
Total consumption	5.7	6.3	5.1	3.0	5.4	3.7	1.7	4.1	6.3	4.7	-2.5	0.3
Business fixed investment	11.3	14.7	11.8	-1.1	3.3	6.2	-3.5	-0.7	9.0	12.7	-0.8	-13.6
Equipment	13.7	13.6	13.8	1.1	3.3	7.2	-4.1	-0.1	11.9	15.2	-2.3	-15.7
Nonresidential construction	6.7	16.7	7.7	-5.7	3.3	4.1	-2.2	-2.0	2.5	6.3	3.0	-8.1
Residential Construction	-2.7	-0.6	-9.5	-6.8	14.7	2.4	-6.6	30.7	18.3	-3.9	-28.1	-20.3
Federal government	-2.5	-0.3	13.1	14.1	4.6	-5.9	-12.4	-5.3	0.1	-6.0	-1.4	3.5
State and local governments	6.0	6.8	7.5	7.4	6.3	3.8	3.3	5.4	4.6	6.0	2.6	1.5

CHAPTER 2

IF NOTHING HAD GONE WRONG: THE BALANCED GROWTH PATH

1. Introduction

The American economy was in a state of underemployment equilibrium from 1958 to 1964. Unemployment exceeded 5% throughout the period, and there was a middling recession in 1960-61. The economic policy debate was principally concerned with economic stimulus: conservative beliefs held back government action, and it was not until 1963 that Walter Heller, the Chairman of the Council of Economic Advisers, persuaded the country and the President that a large tax cut was needed to restore full employment (figure 2.1). After President Kennedy's assassination, Lyndon Johnson made the tax cut proposals his own, and quickly maneuvered them through the Congress. Beginning in 1964, after lower taxes had become reality, the economy began a rapid economic upswing.

While unemployment was uncomfortably high, the price-wage-productivity relationships were in an extraordinary balance. Wholesale prices

Figure 2.1
Unemployment in excess of the
4% full employment target, 1958-65
(percent of civilian labor force)

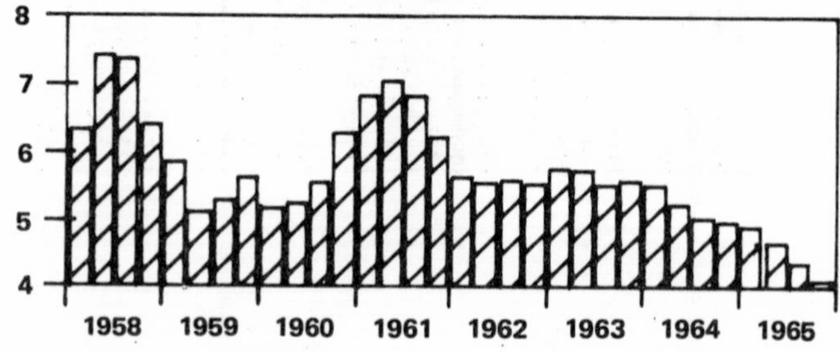

Source: Bureau of Labor Statistics, U.S. Department of Labor

were constant for six years, the longest period of precise price stability in the entire two centuries of this index. Wages followed the productivity trend closely, keeping unit labor costs stable (figure 2.2). Materials prices, including agricultural commodities, showed rather modest changes with a barely perceptible down trend. Monetary policy was relatively easy, with short-term interest rates, such as Treasury bills, fluctuating in the range of 1.0% to 4.2%. The average rate of growth of the money supply was 2.3% over a seven-year interval.

Fiscal policy, on the average, was restraining, with the average full employment surplus equal to 1.2% of the potential GNP (figure 2.3). In the final years of the Eisenhower administration, the largest full employment surplus of the postwar period was allowed to develop, helping to produce the 1960-61 recession. Increased spending over the Berlin crisis and the introduction of the investment tax credit and liberalized depreciation reduced the full employment surplus briefly to less than 1% in 1962, but it rose once more because of the progressive income tax. The 1964 tax reduction brought the full employment budget into almost precise balance.

In retrospect, the period 1958 to 1963 was one of timid economic policies which did not test the economic system by asking it to produce near its potential. On the other hand, after the February 1958 trough of what had been the most severe of the postwar recessions, the economy never approached a situation of great strength or weakness where a serious risk of downward cumulative movement would be found. The economy was in a zone which was uncomfortable for macro-policymakers, and the political process was in a condition of stalemate which made structural improvements in the performance of the economy little more than debating points of economists.

2. The Baseline Solution: "Smooth Growth"

In order to be able to evaluate the subsequent events, a DRI model solution has been developed in which economic policies follow a "stable framework" pattern from 1964 to 1975. The Federal budget is assumed to be kept near full employment balance, with the rate of increase of expenditures near the growth rate of potential GNP. Thus, the Vietnam War is excluded. Monetary policy increases bank reserves at a slowly accelerating rate, reflecting the slight acceleration of potential GNP caused by the more rapid labor force growth of the late 1960's. This strategy is designed to keep financial markets in rough balance, with nominal interest rates responding moderately to the inevitable pickup in world material prices. There is no energy crisis nor food price explosion in this hypothetical history free of interesting events.

Figure 2.2
Productivity, wages, and wholesale commodity prices, 1958-64
(percent, annual rates of change)

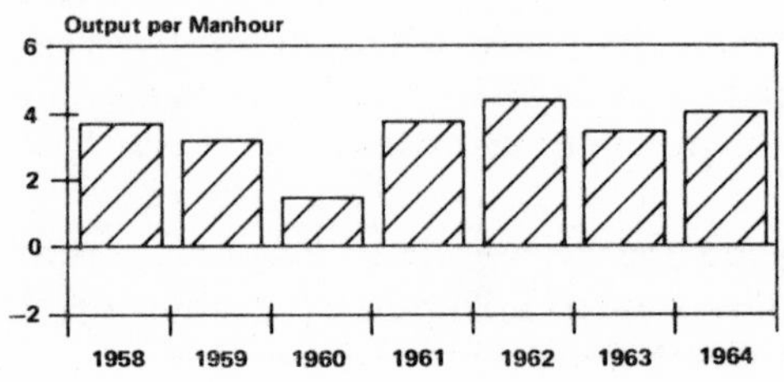

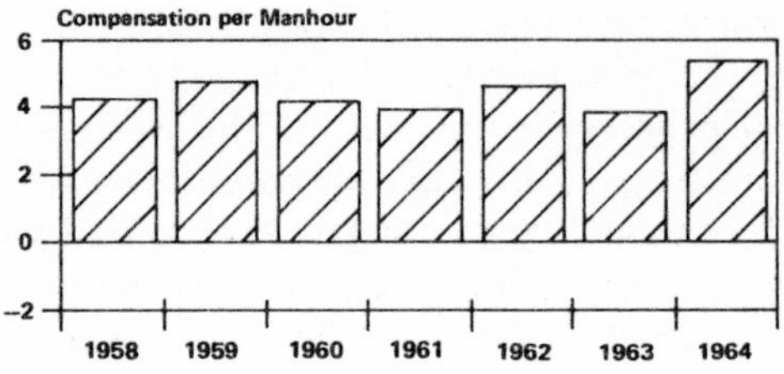

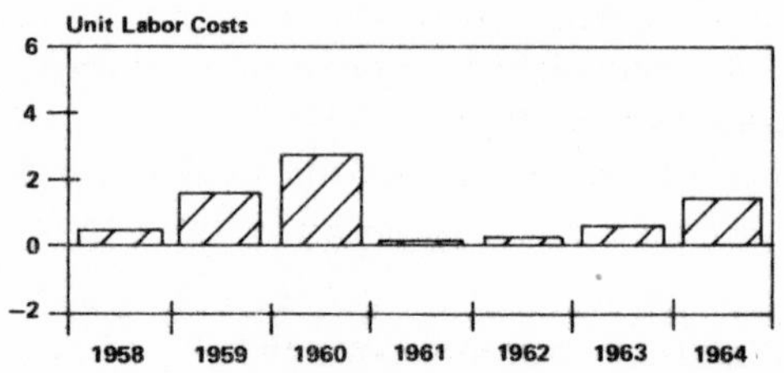

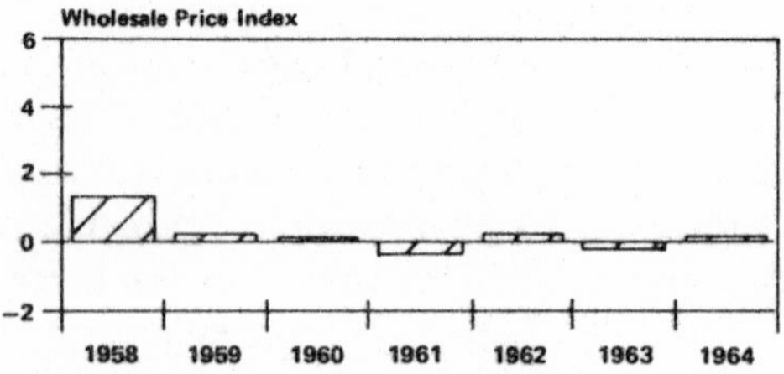

Source: Bureau of Labor Statistics, U.S. Department of Labor

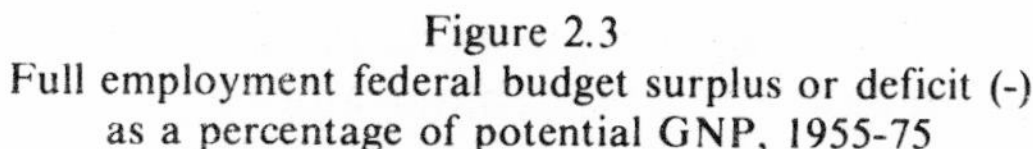

Figure 2.3
Full employment federal budget surplus or deficit (-)
as a percentage of potential GNP, 1955-75

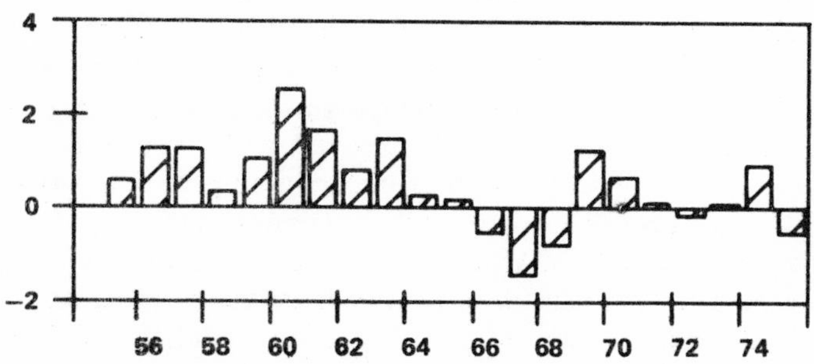

Source: Federal Reserve Bank of St. Louis and Bureau of the Census, U.S. Department of Commerce; calculation by authors.

Given the initial conditions at the point of departure, and stable public policies thereafter, the economy traces a growth path with only mild fluctuations. Moreover, real economic progress would have continued through 1974 and 1975. Earlier business cycle theories have argued that in a situation of uninterrupted growth, business expectations might become too buoyant, that an occasional recession is necessary to bring expectations back down to reality. The model exercise is not consistent with this viewpoint. Under balanced growth, business expectations are fulfilled with reasonable accuracy, so that investment, inventory and employment decisions are largely validated by subsequent market developments. Households enjoy a period of relatively stable income growth, at a rate sufficiently low that it does not encourage an overambitious use of consumer credit.

The results of this baseline simulation are summarized in figures 2.4 to 2.7, and tables 1.2 and 2.1. Unemployment averages 4.6% from 1965 to 1975, teetering near the range where the wage-price spiral accelerates; in the actual history, unemployment dropped to 3.4% during the Vietnam war, pushing the economy out of the zone of price-wage stability. The fraction of the real gross national product which is plowed back into business fixed investment averages a high 11.0%.

The economy would not have remained free of all variation. In particular, the initial conditions in 1964 had some of the makings of a boom in them. Business fixed investment was just beginning to benefit from the 1962 investment tax credit and a return to high industrial capacity utilization. This investment boom would have run out of steam in 1967 even if nothing else had gone wrong. During 1966 and 1967, the housing industry would have suffered some crowding out from other private demands, and automobile sales would have declined as the result of a stock-flow adjustment.

These adjustment mechanisms would have created a minor slowdown in 1967-68, and a minor upswing beginning in 1969. Thereafter, the economy grows at the trend rate. Real GNP growth averages 4.0% from 1969 to 1975. The year 1972 sees slightly rising unemployment because several sectors of demand, including housing, are not expanding. Thus, it is evident that a minor business cycle would have been experienced principally as a result of stock-flow imbalances that existed at the beginning of the period of analysis.

Another source of instability that develops in the baseline simulation is an imbalance between the growth of overall manufacturing capacity and the capacity of the materials and primary processing industries. This is because the smooth growth solution retains the fixed exchange rate policies of those years, which were, in fact, disequilibrium rates. The rate of return in the basic industries is below normal, causing them to underinvest. This leads to worsening bottlenecks as the economy grows. Consequently, industrial wholesale prices would have risen by 7.8% in 1974. The widening differential between capacity utilization in major materials industries and operating rates for all manufacturing industries is illustrated in figure 2.8.

Figure 2.4
The unemployment rate:
"Smooth Growth" simulation and history, 1964-75
(percent)

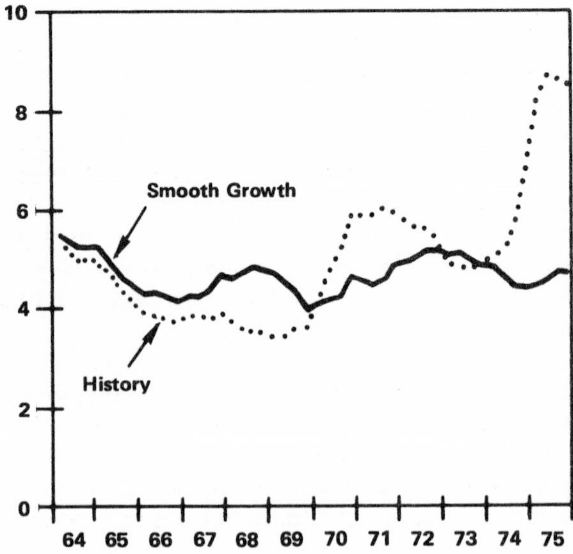

Figure 2.5
Real gross national product
"Smooth Growth" simulation and history, 1964-75
(billions of 1958 dollars)

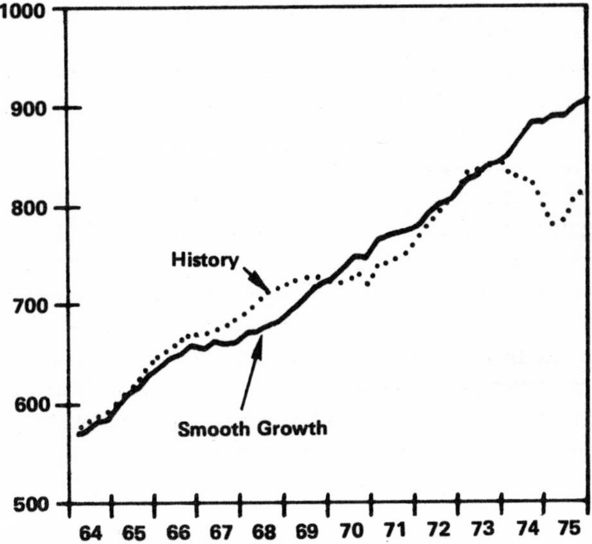

Figure 2.6
Real fixed private nonresidential investment:
"Smooth Growth" simulation and history, 1964-75
(billions of 1958 dollars)

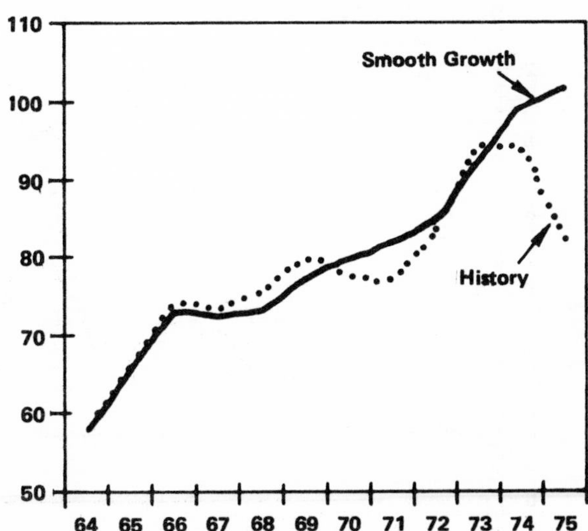

3. Actual Developments Compared to the Smooth Growth Path

The worsening instability of the last ten years can be seen by contrasting the smooth growth solution of the model with actual developments. The principal results of fluctuating activity—rising unemployment and worsening inflation—are too well known to require elaboration. But some of the less visible dimensions of the growing imbalances in the development process must be examined. The increasing violence of fluctuations distorted the development process in several ways.

First, total fixed capital formation was reduced considerably in the 1970's. Comparing history with the smooth growth solution, the fixed capital stock had lost $17 billion (1958 dollars) by the end of 1975, or 1.5% of the total. These losses were concentrated in the primary metals, steel, chemicals, transportation equipment, machinery and electrical equipment industries. Figure 2.6 compares real business fixed investment under the smooth growth simulation with its historical level. The most pronounced difference is in 1975, when real capital spending would have been 24% above recessionary levels under stable economic conditions.

Figure 2.7
Inflation rate, implicit GNP price deflator:
"Smooth Growth" simulation and history, 1964-75
(four-quarter percent change)

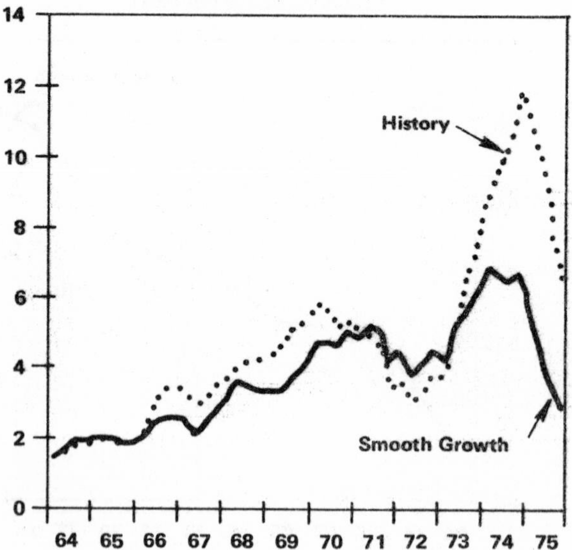

Table 2.1
Solution Summary, "Smooth Growth Path"

	Years											
	1964	1965	1966	1967	1968	1969	1970	1971	1972	1973	1974	1975
GNP and its components—billions of dollars												
Gross national product	627.8	679.9	736.7	767.2	812.8	883.8	967.2	1054.0	1135.9	1252.4	1394.1	1490.5
Real GNP (1958 dollars)	575.9	612.1	648.1	659.3	675.9	709.6	741.2	771.0	797.8	835.0	871.5	897.2
Inventory investment	5.4	8.1	11.4	9.1	6.8	7.6	9.1	12.0	11.3	15.9	20.9	17.8
Net exports	7.2	7.3	7.4	7.4	7.3	6.8	6.3	5.7	2.9	2.4	2.3	2.5
Prices and wages—annual rates of change												
Implicit price deflator	1.7	1.9	2.3	2.4	3.3	3.6	4.8	4.8	4.2	5.3	6.6	3.9
Consumer price index	1.5	1.8	2.4	2.5	3.9	4.3	5.1	4.6	3.7	4.6	5.7	5.5
Wholesale price index	1.3	1.6	1.6	0.7	1.9	2.7	4.5	3.4	3.7	5.1	6.7	1.0
Average hourly earnings index	2.7	3.7	3.8	4.3	5.1	5.1	5.8	7.1	6.8	6.6	7.3	6.3
Key economic measures												
Unemployment Rate (percent)	5.4	4.8	4.2	4.4	4.8	4.4	4.3	4.6	5.1	5.0	4.6	4.6
Industrial production (67=1)	0.803	0.872	0.948	0.962	0.973	1.033	1.094	1.147	1.187	1.257	1.324	1.365
Annual rate of change	5.2	8.6	8.8	1.4	1.1	6.1	6.0	4.8	3.5	5.9	5.3	3.1
Housing starts (millions)	1.51	1.44	1.33	1.37	1.49	1.48	1.70	1.92	1.85	2.14	2.19	1.81
Unit car sales (millions)	8.3	9.4	8.7	8.0	8.9	9.6	9.7	11.1	10.6	11.6	10.6	11.8
Federal budget surplus (NIA)	-3.4	0.8	0.3	-5.9	-7.0	-5.6	-6.9	-10.3	-18.0	-17.9	-15.4	-21.9
Money and interest rates												
Money supply (M1)	159.5	166.3	173.1	177.1	186.4	199.1	212.2	226.7	239.6	257.4	275.0	284.5
Annual rate of change	3.5	4.2	4.1	2.3	5.3	6.8	6.6	6.8	5.7	7.4	6.8	3.5
New high-grade corp. bond rate (percent)	4.43	4.68	5.32	5.45	6.03	6.71	7.42	7.31	7.33	7.33	8.08	7.70
Federal funds rate (percent)	3.68	4.18	4.59	4.93	5.59	7.02	6.67	7.11	6.26	6.65	6.61	4.34
Prime rate (percent)	4.61	4.64	5.39	5.91	6.26	7.28	7.14	7.32	6.78	6.76	7.89	6.33
Incomes—billions of dollars												
Personal income	494.6	534.7	582.4	612.5	652.6	715.7	786.4	852.9	929.5	1026.2	1121.9	1182.3
Real disposable income	406.2	431.7	459.3	474.8	488.4	515.6	543.9	566.7	593.5	624.5	640.2	652.0
Annual rate of change	6.5	6.3	6.4	3.4	2.9	5.6	5.5	4.2	4.7	5.2	2.5	1.8
Saving rate (percent)	6.0	6.1	6.7	7.4	6.6	6.3	7.5	7.9	7.7	8.8	8.3	6.7
Profits after tax (percent change)	11.9	15.8	5.4	-8.2	5.0	3.0	6.7	13.7	6.5	13.3	18.1	14.9
Details of real GNP—annual rates of change												
Gross national product	4.5	6.3	5.9	1.7	2.5	5.0	4.4	4.0	3.5	4.7	4.4	2.9
Total consumption	5.2	6.1	5.7	2.5	3.8	5.9	4.2	3.8	4.9	3.8	3.1	3.8
Business fixed investment	10.9	13.9	11.1	-0.7	1.1	5.7	3.0	2.1	3.9	9.1	7.2	2.9
Equipment	13.1	12.8	13.3	1.7	0.3	7.0	4.2	3.3	4.5	10.1	7.7	2.2
Nonresidential construction	6.7	16.1	6.9	-5.7	3.0	2.7	0.2	-0.8	2.4	6.5	5.9	4.6
Residential construction	-3.4	-2.3	-4.0	0.3	2.6	0.6	9.9	13.1	-1.7	8.8	5.9	-12.1
Federal government	-3.9	-0.2	-0.2	-0.1	-0.1	-0.0	0.0	0.1	0.1	0.2	0.6	1.2
State and local governments	5.6	7.6	7.4	6.0	2.8	5.0	9.2	5.6	1.7	4.9	9.1	6.0

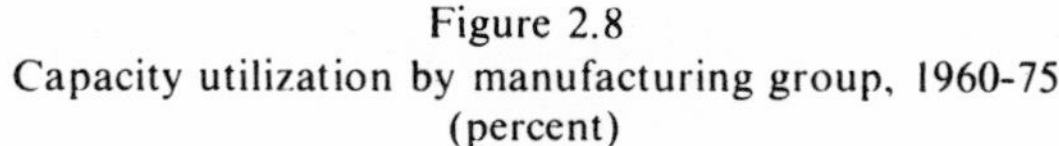

Figure 2.8
Capacity utilization by manufacturing group, 1960-75
(percent)

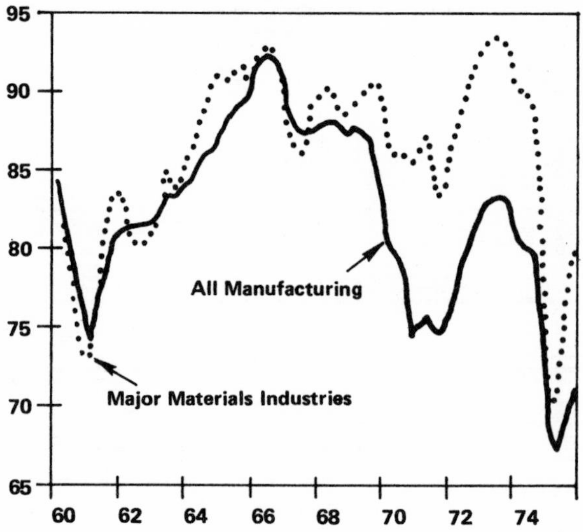

Source: Board of Governors of the Federal Reserve System

Second, by late 1975, the housing stock had been reduced by 1.1 million units, or 1.5%, as a result of the instability. The repeated credit crunches disrupted the flow of capital to the housing industry, and caused many builders to leave the business. Although the easy money and overly rapid expansion of the economy in 1972-73 created an unsustainable housing boom which carried starts to a peak level of 2.42 million, the net result of the fluctuating conditions was to produce less housing.

Third, the average rate of inflation from 1965 to 1975 was 3.9% under smooth growth, compared to an actual result of 5.0%. Moreover, the variability of inflation is lower in the alternative, as shown in figure 2.7. A considerable acceleration from the preceding era of price stability, caused by an end to raw material declines and a slight acceleration of the wage-price mechanism, was unavoidable. Instability added to inflation through supply bottlenecks and the increase in the severity of inflation expectations.

Finally, and most importantly, the economic situation at the end of the period was very, very different under the smooth growth alternative. The unemployment rate would have remained near 4.6% throughout 1975, rather than climbing to 9% in the spring. The economy would still have been developing in a handsome pattern during 1975.

CHAPTER 2

TECHNICAL APPENDIX

THE TECHNIQUE OF THE SMOOTH GROWTH PATH SOLUTION

1. Treatment of Errors

A realistic representation of the economy must include the existence of errors in our model representation of its structure. The equations contain error terms during the period of fit which are considered random in the statistical theory, but which usually have a substantive, but nonrecurring character. There are also errors in the measurement of the variables, some of which are removed through later data revision by the government agencies.

In order to test whether an economy has an inherent tendency to grow along a balanced, stable growth path, one has to allow for the existence of these statistical errors. This was done as follows: first, the errors of each individual equation during the period of fit were treated as individual time series and were fed back into the complete historical system solutions. This is a check on the mechanical accuracy of the model. With the error terms included, the model must reproduce the actual historical values to a high degree of accuracy. The errors in the solution were less than 0.5% for all principal variables. These small errors remain in the solution answers because of rounding in the model solution process over an extended period.

Second, actual observed error series were also fed into the balanced growth path simulation to allow them to have their impact on the economy. It was felt that this would be a better baseline for comparison for the other simulations than a more idealized concept in which the world was represented as free of statistical noise, strikes, and other nonrecurring events that produced the error terms in the equations.

If errors had been large and come in runs of the same direction they could, in principle, have created cyclical paths of their own. As Frisch showed 40 years ago,[1] errors can be an independent source of instability. Frisch formulated a model in which a succession of erratic shocks could sustain a cyclical pattern of movement. He distinguished the impulse problem of external random shocks to an economic system from the propagation of disturbances, which depends on structural and dynamic characteristics of the economy. The present exercise showed that the errors in the equations, whatever their cause, did not produce major instability, and certainly did not push the economy out of the zone of balanced growth. On the other hand, the error terms perturbed the path sufficiently to create brief and erratic variations for the major variables.[2]

2. *Policy Assumptions for the Balanced Growth Path Solution*

The specific assumptions made for this solution are as follows:

2.1. *Fiscal Policy*

Federal spending on goods and services rises at a trend rate which brings it to the actual 1975 levels. This implies a steady decline in constant dollar military spending between 1963 and 1975, at a rate of 1.4% a year, and an offsetting growth in nonmilitary spending for goods and services at a 3.75% annual rate. The real volume of all Federal purchases was virtually unchanged between the beginning and end of these 13 years. The volume of full employment transfers was assumed to rise by the historical average trend, which was 10% a year. The simulated volume of transfers is modified by the inflation rate and by variations in unemployment. Grants-in-aid to state and local governments were assumed to rise at the historical trend rate of 15.5% annually.

[1]Ragnar Frisch, "Propogation Problems and Impulse Problems in Dynamic Economics," *AEA Readings in Business Cycles,* (ed., R.A. Gordon and L.R. Klein), (1965), Richard D. Irwin, Inc., Homewood, Illinois, p. 155.

[2]In one important regard, this treatment of error terms overstates their impact on the normal growth path of the economy. The analysis assumes, in line with the assumption usually followed in econometric models, that error terms are not correlated with the variables in the equations. In actuality, error terms are likely to be larger when the variables in the model go through extreme changes. Thus, for example, the equation for spending on automobiles is likely to have an abnormally large error during an oil embargo, since the structure of the equation itself, even if it is built with the benefit of hindsight, is not likely to model the full change of that period precisely.

The baseline simulation does show some traces of this relationship between "errors" and "shocks." Thus, even when the shocks have been removed by explicit changes in certain key variables, traces of the shocks remain through their impact on the actual error terms that are fed back into the baseline solution. Despite this "impurity," it is still preferable to model the economy with error terms for the baseline simulation than to assume that errors are not part of the actual economic structure.

The statutory corporate tax rate was held at 48% in the balanced growth simulation. The effective rate of taxation on corporate profits was assumed to follow a smooth downward trend from 41.29% in early 1964 to 33.76% by the end of 1975. The investment tax credit was assumed to remain in effect throughout the simulation interval. Indirect tax receipts and contributions for social insurance are endogenous variables in the DRI model. Personal taxes are assumed to be changed continuously so as to leave the budget on a full employment basis in nearly precise balance. The actual budget deficit, on the national income account basis, ranges from surpluses of less than $1 billion in two of three initial years, deficits between $5 and $8 billion from 1967 to 1970, and deficits between $11 and $20 billion in the final five years. These later deficits are produced by an unemployment rate near 5%, with the full employment budget defined on the usual 4% baseline. The accumulated deficit for the entire 13 years would have been $41 billion smaller than historically, but more than the entire difference is accounted for by the year 1975 when the actual budget deficit reached $72.9 billion under the impact of the economic crisis. During the first 12 years, the difference averages less than $1 billion a year.

2.2. Monetary Policy

The Federal Reserve is assumed to provide a steady growth of nonborrowed bank reserves to support the growth of the money supply. The growth rate is set at 4% in 1964, and gradually edges upward to 6.5% by 1971 in response to the acceleration in potential growth and the unavoidable acceleration of raw material prices. The 6.5% growth rate is maintained through 1975.

The reserve requirement on demand deposits was constrained to follow a gradual downward trend. Historically, the reserve requirement was used as an instrument of monetary policy and varied accordingly. The resultant average growth in the money supply, narrowly-defined, was 5.3% for the period as a whole. If the growth of nonborrowed bank reserves had been held down to the 4% appropriate to the opening years, a credit crunch would have been produced by the late sixties.

2.3. Other Modifications

The energy crisis was excluded from the solution by assuming that the wholesale price index for fuels and related products rose by only 5% a year from 1971 on. The actual average increase for the three-year period 1973 to

1975 was 29%. The effect of the oil embargo on spending behavior was removed by additive corrections of the equations for automobile purchases, consumer spending on gasoline, and housing services during the quarters of the embargo. To remove the price instabilities originating in the farm sector, the wholesale price index for agricultural products was assumed to rise at a 3% rate from the beginning of 1972 through 1975. The actual average rate of increase in farm prices was 14% over this four-year interval.

The observed errors in the equation for manufacturing and trade inventory investment for the first two quarters of 1975 were removed, contrary to the general treatment of error terms. The errors, -$24.6 billion and -$33.6 billion, were of a magnitude to produce a cyclical downturn in the simulation. Their inclusion would have resulted in an implausibly low inventory-sales ratio. Apparently this is one instance where the error term is determined by the violence of change in the independent variables.

Total exports and imports in 1958 dollars and their respective price deflators were exogenized in the balanced growth simulation. Their growth rates were assumed to conform to historical trends, and the instability of recent years was removed. The balance of trade surplus averages $7 billion from 1964 to 1971 and drops to an average of $2.5 billion following the devaluation.

CHAPTER 3

THE VIETNAM WAR

1. Introduction

Between January, 1964 and the summer of 1965, American involvement in Vietnam crept into the forefront of national attention. On July 28, 1965, President Johnson announced his decision to escalate U.S. military operations, and from this point on, the war achieved significant economic proportions.

Johnson's decision was a response to the rapidly deteriorating military and political situation. Morale was plummeting. South Vietnamese civilian and military casualties grew to record rates. By June, there had been fourteen governments in sixteen months, as Catholics and Buddhists engaged in their own civil struggle. The United States had invested 420 dead and nearly $4 billion since the French departure in 1954. In July, Communist forces were building up for a major operation and all U.S. attempts at "unconditional negotiation" were futile. U.S. military strategy was one of "limited action," the middle ground between complete withdrawal and total escalation. So far, the war had been fought "off the shelf:" arms and materiel were transferred to Vietnam from reserves and stockpiles in other parts of the world. Military prime contract awards had remained constant around $2.35 billion a month since January, 1964. Indeed, the Administration budget for fiscal 1966 had called for just a $2 billion decrease in defense spending.

Military hardware was needed to support the President's decision to escalate the U.S. commitment. Prime contract awards climbed from $2.1 billion a month in early 1965 to $3.5 billion by mid-1966. Purchases of goods and services for military purposes increased more gradually, rising from $50.1 billion in 1965 to $78.3 billion by 1968 when the war was absorbing the peak volume of resources (figure 3.1-3.2). Military manpower grew from 2.7 million in July 1965 to 3.5 million in July 1968.

Much attention has been devoted to the well-known failure to enact an across-the-board tax increase in January 1966. After considerable internal debate in the Administration, President Johnson chose a relatively small package of tax increases, confined to the restoration of recent repealed excise tax cuts and a system of graduated income tax withholding.

The reasons for the President's failure to ask for a massive, across-the-board tax increase are well known. Both the course of the Vietnam War and the extent of the 1966 upswing in the domestic economy were uncertain, and the Johnson Administration was reluctant to risk a premature application of fiscal brakes. Second, the tax increase could only be passed as a "war tax." But the only certainty about the war was its unpopularity: 76% of the American public opposed a tax hike. Third, Congressional passage required a major concession from Johnson: any tax increase would have to be tied to spending cutbacks on the new Great Society programs. Johnson had a dream of social progress and refused to surrender the harvest of his legislative achievements: Medicare, Model Cities, War on Poverty programs, civil rights, and pollution control reforms. It was his vain hope that the advice he was getting from the Pentagon was correct, that the Vietnam War would take only a limited commitment of resources and that it would be over before the strains of a "guns and butter" policy became acute.

Figure 3.1
Military prime contract awards for work in U.S., Department of Defense, monthly rates, 1960-75 (billions of dollars)

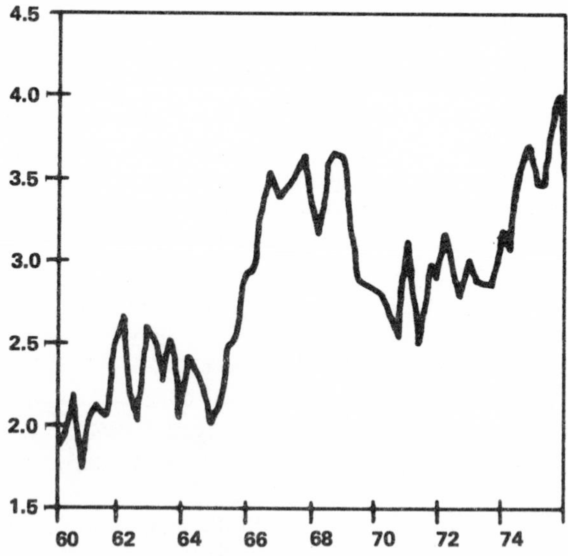

Source: "Defense Indicators," Bureau of the Census, U.S. Department of Commerce

Figure 3.2
Federal government purchases for national defense, constant dollars, 1960-75
(billions of 1958 dollars)

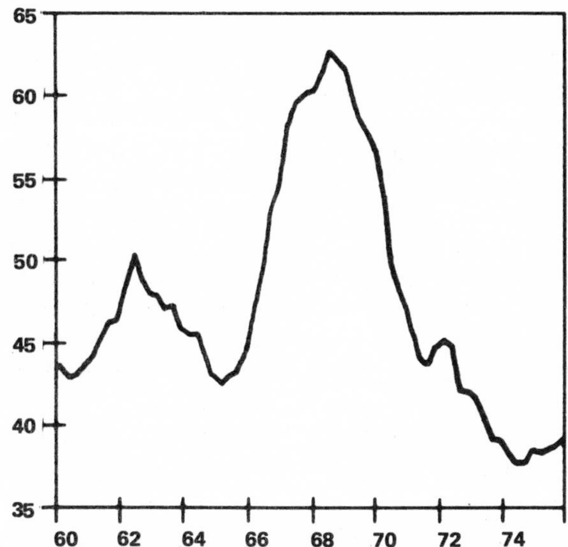

Source: Bureau of Economic Analysis, U.S. Department of Commerce

The Federal Reserve, worried about the emerging signs of inflation, rebelled in December of 1965 and raised its discount rate to commercial banks. A credit crunch developed in 1966, raising interest rates and driving down final sales. Housing starts plummetted from 1.7 million units to 1.1 million units. By 1967 there was an inventory correction and industrial production declined or held constant for a period of 15 months. The episode was not labelled a "recession" because the escalation of the War overcame the slack in the private sector and unemployment did not develop.

By 1968, the inventory correction was completed and the economy took off on a new growth spurt, this time with more inflation. Meanwhile, the case for a tax increase became so overwhelming that a 10% surcharge was enacted a few months before the presidential election. But by that time it was much too late. The boom topped out quickly after the Federal Reserve tightened up once more. The surcharge had to be removed during the 1970-71 recession.

Many observers have blamed the subsequent history of economic instability and inflation on the Vietnam War, and in some extreme versions, the blame is attached mainly to the failure to have a tax increase in January

1966. While the failure to enact the tax increase was a colossal error, it is simplistic to focus all attention on that single decision. The impact of a war on the economy is not limited to the macroeconomic effects of total government spending and receipts. Military production draws on relatively few industries, confronting them with an increase in demand to which they cannot respond smoothly and quickly. Thus, sectoral excess demands are created by war. In addition, wars breed expectations of instability and inflation, create uncertainties in the financial markets, and produce international capital flows that can easily be destabilizing. The Korean War saw much stronger fiscal policies, with large and immediate tax increases in the fall of 1951 and again in 1952. But it was still a major shock to the American economy and set loose an inflation that raised the price level by 7% within just nine months.

Whether the Vietnam War as a whole can be blamed for the entire subsequent history of instability is a broader and more difficult question. In a historical perspective, the War toppled the Democrats from the White House in 1968 and led to a change in the approach to economic policy. A different team might have avoided some of the mistakes of the Republican administration, but it probably would have managed to make some mistakes of its own invention. The associated loss of U.S. power on the world scene may have made it possible for the oil producers to engage in the embargo. And our relations with the Soviet Union might have been sufficiently different that we would not have been so eager for a spirit of detente at any price which brought about the ill-fated Russian wheat deal of 1972.

But these are only speculations. It is possible to assess rather more precisely the direct impact of the War on the economy through the model simulation technique.

2. *Simulation Results: "No Vietnam War"*

To identify the impact of the War on the economy, a simulation was performed assuming that there was no War, but that the other destabilizing elements in our economic history did occur. Federal military expenditures in constant dollars are assumed to decline smoothly at a 1.4% annual rate beginning in 1964, with defense contracts and military employment following a steady trend.

From 1965 through 1971, the principal movements of the economy can be explained by the Vietnam War. The results of the simulation are summarized in figures 3.3-3.7 and table 3.1. The surge of defense orders of 1965-66 produced a general economic boom, including considerable overinvestment in business inventories. This expansion contributed to a surge in civilian

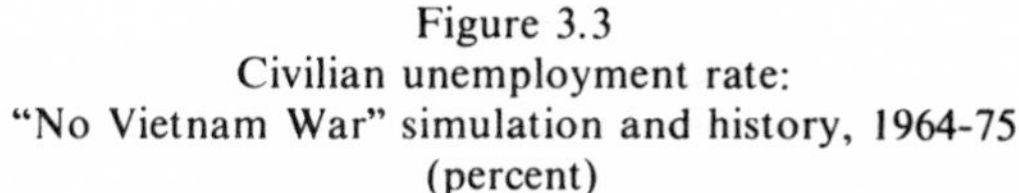

Figure 3.3
Civilian unemployment rate:
"No Vietnam War" simulation and history, 1964-75
(percent)

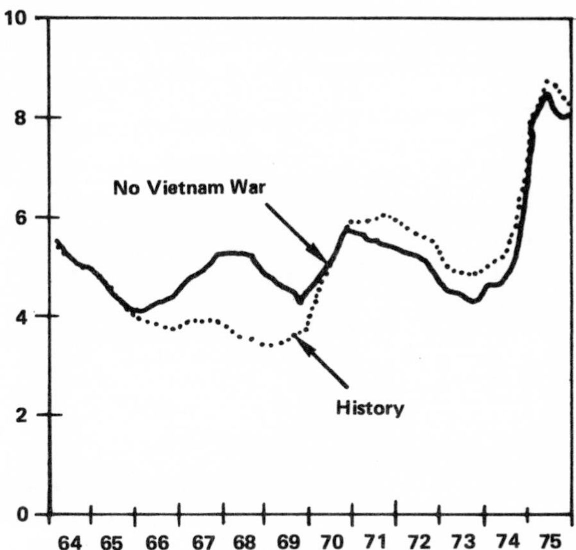

employment of 4.3 million people in the space of just two years. Meanwhile, the Armed Forces were adding 600,000 individuals to their rolls (figure 3.3). The War's impact on the macroeconomy reached a peak in 1968, accounting for an additional 4.6% in real GNP in that year. Without the stimulus of War expenditures, the economy would have entered a protracted growth recession in the spring of 1966, advancing only 2.1% over seven quarters. By mid-1968, the unemployment rate would have been 5.2%, rather than the actual 3.6%. This growth recession would have been created by the tight money policies, and by an end to the investment upswing of the 1962-66 period.

The War had adverse effects on residential construction during the sixties, as military expenditures absorbed a large share of the economy's savings flows at the expense of mortgage lending and private homebuilding. The alternative simulation indicates that an additional 350,000 homes would have been built from 1965 to 1969 without the War. Subsequently, the housing boom of the early 1970's would have been moderated by the greater availability of housing. From 1970 to 1975, there are a total of 150,000 fewer housing starts under the alternative. The cumulative impact of the War was higher long-term interest rates, a reduction in mortgage activity and less investment in residential construction over the past decade.

Figure 3.4
Wholesale price indexes for
farm products and industrial commodities, 1960-75
(1967=1)

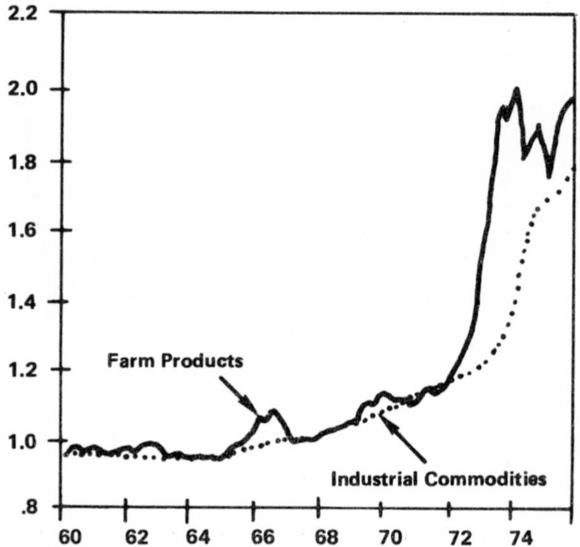

Source: Bureau of Labor Statistics, U.S. Department of Labor

Sensitive commodity prices began to depart from stability as early as mid-1965, and accelerated more in 1966. This in itself is not surprising, since commodity prices always move in response to the business cycle. But as the War demands made themselves felt, wholesale prices rose considerably more than normal, as figure 3.4 shows. At first, price changes generally remained quite modest by contemporary standards, aided by the guidepost interventions in which the power of the presidency was applied to the stabilization of a short list of key prices in the industrial economy. Agricultural policy, during a brief interval, was directed at price stability rather than farm incomes, helping to take at least a portion of the inflationary surge out of food prices. As the War went on and the President's popularity disappeared, the effectiveness of these policies diminished and the inflation gradually worsened. The wage round of 1964-65 was still in proximity of the 3.2% productivity guidepost, but beginning with the New York subway workers in early 1966 and the airline mechanics in the summer of that year, wage settlements accelerated to the 5 to 6% range, and a catching up process spread to other unions and unorganized workers.

Table 3.1
Solution Summary, "No Vietnam War"

	Years											
	1964	1965	1966	1967	1968	1969	1970	1971	1972	1973	1974	1975
GNP and its components—billions of dollars												
Gross national product	631.9	684.5	734.1	757.1	803.5	867.2	918.8	1001.1	1092.9	1226.2	1328.3	1400.8
Real GNP (1958 dollars)	580.6	617.3	644.7	649.7	674.3	709.4	724.2	759.9	804.1	852.4	833.8	806.1
Inventory investment	5.9	9.7	11.5	6.7	5.4	9.1	7.9	8.7	10.7	17.1	13.9	-12.3
Net exports	8.5	6.9	6.5	8.4	7.8	6.7	7.3	2.2	-3.3	6.5	4.5	13.3
Prices and wages—annual rates of change												
Implicit price deflator	1.5	1.9	2.7	2.3	2.2	2.6	3.8	3.8	3.2	5.8	10.8	9.0
Consumer price index	1.3	1.6	3.0	2.2	3.0	3.7	4.5	3.5	3.1	6.3	11.4	9.4
Wholesale price index	0.4	1.9	2.9	-0.7	0.6	2.0	2.8	3.1	4.8	13.8	19.3	9.3
Average hourly earnings index	2.7	3.8	3.9	4.2	4.7	4.5	4.8	5.7	5.7	6.2	8.5	9.1
Key economic measures												
Unemployment Rate (percent)	5.2	4.5	4.3	4.9	5.1	4.5	5.1	5.4	5.0	4.4	5.1	8.1
Industrial production (67=1)	0.814	0.888	0.936	0.926	0.956	1.051	1.068	1.098	1.176	1.283	1.266	1.147
Annual rate of change	6.6	9.2	5.3	-1.0	3.3	10.0	1.6	2.8	7.2	9.1	-1.4	-9.4
Housing starts (millions)	1.54	1.45	1.31	1.38	1.55	1.57	1.43	2.01	2.25	1.95	1.33	1.27
Unit car sales (millions)	8.5	9.7	8.8	7.8	9.3	9.7	9.3	11.5	11.4	11.5	9.0	8.9
Federal budget surplus (NIA)	-2.6	1.0	4.9	-0.9	2.3	15.2	-2.7	-10.2	-7.4	-0.6	-4.9	-66.4
Money and interest rates												
Money supply (M1)	160.2	167.1	173.8	177.5	187.1	197.7	206.8	222.6	235.4	253.1	269.1	279.2
Annual rate of change	4.0	4.3	4.0	2.1	5.4	5.7	4.6	7.6	5.8	7.5	6.3	3.8
New high-grade corp. bond rate (percent)	4.39	4.55	5.22	5.41	5.58	6.13	6.68	6.33	6.38	7.25	8.87	9.16
Federal funds rate (percent)	3.44	4.07	3.55	3.12	3.54	6.35	5.67	3.82	4.01	8.57	9.80	5.21
Prime rate (percent)	4.46	4.55	4.58	4.67	4.73	6.51	6.56	4.76	4.77	7.77	10.29	7.36
Incomes—billions of dollars												
Personal income	497.2	538.8	579.0	606.3	645.8	696.6	750.7	811.1	890.0	998.8	1090.7	1170.0
Real disposable income	407.9	434.6	452.3	462.4	478.6	498.4	524.1	552.5	580.3	621.6	602.5	606.2
Annual rate of change	7.0	6.6	4.1	2.2	3.5	4.2	5.1	5.4	5.0	7.1	-3.1	0.6
Saving rate (percent)	6.0	6.0	6.0	6.7	5.6	4.6	6.4	6.8	5.9	7.9	7.3	7.8
Profits after tax (percent change)	16.2	20.1	-1.3	-14.2	-0.4	2.4	-4.4	21.4	19.1	25.7	15.0	-11.7
Details of real GNP—annual rates of change												
Gross national product	5.4	6.3	4.4	0.8	3.8	5.2	2.1	4.9	5.8	6.0	-2.2	-3.3
Total consumption	5.7	6.4	4.1	1.4	4.6	5.1	3.2	5.1	6.0	4.7	-2.4	0.3
Business fixed investment	11.2	14.8	11.2	-1.9	2.6	8.3	0.0	1.0	8.7	12.0	-0.4	-14.7
Equipment	13.6	13.9	12.9	-0.2	2.2	10.2	0.0	1.3	10.6	14.7	-1.2	-16.3
Nonresidential construction	6.7	16.7	7.7	-5.3	3.5	4.1	-0.0	0.2	4.5	5.3	1.7	-10.5
Residential construction	-2.3	-2.2	-4.3	-1.5	5.9	7.5	-11.0	28.6	14.4	-5.5	-26.0	-15.1
Federal government	-3.3	0.6	-1.2	0.2	0.8	-2.8	-2.3	2.7	0.7	-1.3	1.1	1.4
State and local governments	6.4	6.5	8.1	5.3	3.7	4.5	5.2	8.4	4.4	5.4	3.4	1.6

When the new Administration took office in January 1969, it abandoned all guidepost policies to curtail specific price and wage increases. This was an ideological matter. The immediate result was a quick bulge of price increases and an accelerating inflation as the economy charged forward at a considerable clip.

The simulation indicates that, with the War-related pressures removed, the U.S. would have enjoyed an annual inflation rate below 4% through 1972 (figure 3.5). Over the three-year period 1968-70, the inflation rate averages 2.9%, nearly 2% below the actual experience. The lower inflation in the alternative simulation removes pressures on interest rates. Thus, the tightening of monetary reserves by the Federal Reserve in 1967 and 1969 leads to milder credit strains (figure 3.6). There is a brief slowdown in late 1969, but the 1969-70 recession is averted and the growth paths in the alternative and baseline solutions cross in mid-1970.

The simulation also portrays a vigorous upswing in the early 1970's. Real GNP advances 4.9% in 1971, 5.8% in 1972, and 6.0% in 1973. The expansion is led by growth in consumer spending on automobiles and home furnishings, homebuilding, expenditures of state and local governments and Federal nonmilitary purchases.

Figure 3.5
Inflation rate, implicit GNP deflator:
"No Vietnam War" simulation and history, 1964-75
(percent)

Figure 3.6
Interest rate on new high-grade corporate bonds:
"No Vietnam War" simulation and history, 1964-75
(percent)

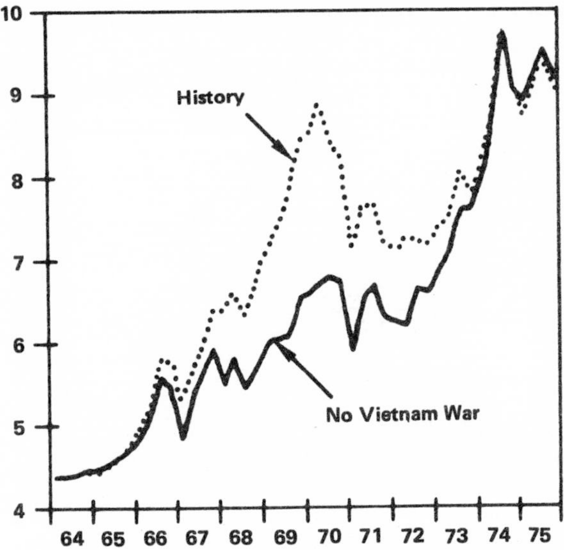

By 1972, easy credit conditions stimulate a resurgence in investment. Real business fixed investment rises 8.7% in 1972 and 12.0% in 1973 in the "No War" simulation. The devaluations of the dollar would have prolonged the investment boom.

The alternative paths of business investment are compared in figure 3.7. Without the War, real expenditures on plant and equipment would have averaged 4.9% higher over the first half of the 1970's.

The economic growth of the early 1970's would have been fostered in part by the worldwide business cycle upswing. Without the War a lower U.S. price level would have stimulated a higher volume of exports. As a result of this cross-sectoral strength, real GNP in the alternative averages 1.5% above its historical level from 1972 to 1974.

By 1974, the expansion would have ended even without the Vietnam War legacy. Other forces in the economy had begun to prevail. The surge in food prices at the start of 1973 quickly put a damper on consumer sentiment. In the alternative simulation, car sales peak in the first quarter of 1973. The savings rate jumps from 5.9% in 1972 to 7.9% in 1973. (This compares with actual savings rates of 6.6% and 8.2% in the respective years.)

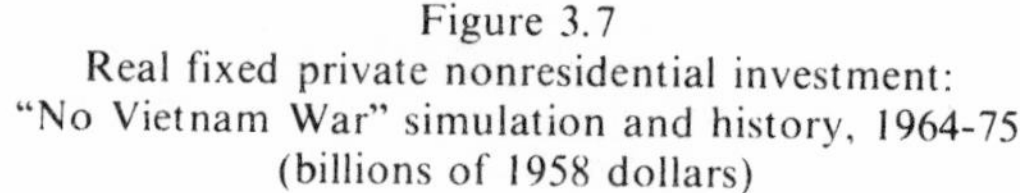

Figure 3.7
Real fixed private nonresidential investment:
"No Vietnam War" simulation and history, 1964-75
(billions of 1958 dollars)

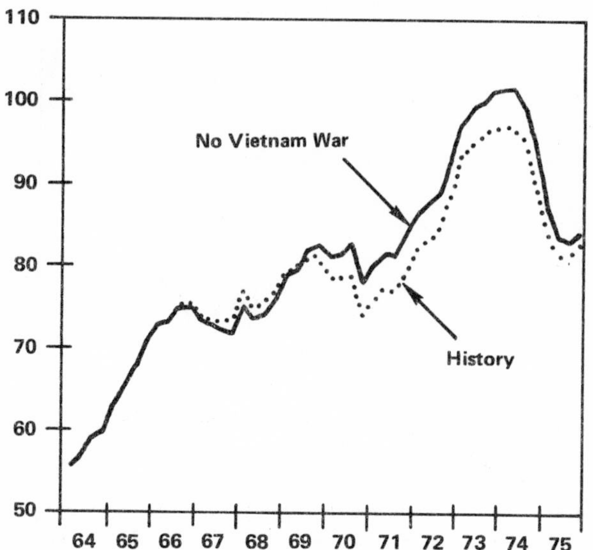

Price movements in the 1970's resemble the historical patterns, as shown in figure 3.5. The burst of prices in the food and energy sectors, superimposed on policies of monetary restraint, creates a severe credit crunch. By 1975, the macroeconomy is in approximately the same situation with or without the War. In the alternative, the unemployment rate peaks at 8.4%, half a percentage point below the actual result. Real GNP declines 3.3% in 1975, but remains 1% above the historical level. The difference reflects the potential long-term benefits of a more stable economy without the War.

In conclusion, the Vietnam War was the decisive economic event for the period 1965 to 1972. Without the War, a good expansion could have proceeded over that entire interval, with the inflation kept outside of the range that is disturbing to the public and to policy, and with the economy benefitting from the devaluations. Capital formation would have been substantially higher and the recession of 1970-71 would have been avoided.

But beginning in 1973, the War ceased to be the determinant of the economy. Food, energy, inflation and tight money took over and would have produced the 1973-75 recession in about the same vivid terms as actually occurred.

3. Simulation Results: If The War Had Been Paid For

A second simulation assesses the consequences of the failure to enact a tax increase to finance the Vietnam War (table 3.2). This simulation was created by imposing a personal tax increase on the historical baseline simulation of the precise magnitude required to keep the Federal budget in full-employment balance from 1966 to 1968. During 1966, when the principal impact of defense spending was through a surge of orders rather than expenditures recorded in the national income accounts, a tax increase of $6 billion was assumed. This could have been accomplished by a 10% surcharge, wich was one of the proposals under debate. By 1967, military expenditures had risen and an additional $11 billion in personal taxes was required to bring the full-employment budget into balance. An actual surcharge was enacted in the second half of 1968 and so, from that point forward, the actual tax policy is used.

If the War had been financed by higher personal income taxes, the overall performance of the economy over the past decade would have been somewhat better. The increase in the consumer price index between 1965 and 1969 would have been cut from 16.3 to 14.2% (figure 3.8). Unemployment would

Figure 3.8
Inflation rate, implicit GNP deflator:
"Taxing the War" simulation and history, 1965-75
(four-quarter percent change)

Table 3.2
Solution Summary, "Taxing the War"

	Years									
	1966	1967	1968	1969	1970	1971	1972	1973	1974	1975
GNP and its components—billions of dollars										
Gross national product	740.9	773.0	833.6	902.1	957.0	1047.4	1159.1	1296.7	1403.6	1463.8
Real GNP (1958 dollars)	650.6	660.8	691.8	721.7	728.9	762.5	811.3	851.8	829.9	791.9
Inventory investment	14.1	6.5	4.9	7.7	6.4	9.2	11.8	17.0	14.3	-16.7
Net exports	5.8	6.9	4.8	3.4	4.2	-0.8	-7.8	2.6	0.9	12.0
Prices and wages—annual rates of change										
Implicit price deflator	2.7	2.7	3.0	3.7	5.1	4.6	4.0	6.6	11.2	9.2
Consumer price index	2.9	2.4	3.5	4.6	5.5	4.3	3.8	6.9	11.7	9.6
Wholesale price index	2.9	-0.4	1.5	2.9	3.6	3.7	5.4	14.1	19.4	9.3
Average hourly earnings index	3.9	4.5	5.3	5.5	5.9	6.8	6.7	7.1	9.1	9.5
Key economic measures										
Unemployment Rate (percent)	4.0	4.5	4.3	3.8	4.8	5.3	4.8	4.3	5.2	8.6
Industrial production (67=1)	0.955	0.953	1.004	1.090	1.084	1.112	1.209	1.293	1.264	1.122
Annual rate of change	7.6	-0.2	5.4	8.6	-0.5	2.6	8.6	7.0	-2.2	-11.3
Housing starts (millions)	1.13	1.20	1.42	1.51	1.52	2.16	2.42	2.01	1.34	1.07
Unit car sales (millions)	8.6	7.8	9.3	9.8	9.0	11.0	11.5	11.5	8.9	8.2
Federal budget surplus (NIA)	3.1	-7.5	-7.2	5.4	-9.8	-14.9	-8.4	0.9	-2.4	-75.3
Money and interest rates										
Money supply (M1)	173.1	177.8	188.8	200.8	210.9	228.2	245.0	263.9	280.5	290.1
Annual rate of change	3.6	2.7	6.2	6.4	5.0	8.2	7.4	7.7	6.3	3.4
New high-grade corp. bond rate (percent)	5.50	5.76	6.19	7.06	7.90	7.07	7.18	7.95	9.51	9.39
Federal funds rate (percent)	5.16	4.24	5.55	8.10	7.04	4.39	4.43	8.61	10.38	5.71
Prime rate (percent)	5.65	5.66	6.24	7.79	7.74	5.43	5.17	8.01	10.67	7.86
Incomes—billions of dollars										
Personal income	582.9	617.6	668.9	727.3	787.5	853.1	943.6	1057.9	1155.7	1231.7
Real disposable income	450.0	460.9	484.1	506.1	532.8	561.4	590.8	628.0	607.7	605.6
Annual rate of change	3.6	2.4	5.0	4.5	5.3	5.4	5.2	6.3	-3.2	-0.3
Saving rate (percent)	5.9	6.5	5.9	5.2	7.4	7.7	6.5	8.5	8.0	8.5
Profits after tax (percent change)	2.3	-11.0	2.6	0.2	-7.2	22.8	24.9	21.2	15.1	-15.7
Details of real GNP—annual rates of change										
Gross national product	5.4	1.6	4.7	4.3	1.0	4.6	6.4	5.0	-2.6	-4.6
Total consumption	3.7	1.7	5.7	5.3	2.8	5.1	6.6	4.0	-2.7	-0.7
Business fixed investment	11.0	-2.9	1.9	7.7	-1.0	2.1	11.1	12.2	-1.4	-15.1
Equipment	12.8	-1.0	2.0	9.3	-1.3	2.3	13.5	14.6	-2.6	-16.9
Nonresidential construction	7.3	-6.8	1.7	4.0	-0.1	1.5	5.5	6.3	2.0	-10.4
Residential construction	-12.4	-7.8	12.7	7.9	-2.8	32.2	17.0	-8.2	-25.7	-26.0
Federal government	13.1	14.1	4.6	-5.9	-12.4	-5.3	0.1	-6.0	-1.4	3.5
State and local governments	7.2	6.6	4.6	3.8	6.2	6.9	4.5	6.2	3.5	-0.8

have stayed half a percentage point higher from 1966 to 1968, somewhat reducing wage and other inflationary pressures (figure 3.9). Thereafter, unemployment would have averaged 0.6 percentage points lower from 1971 to 1974, until that beneficial effect converted itself into more rapid wage increases. By 1975, the real economy is at the same level with or without the tax increase.

The basic movements of the economy would not have been substantially different. Real growth would have been very high for a brief period, the 1967 credit crunch and mini-recession would still have taken place, and 1968 would have been another boom year.

There are three reasons for this very limited impact of a better tax policy. First, the economy was well into an upswing independent of the War. After five years of subnormal growth, high unemployment and depressed investment, the economy was ready for a capital goods boom. The years 1965 and 1966 saw an annual average rate of increase in business fixed investment of 13%. Perhaps the War fostered this investment boom, particularly in its later stages; but that stimulus would have occurred even if personal taxes had been raised.

Figure 3.9
Civilian unemployment rate:
"Taxing the War" simulation and history, 1964-75
(percent)

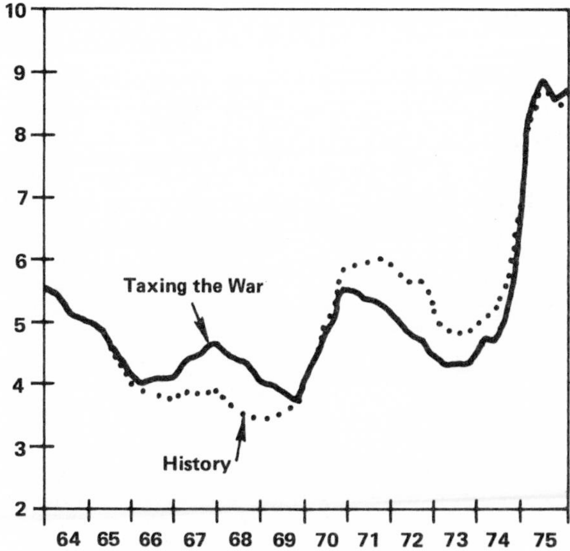

Second, the 1965-66 expansion was partially fueled by enormous inventory accumulation. As the War placed large demands on industry in the opening months of 1966, utilization rates rose and delivery periods lengthened very suddenly. Industry scrambled to try to obtain the materials necessary for production, creating industrial price pressures, and, at least briefly, a "shortage" economy. Credit conditions tightened during the scramble for supplies, slowing the growth of final sales. The stock market collapsed in May 1966 and the consumer saving rate rose gradually from 6 to 7½%. Housing starts declined as the public shifted funds from savings institutions to money market paper. The year 1967 saw the inventory correction in which the unwanted buildups of late 1966 were gradually absorbed.

Finally, a personal tax increase would not have changed the basic movements of the economy because there are time lags in its effects. Usually, households do not adjust their spending behavior to the changed taxes immediately. Even if the adjustment lag was only a quarter or two, the economy accelerated so quickly in 1966 that much of the impact would have come too late. The impact of the War on the economy actually began in the second half of 1965, when defense orders began to surge. The tax cut was an issue for the budget that the President was to submit in January, 1966. If it had been enacted promptly—the simulation assumes it to be effective January 1, 1966—it would have curtailed consumer spending later in 1966. The reduction would have been greatest in 1967, by which time the economy was in a minor recession. The capital goods boom, the surge in defense orders, and the inventory hoarding all would have largely run their course before the tax cut had its real effect.

To attribute a greater effectiveness to the foregone tax cut, one has to assume that it would have affected business expectations sufficiently to moderate the capital goods boom and inventory hoarding. The model exercise does not show much of an impact on inventory or investment behavior, but confines the benefit of the tax cut to the macro dimensions of total real GNP, consumption, unemployment, wage increases and prices.[1] It was the War that overheated the economy, not the error in fiscal policy.

[1]The same general conclusions are reached by the NSF-NBER Model Seminar Study. This project applied four different macromodels to this issue, including the models of the Bureau of Economic Analysis, Wharton and DRI. See Albert A. Hirsch, "Econometric Review of Alternative Policies, 1966-75," presented at the Dallas Meeting of the American Economic Association, December 28, 1975.

CHAPTER 3

TECHNICAL APPENDIX

The two simulations were created by imposing modifying assumptions on the baseline solution described in Chapter 1. The baseline simulation contains the null errors of each equation and closely replicates the historical data. The specific assumptions of each simulation are described below.

1. "No Vietnam War"

1.1. Fiscal Policy

The parameters relating to Federal government military expenditures are assumed to trace a steady growth path from 1964 to 1975. By comparison with the baseline simulation, it is possible to isolate the macroeconomic effects of the War.

It is assumed that real Federal military purchases of goods and services (*GMLF58*) would have declined steadily at a 1.4% rate from the end of 1963 through 1975. Under this assumption military purchases in constant dollars are approximately equal to historical values at the beginning and end of the solution interval. The expenditure bulge of the Vietnam War period is removed. The variable *GMLF58* takes the following values:

	1966	1967	1968	1969	1970
Alternative	$42.8	42.2	41.7	41.1	40.5
History	51.1	59.6	61.9	68.3	49.9
Difference	-8.2	-17.3	-20.3	-17.2	-9.4
	1971	**1972**	**1973**	**1974**	**1975**
Alternative	39.9	39.4	38.8	38.3	37.7
History	44.4	43.5	40.0	38.1	38.7
Difference	-4.5	-4.1	-1.2	0.2	-1.0

Prime contract awards (in current dollars) are assumed to increase at a constant 4% rate over the 1964-75 period. Their value rises from $2.365 billion per month in 1964 to $3.640 billion monthly in 1975. In the DRI model, prime contract awards affect inventory investment.

Military employment under the Defense Department is assumed to decline at an annual rate of 2%.

The 10% personal tax surcharge effective in fiscal years 1969 and 1970 was removed through an additive factor on Federal government personal tax receipts. The tax reduction amounts to $7.6 billion in fiscal 1969 and $8.0 billion in fiscal 1970.

1.2. Monetary Policy

The monetary policy instrument in the DRI model is bank reserves held against private deposits *(RPD's)*. In this simulation, the growth of *RPD's* followed its historical path, except in periods in which this strategy caused the Federal funds rate to fall below an arbitrary lower bound, set at 3%. To implement this rule, the growth of *RPD's* was lowered in the 1967-68 period and again in the years 1971 and 1972. *RPD's* were unchanged in the 1964-66 interval. The level of *RPD's* averages 1.8% below its historical path in the 1967-70 period and 2.5% below the actual from 1971 to 1975. Interest rates are lower throughout the simulation interval as a result of lower inflation rates and the absence of excess demands associated with the Vietnam War.

2. *"If the War Had Been Paid For"*

2.1. Fiscal Policy

In the second fiscal policy simulation, it is assumed that personal taxes were increased over a three-year period, 1966-68, to finance the war. Personal tax receipts were adjusted by the following increments (billions of dollars) to achieve a balanced full-employment budget in each quarter:

1966:1	1966:2	1966:3	1966:4	1967:1	1967:2
$5.8	6.1	6.3	6.5	10.4	10.3

1967:3	1967:4	1968:1	1968:2	1968:3	1968:4
11.0	11.1	9.7	11.3	3.3	0.4

2.2. Monetary Policy

Bank reserves held to support private deposits were adjusted to leave the Federal funds rate within a narrow range of its actual values from 1966 through 1975. This procedure is intended to leave the degree of monetary accommodation or restraint unchanged.

CHAPTER 4

FISCAL POLICIES, 1969-74: POLITICAL BUSINESS CYCLES?

1. Introduction

In recent years, the charge has been leveled that fiscal policy is manipulated on a four-year political cycle to help presidents promote their reelection. Some degree of cynicism has always been justified: in the year before an election, presidents and Congresses have routinely pursued more generous expenditures policies in such traditional areas as agriculture, social security, public works and welfare. Such outlays, usually changes in timing, are a part of the cost of a pluralistic democracy. They reduce the average efficiency of resource use in the public sector but are of sufficiently small magnitude to be lost in macroeconomic analysis.

In the past, the political element in business cycles has, at most, had a minor influence in the United States. This conclusion is supported by a review of attitudes and policies during the postwar presidential election years. In 1948, President Truman and his economic advisers did not recognize the recession that was developing and took no major actions to reverse it. Moreover, the economic report of January 1949, written after the election, was heavily preoccupied with inflation. In the 1952 election year, the economy was in a lull following the Korean War boom, with unemployment low but industrial production stagnant. President Truman resisted Congressional attempts to reduce business taxation. Later, the Congress took the initiative in removing the excess profits tax and reducing the level of general taxation in time to help reverse the 1954 recession. President Truman undertook no actions to reaccelerate the economy to help Adlai Stevenson stand a better chance in his campaign.

President Eisenhower enjoyed a period of prosperity during the 1956 election year which helped to create an atmosphere of accomplishment and satisfaction. His economic policies were conservative and there was little reason for major fiscal policy initiatives that year.

In 1960, when the economy once more slid into recession before the election, the Administration resolutely denied its presence. Moreover, John Kennedy did not assert the existence of recession until his post-election task force reported in January 1961. The budget policy of the closing Eisenhower years had produced the largest budget surpluses of the postwar period. These restrictive budgets, the prematurely tight money policies of 1959, and an extended steel strike broke the forward momentum of the economy. The ensuing 1960 recession was one of the factors in helping John F. Kennedy narrowly defeat Richard M. Nixon.

Lyndon Johnson was helped in his landslide reelection of 1964 by the extraordinary economic growth of that year. The great tax cut of the spring of 1964 proved to be good politics. But the tax cut was a presidential initiative at least two years earlier and it was only the resistance of the business community and the Congress which delayed its enactment to the election year. The antithesis of the political business cycle policy was observed in 1968, when Lyndon Johnson finally imposed the Vietnam surcharge on personal and corporate income taxes a few months before the election. Hubert Humphrey had little reason to be grateful to the Administration in his election campaign.

Gerald Ford also did little to use economic policies to aid his 1976 election campaign. His fiscal policy was marked by vetoes of congressional spending initiatives. Further, an inexplicable underspending of actual budget plans by about 3% in the second and third quarters of 1976 helped slow the economic recovery and contributed to rising unemployment.

2. Fiscal Policy During the Nixon Administration

When the Nixon Administration first took office in 1969, it adopted the policy of "gradualism," designed to moderate inflation through demand management. The policy of gradualism combined fiscal and monetary restraints, designed to edge unemployment up from 3.3% at the time the President took office, to 4.5% in the course of a year or two. By slowing the overheated economy and eliminating excess demand, the rate of inflation would be reduced and inflationary expectations broken.

In actuality, it proved impossible to manage final demand so precisely. On a full employment basis, the budget policy was quite restrictive, as figure 4.1 illustrates. More importantly, it was impossible to fine-tune monetary policy. Federal Reserve policy became more restrictive, holding money supply growth to 2.3% in the last half of 1969. A credit crunch developed, which in turn produced a stock market collapse and made business highly illiquid.

Figure 4.1
Full employment federal budget
surplus or deficit (-), 1969-75
(billions of dollars)

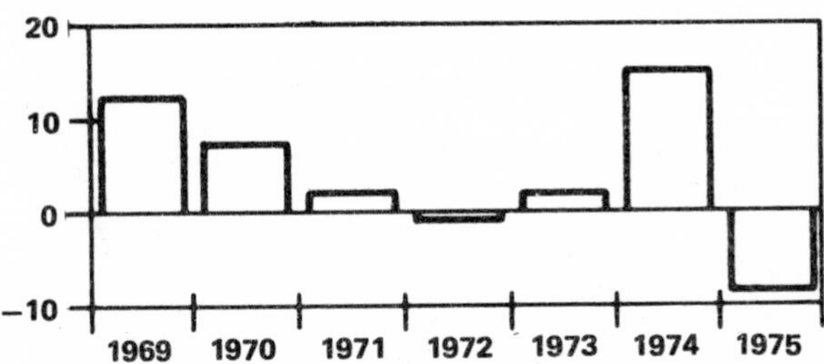

Source: Federal Reserve Bank of St. Louis

Fears of bankruptcy after the failure of the Penn Central Railroad and the loss of access to usual sources of business capital forced massive layoffs, a period of stagnation in production, and ultimately a full-scale recession. Unemployment peaked at 6.1% in December of 1970, and remained at the 6% level throughout 1971. It was a mild recession because inventory policies had remained cautious after the large inventory errors of 1966-67, so there was little surge in this usually volatile item.

The recession did not cure the inflation. Such hopes were disappointed by a major catchup element in the wage settlements of 1969-70. Inflation expectations were aroused and the settlements actually accelerated slightly despite the rise in unemployment (figure 4.2). The persistence of inflation despite recession, creating the newly fashionable concept of "stagflation," created much concern in the mind of the public and businesses.

As the economy remained in a rather weak condition, the President's patience ran out, and in August 1971 he launched the New Economic Policy, a comprehensive package of policy measures. The program had three major components: fiscal stimulus with accommodation from the monetary authorities, designed to reduce unemployment immediately; a wage-price freeze to break stubborn inflationary expectations; and the devaluation of the dollar to improve the balance of trade. The principal fiscal initiatives in the New Economic Policy, as finally enacted, were (1) a 7% business investment tax credit, (2) repeal of the 7% excise tax on automobiles and the 10% excise tax on light trucks, (3) personal income tax reductions through increases in the personal exemption and the minimum standard deduction, (4) a temporary surcharge on dutiable imports at a rate of 10%, and (5) provision

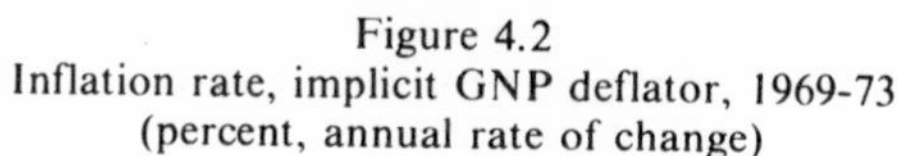

Figure 4.2
Inflation rate, implicit GNP deflator, 1969-73
(percent, annual rate of change)

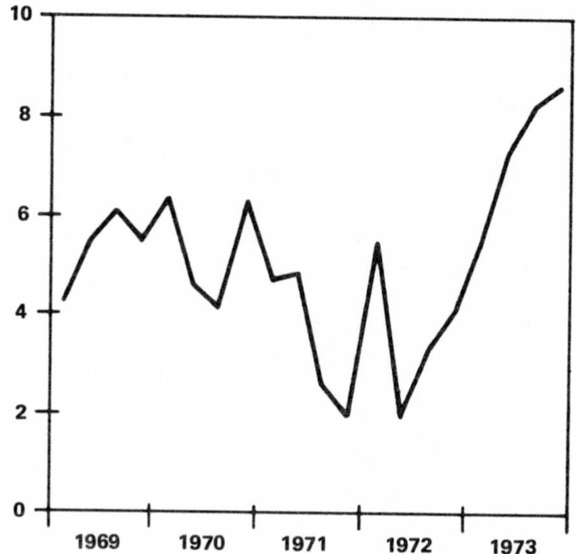

for favorable tax treatment of Domestic International Sales Corporations.[1] Tax law changes were estimated to cut revenues by $8.9 billion in 1972. However, a simultaneous increase in the Social Security base reduced the net fiscal stimulus to $3.7 billion.[2]

The President's New Economic Policy was extremely effective.[3] In the 15-month period beginning in October 1971, the economy grew at a 7.1% rate and the unemployment rate dropped from 6.1% to 5.1%. The improving economic conditions sparked a revival in consumer confidence. The savings rate fell from 8.1% in 1971 to 6.5% in 1972. Real consumption rose 6.2% in 1972. Meanwhile, the investment tax credit contributed to a 9.1% increase in real business fixed investment.

Another favorable sign was the slowdown in inflation. The 90-day freeze was nearly fully effective for a time and was followed by looser controls on wages, prices and dividends. The rise in consumer prices averaged only 3.2%

[1] *Economic Report of the President, 1971*, U.S. Government Printing Office, (1971), Washington, D.C., pp. 69-71.

[2] *Ibid.*, p. 106.

[3] For a contemporary analysis, see O. Eckstein, "The New Economic Program of August 15, 1971," *Parameters and Policies in the U.S. Economy*, (1976), North Holland, Amsterdam, pp. 331-339.

from the fall of 1971 through the end of 1972, compared to 4.3% in the preceding four quarters. Market forces also played an effective role in controlling inflation, as some industries were unable to implement price increases approved by the Cost of Living Council.

But within weeks after the 1972 election, the economic situation deteriorated. Money growth had exceeded targets throughout 1972, and the Federal Reserve reacted by tightening the supply of bank reserves. The explosion in agricultural prices began reaching consumers before the end of the year. In January 1973, the Administration introduced Phase III, a weakened version of wage and price controls. Within two months of the election, inflation accelerated, interest rates moved upward, and the great postwar economic crisis began.

3. The Alternative Simulation: "Stable Fiscal Policies, 1969-74"

To assess the role of fiscal policy in the onset of the crisis, a simulation was run in which the actual fiscal policy was replaced with a continuing balance in the full-employment budget from mid-1969 up until the 1975 tax cuts (table 4.1). The expenditure assumptions were not changed, but personal taxes were adjusted continuously to bring the full-employment budget into balance. Monetary policy instruments were adjusted to leave short-term interest rates at their historical values.

The alternative policy would have been more stimulative during the initial years of the Nixon Administration, the period of gradualism (figure 4.3). Only in the final quarter of 1972 and in early 1973 would fiscal policy have been somewhat more restrictive.

As a result, unemployment would have been less severe during the 1970 recession (figure 4.4), reduced from its actual level by 0.4 percentage points in 1970 and 0.3 percentage points in 1971. In subsequent years, the differences would have been small, with unemployment slightly higher in 1973 and lower again in late 1974. The additional fiscal stimulus would have produced a slightly higher inflation in 1971 and 1972 (figure 4.5). By 1973, the price level is 1% above the actual mark. The inflation rate follows its historical pattern from that point on.

The economy would have grown at a slightly more moderate pace from 1971 to 1973. At the beginning of the 1974-75 recession, the actual full-employment budget was in surplus, and the economy would have benefitted from a stable fiscal policy. However, by 1975, the economy had deteriorated to such an extent for other reasons that a balanced full-employment budget would obviously have been inappropriate.

This simulation conveys the same message as the analysis of the failure to increase taxes in the critical stages of the Vietnam War. The implementation of a stable fiscal policy would not have been decisive in changing the rhythm of the business cycle, either with regard to unemployment or with regard to inflation. Indeed, in the case of the Nixon Administration's fiscal policies, the difference between the "stable framework," full-employment budget balance policies and the actual policies was moderate relative to the dimensions of the economy. The favorable economic conditions just prior to the 1972 election

Table 4.1
Solution Summary, "Stable Fiscal Policies, 1969-74"

	Years					
	1969	1970	1971	1972	1973	1974
	GNP and its components—billions of dollars					
Gross national product	934.9	989.8	1068.6	1168.2	1303.3	1420.8
Real GNP (1958 dollars)	729.5	731.0	751.9	792.1	836.4	829.1
Inventory investment	8.1	5.8	7.2	8.4	14.3	14.4
Net exports	1.4	2.2	-1.4	-6.5	4.3	-0.3
	Prices and wages—annual rates of change					
Implicit price deflator	4.8	5.7	4.9	3.8	5.7	10.0
Consumer price index	5.4	6.1	4.6	3.6	6.3	10.9
Wholesale price index	3.8	3.8	3.6	4.7	13.0	18.8
Average hourly earnings index	6.6	6.9	7.3	6.8	6.6	8.3
	Key economic measures					
Unemployment Rate (percent)	3.4	4.6	5.6	5.5	5.0	5.4
Industrial production (67=1)	1.117	1.094	1.086	1.151	1.244	1.264
Annual rate of change	5.9	-2.1	-0.7	6.0	8.1	1.6
Housing starts (millions)	1.51	1.47	2.04	2.35	2.04	1.36
Unit car sales (millions)	9.7	8.6	10.3	10.7	11.3	9.1
Federal budget surplus (NIA)	3.4	-16.2	-22.1	-16.7	-7.6	-22.3
	Money and interest rates					
Money supply (M1)	207.2	217.8	233.1	247.7	265.8	282.9
Annual rate of change	6.7	5.1	7.0	6.3	7.3	6.4
New high-grade corp. bond rate (%)	7.64	8.52	7.55	7.41	7.81	8.95
Federal funds rate (percent)	8.22	7.21	4.81	4.53	8.78	10.63
Prime rate (percent)	7.95	7.94	5.82	5.36	8.06	10.89
	Incomes—billions of dollars					
Personal income	752.4	815.2	874.3	956.5	1066.0	1166.0
Real disposable income	519.7	544.9	562.4	583.9	622.7	618.4
Annual rate of change	4.1	4.9	3.2	3.8	6.7	-0.7
Saving rate (percent)	6.4	8.6	8.5	7.0	8.7	8.7
Profits after tax (percent change)	-3.7	-9.9	14.7	20.8	26.1	22.4
	Details of real GNP—annual rates of change					
Gross national product	3.2	0.2	2.9	5.3	5.6	-0.9
Total consumption	4.5	2.4	3.3	5.5	4.5	-0.6
Business fixed investment	6.1	-2.1	-0.6	7.7	11.6	0.9
Equipment	7.1	-2.4	-0.2	10.0	14.1	0.2
Nonresidential construction	3.9	-1.5	-1.5	2.4	5.4	2.8
Residential construction	2.8	-4.7	28.4	17.0	-4.5	-25.6
Federal government	-5.9	-12.6	-5.7	-0.3	-6.3	-1.4
State and local governments	3.7	3.9	5.6	4.0	6.0	2.4

Figure 4.3
Real gross national product:
"Stable Fiscal Policies" simulation and history, 1969-73
(billions of 1958 dollars)

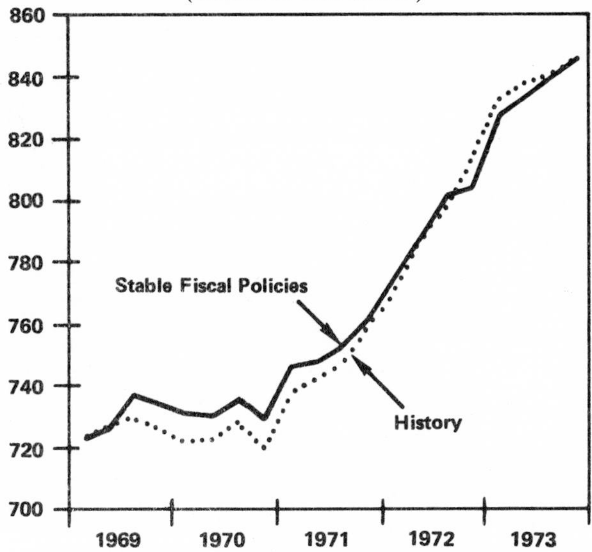

Figure 4.4
Civilian unemployment rate:
"Stable Fiscal Policies" simulation and history, 1969-73
(percent)

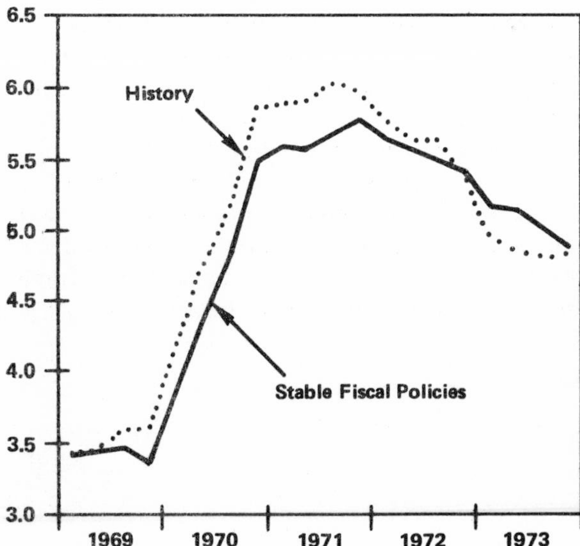

Figure 4.5
Inflation rate, implicit GNP deflator:
"Stable Fiscal Policies" simulation and history, 1969-73
(four-quarter percent change)

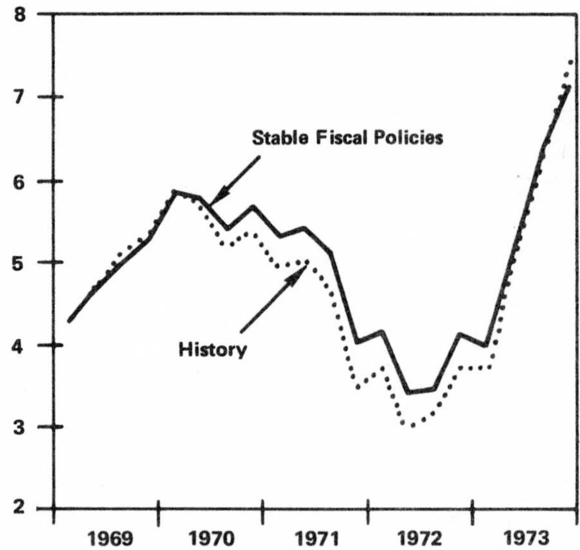

were related less to the overall budget magnitudes than to the more specific elements of the New Economic Policy, including the dollar devaluation and the temporary gains on the inflation front obtained through the price-wage controls. Improved inflation meant better consumer confidence, record retail sales and an overall growth rate of the real GNP of 7% over six quarters. Federal Reserve policy was also more important than overall fiscal policy in these years, with the restrictive stance of 1969 helping to create the 1970 recession, and the policy of low interest rates and high money supply growth of 1971-72 contributing to the investment boom. The evidence for the years 1969 to 1974 does confirm earlier results that a "stable framework" policy would have produced better results than the actual budget policies.

CHAPTER 4

TECHNICAL APPENDIX

The preceding policy simulation examines the effectiveness of the "balanced full-employment budget" as an economic stabilizer. The DRI Full-Employment Budget Model was used to compute a full-employment budget surplus on a National Income Accounts basis from simulation values for Federal revenues and expenditures. The model calculates the flows of revenues and expenditures which would prevail under given fiscal policy parameters if the economy were at full employment, defined here by the 4% unemployment guideline. The variable for Federal personal tax receipts *(TPGF)* in the DRI model was adjusted to bring the full-employment budget into balance. This was accomplished through an iterative procedure, alternatively solving the DRI model and the satellite Full-Employment Budget Model. The increments to actual personal tax receipts (in billions of dollars at annual rates) are as follows:

1969:3	1969:4	1970:1	1970:2	1970:3	1970:4
-$12.3	-13.0	-11.0	-5.8	-6.0	-9.1

1971:1	1971:2	1971:3	1971:4	1972:1	1972:2
-7.6	-2.2	-3.0	-1.5	-9.1	-0.4

1972:3	1972:4	1973:1	1973:2	1973:3	1973:4
-8.5	+15.5	+5.4	-0.2	-6.8	-8.5

1974:1	1974:2	1974:3	1974:4	1975:1
-15.9	-22.2	-20.7	-18.5	-16.6

The actual tax rebates and reductions implemented in the second quarter of 1975 were retained in the simulation. The 1975 tax reductions created full-employment budget deficits of -$41.3 billion in 1975:2, -$3.9 billion in 1975:3, and -$4.5 billion in 1975:4.

Nominal Federal government purchases of goods and services were exogenized at historical levels.

Monetary policy was assumed to accommodate the tax changes. Bank reserves against private deposits *(RPD's)* were adjusted continuously to leave the Federal funds rate within a narrow range of its historical values.

CHAPTER 5

PRICE CONTROLS AND THEIR AFTERMATH, 1971-74

1. Introduction

The rate of inflation in the summer of 1974 was accentuated by the termination of the price control program initiated in August 1971. From February to August of 1974, the wholesale industrial price index rose at a 35% annual rate. The unfortunate coincidence of an industrial price explosion with the Federal Reserve's all-out campaign to slow the growth of the money supply produced a financial crisis in the fall of 1974.

Several studies have analyzed the impact of the price controls program.[1] These studies generally find that controls had a helpful impact on inflation in the 1971-73 period, and the authors generally conclude that the impact on prices was greater than the impact on wages. Robert J. Gordon found that "Controls worked not by moderating the behavior of wages relative to prices, but rather by squeezing profit margins sufficiently to hold prices below their free market values."[2] He predicted that the end of controls would be followed by a period of catch-up in prices to reestablish profit margins.

John Dunlop, who served as Director of the Cost of Living Council from January 1973 through June 1974, offers the following appraisal of price controls:

> My general conclusion is that controls had significant price and wage effects in some particular industries, construction and medical care being noteworthy. The existence of controls in place also significantly restrained inflation when the international price surge developed from the embargo in the last quarter of 1973. The initiatives to change government agricultural policies in 1972 and

[1]John T. Dunlop, "Inflation and Incomes Policies: The Political Economy of Recent U.S. Experience," (1974), Eighth Monash Economics Lecture, Monash University, Clayton, Victoria, Australia, September 9; R.J. Gordon, "The Response of Wages and Prices to the First Two Years of Controls," *Brookings Papers on Economic Activity*, (1973), pp. 765-778; R. Lanzillotti, M. Hamilton and R.B. Roberts, *Phase II in Review: The Price Commission Experience*, (1975), The Brookings Institution, Washington, D.C.

[2]R.J. Gordon (1973), p. 777.

> 1973 to increase to crop output and imports were vital. . . . The impact more generally on wages and prices was of a small but perceptible order. For the longer run many of the most significant effects of controls are likely to be in the area of structural changes.[3]

The long-run benefits of wage stabilization policies, in Professor Dunlop's view, are the development of voluntary procedures for settling labor-management disputes and other reforms in collective bargaining which might reduce the economy's inflation bias.

In this study, the Data Resources econometric model is used to simulate a complete path for the economy, assuming that there were no price controls. This exercise is designed to identify the net impact of the program, both in its imposition and its end. Previous studies generally used individual equations for prices and wages, in some cases linking them in a small-scale wage-price model, to seek to identify the net effects. The use of a full macroeconometric model shows more repercussions and does not assume, for example, that the real path of development for the economy would have been unchanged or that monetary conditions would have been left the same. On the other hand, it must be recognized that even the 900-equation model does not capture the entire range of effects created by price controls. Even this study does not allow explicitly for the worsened shortages of materials caused by diversions of supplies into uncontrolled export channels. Nor does it allow explicitly for the deterioration in "vendor performance" in the industrial markets; this measure of delivery periods reached its worst point since the Korean War during the price control program, contributing to the inventory cycle.[4]

2. *The Four Phases*

The various phases of price controls spanned the period from August 15, 1971 to April 30, 1974. Phase I, a 90-day freeze on wages, prices and rents, was announced as part of the New Economic Policy. The President acted on authority granted by Congress, despite the Administration's objections, twelve months earlier.

The imposition of the wage-price freeze was perhaps the most surprising

[3]John T. Dunlop (1974), p. 10.

[4]The 1976 version of the Data Resources Quarterly Model has been used because it provides a more complete representation of the impact of controls on individual commodity prices. This later version of the model also incorporates a host of data revisions, including the national income and product accounts rebenchmarked from 1958 to 1972. Thus, the simulation results are not strictly comparable to other solutions reported here.

element of President Nixon's policy package. In his Economic Report to Congress in February 1971, President Nixon declared "Free prices and wages are the heart of our economic system; we should not stop them from working even to cure an inflation fever."[5] The Administration had steadily asserted a strong belief in free markets, and condemned the government intervention of even the mildest forms of incomes policy. However, the policy of "gradualism" had failed to reduce the inflation rate from the 5 to 6% range as the economy emerged from the 1970 recession. With wage settlements of the 1970-71 round exceeding 7%, a sense of discouragement developed over the long-run inflation prospects and the future of the economy. Dr. Arthur Burns, Chairman of the Federal Reserve Board and proponent of free markets, took the position that monetary policy would require major assistance from other branches of government in the battle against inflation, although he did not publicly advocate a controls system. The labor movement had neutralized its influence by endorsing controls provided they were applied equally to wages and prices. Finally, members of the Business Council, a prestigious group of corporate executives, are reported to have asked the President to impose controls, hoping to limit wage gains. Their action was an indication of the pessimism that existed among the leadership of American industry. But controls were destined to introduce new disruptive elements into business decision-making.

Phase I was timed to minimize the difficulties in the transition to controls. The industrial wage round of 1970-71 had just been completed with the signing of a three-year contract in the steel industry. The principal open situations were the collective bargaining agreements of teachers that would become effective with the opening of the school year in the fall. Initially, policy was tough in these cases, but eventually the teachers were granted most of the benefits originally negotiated.

During the freeze, prices and wages exhibited very slight increases. The wholesale price index, which had risen 17.7% in the previous twelve months, advanced at a 1.0% rate from August to November 1971. Consumer prices increased at a 2.0% rate during the same three-month period. The rise in wages slowed to 3.1% from 6.9% in the previous year.

With their success in moderating inflation, "controls proved initially surprisingly popular and acquired a life and constituency of their own. The Administration was to rediscover the truth that it is harder to get out of controls, one might add, gracefully, than to impose them."[6]

After three months, the freeze was followed by Phase II, which remained in

[5] *Economic Report of the President, February 1971*, p. 7.
[6] John T. Dunlop (1974), p. 5.

effect until January 1973, past the 1972 election. Under Phase II, the Cost of Living Council and its principal agencies, the Price Commission and the Pay Board, were created to design and administer regulations for prices, wages, rents, dividends, and profit margins. A staff of 800 was hired for the Cost of Living Council and an additional 3,000 Internal Revenue Service employees were assigned to enforce the stabilization program. The Federal Government's administrative costs of price controls totalled $125.1 million in fiscal 1972 and 1973.[7]

The objective of Phase II regulations was to reduce the inflation rate to the 2-3% range. Price increases were restricted to dollar-for-dollar pass-throughs of allowable costs, defined as unit labor costs, unit material costs, unit operating costs and unit overhead costs. However, a firm's price increases were restricted to the range in which its profit margin on sales would not exceed the average of the best two of three fiscal years prior to August 1971. Prenotification of price increases was required of companies with sales of $100 million. A special feature of controls was "term limit pricing," an option for multiproduct firms which simplified the procedure for approving price adjustments. Under term limit pricing agreements, firms were required to restrict weighted-average price increases to 2% of sales. In March 1972, this ceiling was lowered to 1.8% and a limit of 8% was placed on individual products covered within a term limit pricing agreement. This aspect of Phase II regulations has been criticized as being too generous.[8]

Under Phase II, the Pay Board set standards for wages and compensation. Wages and salaries were allowed to rise as much as 5.5% a year, while the upper limit for fringe benefits was 6.2%. Assuming a 3% trend rise in productivity, the Pay Board reasoned that a 5.5% rate of increase in wages would limit the rise in unit labor costs to 2.5%. This would be consistent with the Price Commission's 2-3% inflation target.

Phase II achieved limited success in reducing inflation. From November 1971 to December 1972 the rise in the consumer price index was held to 3.4%. Wholesale industrial prices increased at a 3.7% rate. There was a post-freeze bulge in wages in December of 1971. Wages rose 7.3% during 1972, a pace little different from the precontrols experience. Wholesale agricultural prices were exempt from Phase II regulations, and surged 18.8% over the twelve months ending in December of 1972.

Phase III of price controls was announced on January 11, 1973 and lasted only five months. The government continued to set standards for price changes, but compliance was quasi-voluntary. Phase III, intended to ease the

[7]R. Lanzillotti, M. Hamilton and R.B. Roberts (1975), p. 190.
[8]R. Lanzillotti, M. Hamilton and R.B. Roberts (1975), pp. 40-50.

transition back to free markets, was ineffective. Generally, regulations were vague enough to encompass whatever companies might do. By this juncture, capacity shortages were surfacing amidst the increasing worldwide demands for primary materials. Farm prices soared as poor weather caused a decline in world agricultural production. In the five months of Phase III, wholesale prices surged upward at an annual rate of 19.7%, while consumer price inflation accelerated to an 8.3% rate. The worsening inflation and movements in Congress toward a legislated wage-price freeze led President Nixon to impose a sixty-day price freeze on June 14, 1973, "against the unanimous advice of his economic advisers."[9] Wages and raw agricultural prices were exempted from the freeze. Phase IV brought a return to mandatory controls on August 12, 1973. Its regulations again limited price increases to dollar-for-dollar cost pass-throughs and required pre-notification by large firms.

As support for the controls program was fading, John T. Dunlop, the administrator, began a series of sector-by-sector negotiations designed to bring an orderly end to controls. In return for an early release from price controls, firms agreed to limit subsequent prices and, in some cases, to increase productive capacity, implement collective bargaining reforms and limit exports. The decontrol process began in October 1973 with the fertilizer industry. Subsequent agreements were negotiated with the cement, automobile, paper, furniture and rubber industries. On April 1, 1974, the decontrol of 165 sectors of the economy was announced. When the control authority expired, the commodities remaining under control accounted for only 12.1% of the CPI.[10]

Phase IV was badly affected by the Arab oil embargo and fuel price increases. The supply-demand imbalances created by price controls and worldwide economic expansion added to the pressure on prices. Indeed, inflation reached the double-digit range several months before the expiration of Phase IV on April 30, 1974.

The political support for controls also weakened. President Nixon sought extension of the legal authority in his January messages. But as the risk of his impeachment grew, he sought the support of the conservative wing of the U.S. Senate to retain office. His support for extension of price control authority was quietly withdrawn and it was allowed to die.

In summary, the price and wage controls were imposed quite rigidly, apparently with high effectiveness in the first few months of the program. They then went through a series of strategic retreats, with the entire program (except energy prices) expiring on April 30, 1974. The subsequent explosion

[9]John T. Dunlop (1974), p. 8.
[10]John T. Dunlop (1974), p. 9.

of industrial prices was one of the contributing elements to the double-digit inflation and the subsequent collapse.

3. Model Simulation: "No Price Controls, 1971-74"

This simulation retraces the history of the years 1971 to 1975 on the alternative hypothesis that the controls were never imposed. Price controls enter the Data Resources model in various equations. Typically, controls enter as a dummy variable for the period from the third or fourth quarter 1971 to the third quarter of 1974 with the following condition imposed as a constraint: the sum of the values of the dummy variable over the full period must be equal to zero (see figure 5.1). This implies that, in the long run, relative price-cost relationships are unaffected by the controls episode, although it may have taken several quarters after the end of controls before normal equilibrium was restored. A normal equilibrium does not mean that the absolute levels of wages or prices are constrained to be unchanged, nor that the arithmetic relationships between prices and costs or the average return on capital be the same. The equations will still modify these outcomes through differences in demand conditions, differences in utilization rates created by variations of investment, and by various other factors during the control years.

The absence or presence of statistically significant effects from controls is initially determined in the estimation process of the individual equations. Dummy variables are constructed after an analysis of single-equation error terms. Where prices were not significantly affected by the coming or going of

Figure 5.1
Price controls dummy variable

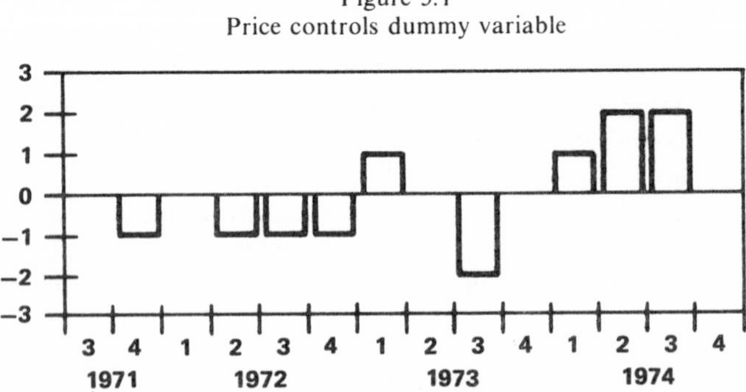

Variable = 0 in all other periods

controls, the dummy variables simply are not significant and do not appear. Thus, in all the equations in which a price control dummy is entered, the statistical record suggests that at least the timing of pricing was changed in an identifiable fashion. In addition, consumer confidence, wages and several categories of spending were affected, typically adversely. The equations for which the price control effects were found were the following:

Wholesale Prices
Processed foods
Textiles
Chemicals
Rubber and plastics
Paper, pulp
Metals
Machinery and equipment
Transportation equipment

Other Variables
Hourly earnings index
Consumer sentiment index

Implicit GNP Deflators
Motor vehicles and parts
Furniture
Other durable consumer goods
Food and beverages
Clothing
Gasoline and motor oil
Other consumer nondurables
Household operation
Other consumer services
Residential investment
Producers durable equipment investment

In the model simulation, "No Price Controls, 1971-74," the dummy variables representing wage and price controls were set equal to zero over the entire solution interval.

A comparison of the alternative solution with the historical simulation suggests that price controls achieved limited success in reducing inflation in 1972 and 1973; Phase I and Phase II proved to be the only effective segments of the stabilization program. In the solution without controls, the price level, measured by the implicit GNP deflator, is 1.2% higher by the end of 1972 (see figure 5.2). Wages are only 0.4% higher.

Price controls were also successful in reducing inflationary expectations, a major objective of stabilization policy. A survey by the University of Michigan Survey Research Center shows that between February 1971 and May 1972, the percentage of consumers expecting prices to rise by 5% or more in the coming year dropped from 41% to 30%. The favorable change in price expectations had a moderating influence on wage demands, as illustrated in figure 5.3.

The alternative solution shows that the maximum benefits of controls were achieved in the fourth quarter of 1973, when prices would have been 1.4% higher without price controls. By the second half of 1974 the benefits of controls are lost. In 1975 the price level is actually 0.8% worse in the solution because of price controls. Wages, which are strongly influenced by past inflation, are 0.9% higher in 1974 and 0.6% higher in 1975 in the "No Price Controls" simulation. The striking conclusion from this exercise is that the

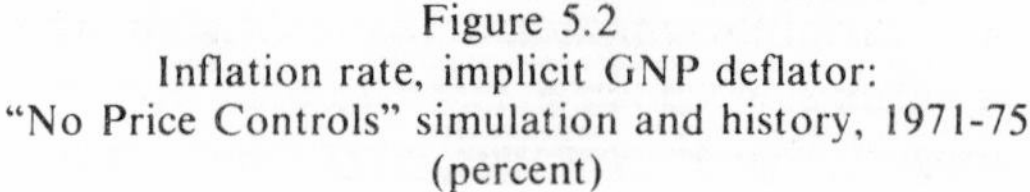

Figure 5.2
Inflation rate, implicit GNP deflator:
"No Price Controls" simulation and history, 1971-75
(percent)

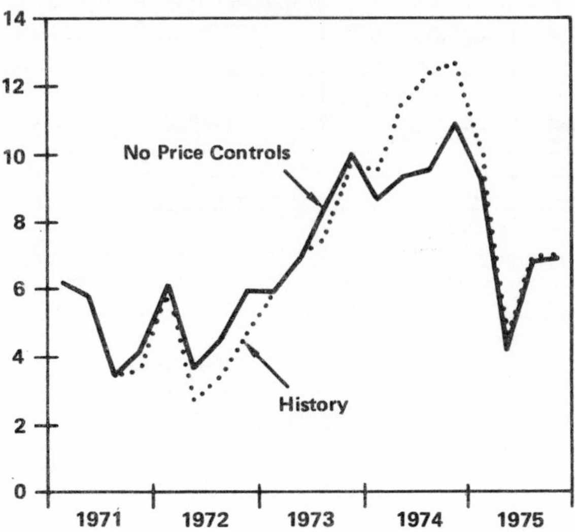

inflation experience would not have been substantially different in the absence of price controls.

Price controls had a greater impact on wholesale prices than on final prices (see figure 5.4). In the alternative without controls, the wholesale price index is 2.5% higher in 1972 and 3.4% higher in 1973. In 1973, wholesale prices for processed foods and feeds are 6.2% above actual levels. Chemical prices are 6.3% higher in 1973; metal prices are 5.8% higher. Other 1973 wholesale prices which are significantly higher in the alternative include rubber and plastics (+5.1%), paper and related products (+4.2%), and machinery (+4.6%).

Capacity utilization is lower in the alternative during this period, particularly in the raw materials industries. With market forces allowed to work, excess demands are less acute. This is illustrated in figure 5.5, which compares vendor performance in the alternative and historical solutions. Vendor performance is the proportion of companies reporting slower deliveries in any given month. Under price controls, vendor performance reached .92 in May 1973, the highest mark recorded since September 1950 during the Korean War. Without price controls, vendor performance would have peaked at .83 and delivery times would have been much shorter in late

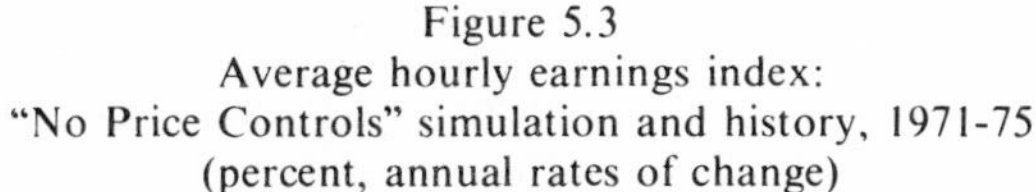

Figure 5.3
Average hourly earnings index:
"No Price Controls" simulation and history, 1971-75
(percent, annual rates of change)

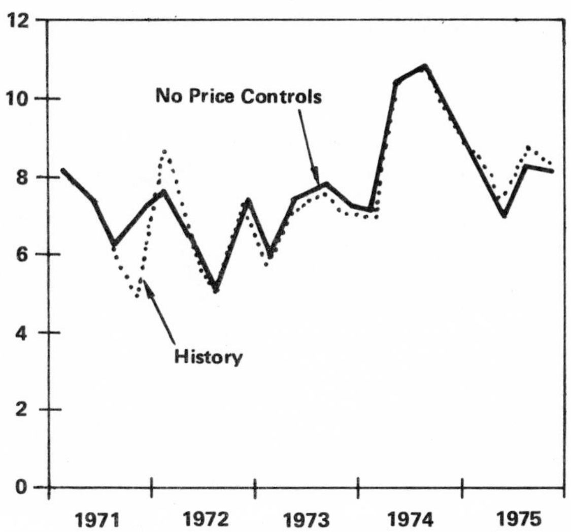

Source of historical data: Bureau of Labor Statistics, U.S. Department of Labor. Index adjusted for overtime and mix.

1973 and early 1974. Price controls were a major cause of the industrial bottlenecks of 1973 and 1974.

The real economy was not significantly altered by price controls. Without controls, higher prices would have lowered real demands from late 1971 through the first quarter of 1974. Spared the disruptive impact of decontrol, the economy would have been somewhat stronger in subsequent periods. In the solution "No Price Controls," real GNP is 0.8% above the historical path by the end of 1975, while the unemployment rate is 0.2 percentage points below the actual.

A comparison of the simulation without price controls and the baseline simulation is presented in table 5.1.

Figure 5.4
Wholesale price index:
"No Price Controls" simulation and history, 1971-75
(four-quarter percent change)

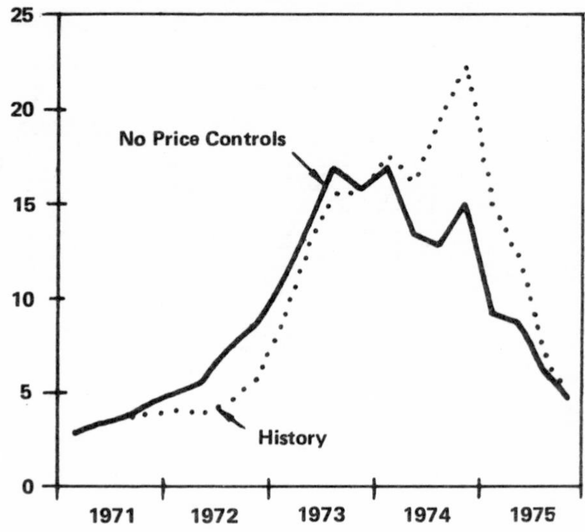

Table 5.1
The impact of price controls
(Percentage difference between levels in "No Price Controls" simulation and historical tracking simulation)

	1971	1972	1973	1974	1975
Prices					
Implicit GNP deflator	0.1	0.8	1.3	0.3	-0.8
Consumer price index	0.1	0.7	1.3	0.6	-0.4
Wholesale price index	0.2	2.5	3.4	-0.6	-2.9
Industrial commodities	0.2	2.5	3.4	-1.2	-3.8
Processed foods	0.4	4.0	6.2	1.7	-0.8
Wages—hourly earnings index	0.1	0.3	0.6	0.9	0.6
Real GNP (1972 dollars)	-0.1	-0.2	-0.3	0.1	0.5
Industrial production	-0.1	-0.4	-0.9	-0.1	0.6

Figure 5.5
Vendor performance:
"No Price Controls" simulation and history, 1971-75
(proportion of companies reporting slower deliveries)

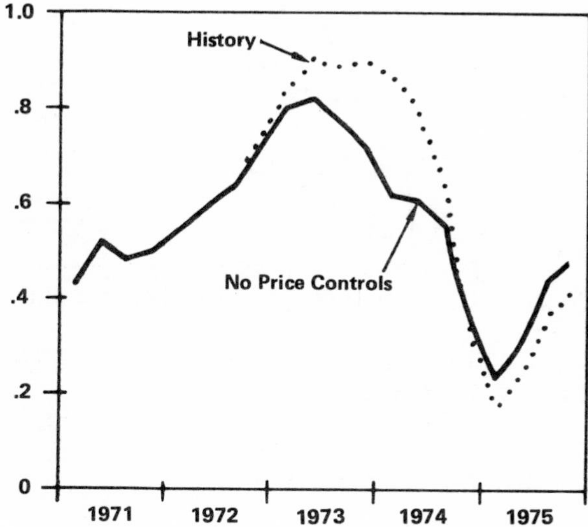

Source of historical data: "Business Conditions Digest," Bureau of Economic Analysis, U.S. Department of Commerce

CHAPTER 5

TECHNICAL APPENDIX

The simulation "No Price Controls" was developed under the assumption that there were no controls on prices, wages, dividends and rents over the period from August 15, 1971 to April 30, 1974. Thus, all dummy variables representing price controls were set equal to zero.

The following equation is representative of the equations for wholesale and final prices in the 1976 DRI model:

$$\begin{aligned} LN(P_i/P_{i,-1}) = {} & a_0 + a_1 LN(r/r_{-1}) + a_2 LN(w_i/w_{i-1}) \\ & + a_3 LN(c_i/c_{i\,-1}) + a_4(CU - CU_{-1}) \\ & + a_5(1-RDELYSLOW)^{-1} + a_6 LN(JQ/JQ_{-1}) \\ & + a_7 DMYCONTROLS \end{aligned}$$

where

LN indicates a variable's natural logarithm,

P_i = price index for commodity group i,

r = rental price of capital,

w_i = unit labor costs = AHE/JQ, where
- AHE = average hourly earnings index,
- JQ = eight-quarter moving average of output per manhour index for the private economy (productivity trend),

c_i = materials cost index, a weighted average of 12 wholesale price indexes and an indirect business tax index,

CU = capacity utilization, major materials industries, Federal Reserve Board,

$RDELYSLOW$ = proportion of companies reporting slower deliveries of materials (vendor performance),

$DMYCONTROLS$ = dummy variables for price controls from August 1971 through April 1974 (Phases I-IV) and the decontrol period. The sum of values for the variable was constrained to equal zero (see text).

The wholesale price indexes for raw agricultural commodities, fuels and power, and lumber were exogenized at their historical values.

CHAPTER 6

THE 1972-73 AGRICULTURAL PRICE EXPLOSION

1. Introduction

The explosion of food prices which began in the summer of 1972 (figure 6.1) was one of the most dramatic elements in the constellation of forces which created the great postwar economic crisis. For two decades prior to 1972, agricultural prices had been declining greatly relative to other commodity prices. Thus, the American people long enjoyed and took for granted a cheap and abundant food supply.

There were other periods in our history in which food supplies were strained in this century, during World War I, 1941-48, 1950-51, and the mid-1960's. In each of these episodes the prospect of a prolonged food scarcity became a global concern. Observers noted with alarm the growing world population, increasing life expectancies and the scarcity of cultivable land.

Crop failures on the Asian continent began to contribute to an acceleration in U.S. food prices during the mid-sixties. China became a major importer of wheat, as did the Soviet Union in the 1963-65 period following disappointing grain crops. India experienced crop failures in 1965 and 1966. In the United States, grain stocks were depleted to accommodate these crop shortfalls. Expansion of the armed services also raised domestic food demand. Consumer food prices rose 6.8% over the twelve months ending in March 1966. But the food "shortage" of the 1960's was short-lived and its impact on our domestic economy was mild in comparison to subsequent events. Worldwide grain production quickly resumed its upward trend, increasing 12% between 1965 and 1967 and permitting a rebuilding of grain stocks. Over the four years up to 1972, the rate of increase in U.S. consumer food prices averaged a moderate 4.3%.

The Russian wheat deal of 1972 has been widely blamed as the principal event that triggered the food price inflation. But the causes go deeper and can only be found in an analysis of the entire world food economy. The world has become dependent upon American agricultural exports. By 1973, the United States provided 44% of all wheat exports, 57% of all feed grain exports, 58%

Figure 6.1
Wholesale price index for farm products
and consumer price index for food, 1953-75
(1967 = 1)

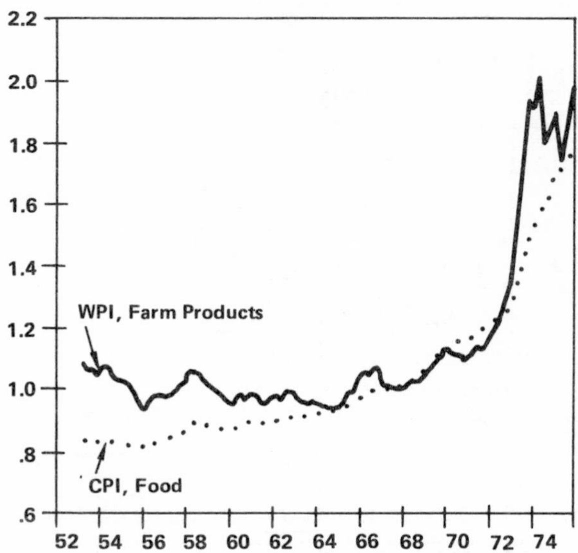

Source: Bureau of Labor Statistics, U.S. Department of Labor

of all oilseed exports such as soybeans, 27% of all cotton exports, and 27% of all rice exports. These are truly astonishing figures, particularly when one considers that only 3½% of the American labor force is employed in agriculture. The combination of our extraordinarily fertile land, the great progress in agricultural technology in the United States, the abundant use of capital and fertilizer, and the healthy working of the profit motive have made the United States the bread basket of the world.

Furthermore, this dependence on the United States is steadily increasing. Many of the less developed countries have chosen to industrialize rather than to develop their agriculture, thereby requiring increasing amounts of agricultural imports. The noncommunist developing countries imported 52 million tons of grain in 1974, in contrast to an average of only 30 million tons over the ten-year period ending in 1972. The low cost of subsidized American grains has made this growing reliance on U.S. exports economically feasible. During the 1960's, over half of U.S. wheat exports were under aid programs. Thus, to a degree, the incentives to devote resources to agricultural research, capital, and fertilizers and to thereby raise production were lacking. The socialist countries, particularly the Soviet Union, similarly are anxious for industrialization, and have squeezed their agriculture to produce a surplus made available to the urban industrial labor force. This was the basic policy of Stalin for twenty years. Although there has been some relaxation in Soviet policy, agriculture remains a neglected sector.

Following World War II, several of the developed countries resumed or initiated protectionist agricultural policies. West Germany and Great Britain supported wheat production at high cost, while Japan subsidized its rice production. The European Economic Community adopted its common agricultural policy to protect French and other farmers against world competition. But even the EEC is experiencing an increasing dependence on the U.S.

There have always been variations in the supply of agricultural commodities because of weather and other natural factors. Over the last 26 years, world food production has risen at an average of nearly 3% a year, according to the World Food and Agricultural Organization. Population has grown about 2% annually, leaving a small margin for an upgrading of eating standards. But year to year, the increase in food production ranges from nothing to over 6%. Usually, the existence of food stocks helps to stabilize prices despite the short-run inelasticity of the demand for food.

But in the period 1972 to 1974, a series of natural disasters affected world food supply. The Soviet Union suffered a massive disaster in grain production in 1972. Whereas in earlier periods, she might have chosen to curtail living standards of her people, in 1972 the Soviet Union decided to purchase massive quantities of grain to maintain her livestock production and continue the increasing provision of meat to her population. Although the same natural conditions also resulted in considerable purchases by the Chinese People's Republic, India and other nations, the purchase of American grain by the Soviet Union was, far and away, the greatest shock to the world trade of foodstuffs. During the 1972-73 crop year, net grain imports by the Soviet Union totalled 19.6 million metric tons, compared to 1.2 million the previous year. The 1972 sales were negotiated at a time when the U.S. was anticipating bumper crops that never materialized. Thus, the Soviet Union paid an average price of $1.62 a bushel for wheat, only half the market price for that year's harvest.

Subsequently, various other crop failures developed. In 1973 the anchovy harvest off the coast of Peru disappeared, apparently because of a shift in ocean currents. The meal of the anchovy is a source of protein used in fertilizer and animal feed. The significance of this loss has undoubtedly been exaggerated: the 1973 loss of production of Peruvian fish meal was equivalent to only 1.2% of world output of all oil meals. The soybean crop in the United States was badly damaged by excessively wet weather in the spring of 1974. In the same year, U.S. corn production fell by 18%, the result of a summer drought and early frosts in the Midwest. The 1973-74 surge in fertilizer prices also pushed up food prices. Depressed rates of return in that industry during the late 1960's discouraged investment in new fertilizer plants. When demand surged in 1973, tight supplies developed. The rise in world oil prices prolonged that rise of fertilizer costs.

These particular historical events have led to widespread fears that there has been a long-term change in world weather conditions, so that it may prove impossible to reconcile rising nutritional standards of a still rapidly growing world population with a slowly growing world food supply. Only time will settle this question. A recent study by S. A. Woods reaches a different conclusion.[1] Dr. Woods performed a series of spectral and cross-spectral analyses of world food production and world food prices. He found a strongly defined three-year cycle in world food supply. The supply cycle produces a price cycle of the same periodicity, and probably the two interact in the cobweb mechanism long reported by agricultural economists. High prices attract additional resources to food production: the number of acres planted increases; the amount of fertilizer that is applied expands; and farmers use their above-average farm income to increase the mechanization of production. As a result, agricultural output grows a year or two later, which then produces lower prices, cuts farm income and reduces the resources devoted to production. Recognition of this three-year cycle should alter the expectations of farmers enough to break it, but in fact this cycle has persisted throughout the postwar period.

Seen in this light, the most recent experience is not that different from what went before. For example, one cannot identify a statistically significant retardation in the growth trend of the world food supply. Nor can any kind of weather cycle be identified which has the three-year periodicity which spectral analysis reveals to be the fundamental agricultural cycle.

The Woods study does identify one factor which, more than any other, explains the extraordinary price response to the three-year production cycle of 1972-74. This is the absence of a stabilizing buffer stock. The response of price to supply is very much affected by the inventory situation of agricultural commodities. Because United States agricultural policy sought for two decades to unload burdensome stocks, we were pleased to get rid of these

[1]Samuel Adams Woods, "Food Cycles and Crises: A Spectral-Analytic Inquiry into the Nature of the World Food Problem," (April 1975), a dissertation presented to Harvard University.

surpluses without thinking through the implication on the world food economy.

The period 1972-73 was also a period of rapid consumer income growth in much of the world. Consequently, the upgrading of food standards with greater meat consumption was accelerated. The governments of the major grain-producing nations—Canada, the United States and Australia—promoted the export of grain for use as animal feed. But compared to the variations in agriculture supply and the impact of the lack of stocks, the world business cycle was probably a relatively minor factor in producing the food disaster. In the United States, for example, the income elasticity of the demand for food is 0.3%. If the world business cycle raised real income growth by 3% above normal, this would imply an increase in food demand of 0.9% beyond trend, a relatively small magnitude in relation to the 4% deviation of supply and the additional effects created by the lack of buffer stocks.

A factor which clearly exacerbated the food price inflation was the pricing policies of foreign governments. D. Gale Johnson has concluded that most of the price response to the worldwide grain shortage occurred in a small segment of the international grain market.

> ...governmental policies in many countries prevented the price system from rationing available supplies. In countries with a large fraction of the world's population, grain prices were not permitted to increase to reflect shortfalls of production and the depletion of grain reserves. Thus, the price-increasing factors were concentrated in the international grain markets, which had to absorb most of the production shortfalls and the expanding world demand... In other words, there was very little sharing of the small reduction in grain production.[2]

In conclusion, when nature reinforced the economic supply-price cycle in the 1972-74 period, government policies and the lack of buffer stocks interacted to produce the worst agricultural price explosion in half a century (figure 6.2).

2. The Impact of the Food Price Explosion on the Economy

By comparing the hypothetical path that the economy would have followed if wholesale agricultural prices had risen at just 3% a year after mid-1971 with a

[2]D. Gale Johnson, *World Food Problems and Prospects,* (1975), American Enterprise Institute for Public Policy Research, Washington, D.C., p. 23.

Figure 6.2
Wheat and coarse grain stocks as a percentage of total disappearance (crop-year basis), 1955-74

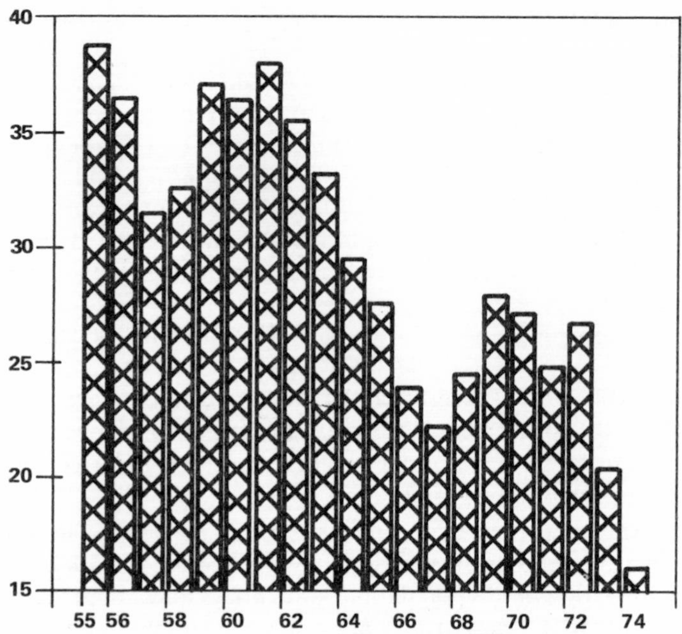

Source: Economic Research Service, U.S. Department of Agriculture

solution based on the actual food price movements, we can identify the differential impact of this particular "shock." Consumer food prices actually rose by 4.3% in 1972, and by 14.4% a year in 1973 and 1974. Thus, while consumers began to notice the upturn in food prices during 1972, the full extent of this phenomenon only became clear at the beginning of 1973. At that point, the surge in food prices became so great that it significantly reduced the growth in real disposable income. By the second quarter of 1973 the consumer spending boom was over. The real gain in consumption slowed from a 7.8% rate in the preceding four quarters to a 0.9% rate during the next two quarters. With housing activity beginning to fade as a result of tighter money and fiscal policies, the whole economy switched from a 7% to a 2% growth path. By the end of 1973, the energy embargo created another massive setback to consumer confidence and the recession was seriously underway.

Figures 6.3-6.5 and table 6.1 show what would have happened to the economy if the food price disaster had not occurred. The rate of inflation would still have been unacceptably high, and consumer prices, which actually

Table 6.1
Solution Summary, "Lower Food Prices"

	Quarters								Years			
	73:1	73:2	73:3	73:4	74:1	74:2	74:3	74:4	1972	1973	1974	1975
GNP and its components—billions of dollars												
Gross national product	1248.1	1279.2	1310.1	1345.2	1362.9	1392.7	1426.0	1434.9	1158.6	1295.6	1404.1	1467.5
Real GNP (1958 dollars)	835.3	843.4	850.5	860.5	850.3	849.8	846.8	826.5	793.3	847.4	843.4	809.9
Inventory investment	10.7	11.8	13.6	31.3	20.0	17.0	12.6	21.4	9.0	16.8	17.8	-13.2
Net exports	-3.9	-4.4	1.0	1.3	3.3	-10.6	-12.7	-9.7	-7.3	-1.5	-7.4	1.1
Prices and wages—annual rates of change												
Implicit price deflator	4.5	6.2	6.4	6.0	10.5	9.3	11.5	13.0	3.4	4.7	8.9	8.8
Consumer price index	4.8	6.2	5.7	6.3	9.3	10.2	13.1	11.6	3.2	4.6	8.9	9.4
Wholesale price index	8.1	9.9	4.2	10.3	23.0	29.0	27.9	13.8	3.4	6.3	18.5	10.2
Average hourly earnings index	5.5	7.0	7.3	6.7	6.4	9.6	10.0	8.7	6.5	6.4	7.8	8.0
Key economic measures												
Unemployment Rate (percent)	4.9	4.8	4.6	4.4	4.6	4.4	4.6	5.6	5.5	4.7	4.8	7.8
Industrial production (67=1)	1.249	1.281	1.314	1.330	1.321	1.332	1.335	1.289	1.158	1.294	1.319	1.177
Annual rate of change	13.0	10.5	10.9	5.0	-2.9	3.4	1.2	-13.2	8.1	11.8	2.0	-10.8
Housing starts (millions)	2.48	2.30	2.19	1.82	1.80	1.73	1.37	1.06	2.37	2.20	1.49	1.16
Unit car sales (millions)	12.6	12.4	12.1	10.4	9.8	10.0	10.9	7.7	10.9	11.9	9.6	8.8
Federal budget surplus (NIA)	-12.4	-8.3	-3.3	0.1	0.4	5.4	1.3	-24.0	-17.4	-6.0	-4.2	-72.1
Money and interest rates												
Money supply (M1)	257.9	262.9	266.2	269.0	272.7	278.4	280.0	281.6	245.8	264.0	278.2	287.9
Annual rate of change	6.6	8.0	5.1	4.3	5.7	8.5	2.4	2.4	6.4	7.4	5.4	3.5
New high-grade corp. bond rate (percent)	7.32	7.37	7.85	7.52	7.86	8.53	9.47	8.76	7.18	7.52	8.66	8.93
Federal funds rate (percent)	5.88	6.70	9.13	8.53	8.38	9.85	12.16	9.10	4.31	7.56	9.85	5.49
Prime rate (percent)	5.64	6.24	8.10	8.74	8.34	9.81	11.69	10.78	5.19	7.18	10.15	7.65
Incomes—billions of dollars												
Personal income	1013.1	1039.1	1066.8	1097.4	1111.1	1136.5	1169.5	1185.8	946.4	1054.1	1150.7	1231.9
Real disposable income	616.4	621.4	626.6	630.4	621.1	618.5	619.1	610.8	581.8	623.7	617.4	622.8
Annual rate of change	10.5	3.3	3.4	2.4	-5.7	-1.7	0.4	-5.3	4.5	7.2	-1.0	0.9
Saving rate (percent)	7.5	7.8	8.0	9.5	9.0	7.7	7.0	9.1	6.6	8.2	8.2	9.2
Profits after tax (percent change)	28.8	28.5	21.2	20.7	20.6	25.0	32.0	-4.0	23.2	24.7	18.0	-14.5
Details of real GNP—annual rates of change												
Gross national product	10.4	4.0	3.4	4.8	-4.7	-0.2	-1.4	-9.2	6.1	6.8	-0.5	-4.0
Total consumption	8.4	1.7	2.4	-5.0	-2.9	4.2	3.6	-13.5	6.2	5.2	-1.0	-0.1
Business fixed investment	24.7	10.3	4.5	4.9	5.6	4.5	-4.5	-18.2	8.9	12.9	2.4	-12.0
Equipment	28.6	11.5	3.0	4.3	2.3	5.5	-1.5	-27.2	11.8	15.5	1.3	-14.2
Nonresidential construction	14.6	6.8	8.7	6.4	14.9	1.7	-12.0	10.5	2.4	6.4	5.6	-6.5
Residential construction	7.8	-3.4	-14.5	-19.4	-33.2	-6.9	-28.3	-48.0	18.7	-0.3	-22.5	-27.7
Federal government	-1.7	-8.1	-10.0	1.5	-0.8	-0.1	1.5	3.9	0.1	-6.0	-1.4	3.5
State and local governments	6.9	10.0	5.5	8.2	2.2	4.6	-0.2	-0.5	4.5	6.9	4.1	1.5

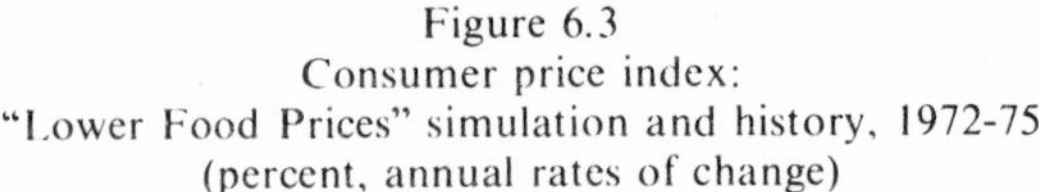

Figure 6.3
Consumer price index:
"Lower Food Prices" simulation and history, 1972-75
(percent, annual rates of change)

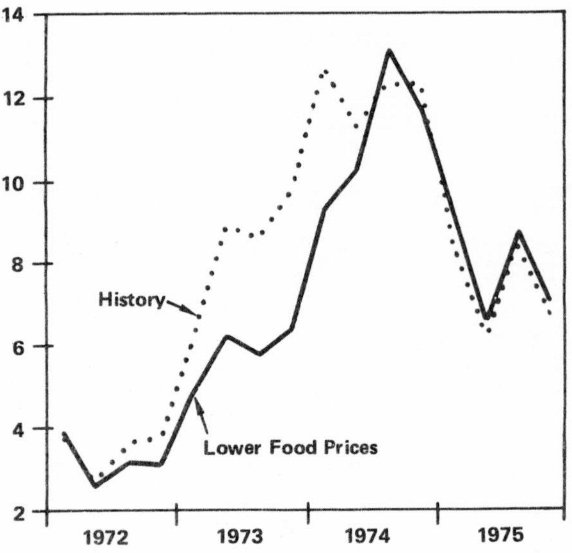

rose at a 10.2% rate from the beginning of 1973 to the end of 1974, would have risen at a 8.3% pace instead. During 1974, when energy inflation and the termination of wage and price controls were important factors, the rate of consumer price inflation would have been 9.4%, instead of the 11.1% rate that was actually experienced.

In terms of real activity, the more volatile elements of consumer durable and nondurable spending would have done significantly better if food prices had not cut purchasing power and created uncertainty. For example, an additional 700,000 automobiles would have been purchased in 1974. Unemployment by the end of 1974 would have been 5.6% instead of the actual 6.6%. By the spring quarter of 1975, unemployment would have peaked at 8.1% instead of an actual value of 8.9%.

Against these negatives has to be weighed the benefit that was obtained from the large volume and high prices of agricultural exports. The surplus of exports over imports, in nominal terms, would have averaged about $7 billion less on the average in 1973 and 1974. The additional exports of agricultural commodities created purchasing power in the hands of American farmers. Thus, the United States showed a very substantial benefit from the food price explosion along with the damage that she suffered.

Figure 6.4
Real consumer spending:
"Lower Food Prices" simulation and history, 1973-75
(billions of 1958 dollars)

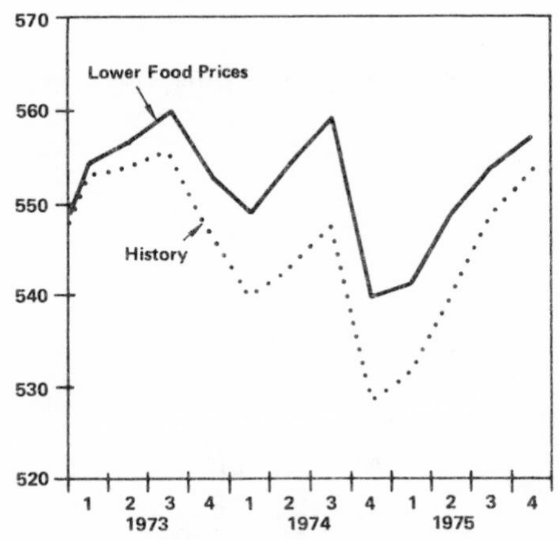

Figure 6.5
Unemployment rate:
"Lower Food Prices" simulation and history, 1972-75
(percent)

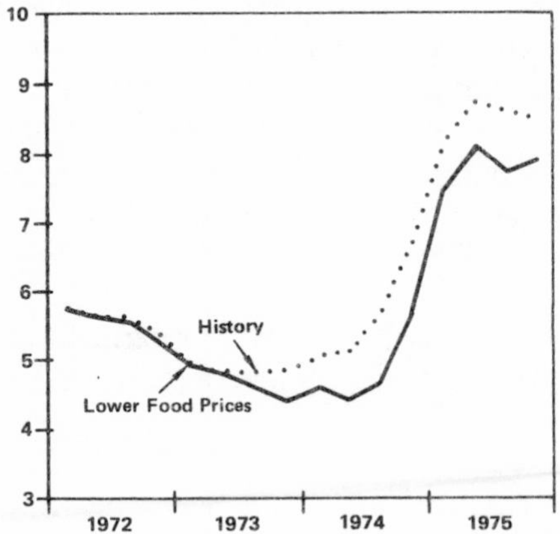

CHAPTER 6

TECHNICAL APPENDIX

Food prices are represented in the DRI model through a stage-of-processing submodel.[3]

Under this approach,

$$(1) \quad p_{ri} = a_{0i} + a_{1i}p_{wi} + a_{2i}l_{ri} + a_{3i}c_{ri} + a_{4i}d_{ri}$$

where

p_{ri} = consumer retail price of product *i,*

p_{wi} = wholesale price of product *i,*

l_{ri} = unit labor cost of *i* at the retail stage,

c_{ri} = other unit costs at the retail stage, including freight, capital and taxes,

d_{ri} = demand pressure variable for *i* at the retail stage.

The wholesale price of the finished product, in turn, is dependent upon the price of semifinished goods, the cost elements at the wholesale stage, and a demand variable representing excess demand. The semifinished product price, in turn, is related, by similar structure, to raw materials prices.

More generally, the price at stage *j* depends on the costs at that stage of processing and demand in its market. The DRI model contains stage-of-processing equations for nine categories of end products, and four stages of processing—raw, semifinished, finished wholesale, and retail. The GNP deflators are calculated from the consumer and finished wholesale prices according to the same general pattern used in the construction of the official deflator statistics.

For purposes of the present exercise, raw agricultural prices are treated as exogenous, although the model contains a behavioral equation linking them

[3]Joel Popkin and Paul H. Earl, "Relationship Between the Behavior of Consumer and Wholesale Prices," (August 1971), Proceedings of the Business and Economics Statistics Section, American Statistical Association, pp. 40-45.

to grain stocks, foreign and domestic demand, and the exchange rate. The assumed agricultural prices are then fed through the stage-of-processing model to calculate retail food prices and the GNP deflators, which, in turn, have an impact on the entire model.

The "Lower Food Prices" simulation was created by imposing the following modifications on the baseline simulation containing the null errors of each stochastic equation:

(1) The wholesale price index for farm products *(WPI01)* is assumed to rise at a 3% annual rate from the first quarter of 1972 through the end of 1975.

(2) Exports of crude foods in 1967 dollars, an exogenous variable, is assumed to increase at a 4.5% annual rate over the 1972-75 solution interval.

(3) The endogenous variable representing exports of manufactured food products in 1967 dollars is constrained to a 3.7% growth path from 1972 to 1975.

(4) Constant-dollar Federal government purchases of goods and services are exogenized at historical levels.

The time pattern of increases in the wholesale price index for processed foods and feeds *(WPI02)* was altered through negative additive factors in the final two quarters of 1974 and positive additive factors in 1975. The adjustments to the first-difference equation for *WPI02* are as follows:

	1974:3	1974:4	1975:1	1975:2	1975:3	1975:4
+*WPI02*	-.04	-.04	.01	.04	.01	.02

This results in a smoother pattern of food price movements. *WPI02* rises 11.0% in 1974 and 7.6% in 1975 in the simulation.

A negative add factor was applied to the equation for corporate profits before tax, including inventory valuation adjustment, over the period 1973 to 1975. This alters the distribution of national income between profits and personal income.

CHAPTER 7

MONETARY POLICIES

1. Introduction

The monetary factor has become increasingly powerful in postwar business cycles. Worsening inflation has induced ever-higher peaks of interest rates. The gradual deterioration of the liquidity position of American business has made it increasingly vulnerable to variations in the cost and availability of external capital. The consumer has been affected by the worsening performance of the stock market. And the housing industry has been the victim of distortions of savings flows through disintermediation in every postwar credit crunch; after 20 years of bad experiences, it has yet to find a solution to this problem.

The swings in credit conditions, from credit crunch to ease and back over the business cycle, are the result of two conflicting sets of forces. On the one hand, the business cycle creates wide variations in the demand for credit. The need for external financing by business approaches its peak near the end of the boom, when labor costs are increasing most rapidly, investment commitments are at their peak, and product sales begin to slacken. On the other hand, monetary policy, which regulates the overall availability of credit, changes its course relatively late in the cycle, tightening up the supply of credit at the very instant when the demand is also at its peak. Conversely, when the cycle is near its trough and private credit demand is weakest, the Federal Reserve has sought to produce an increase in the money supply and in the use of credit. Because there are time lags in the effects of monetary policy ranging from 6 to 18 months, the peak stimulus tends to occur long after the business cycle has entered its recovery phase. Thus, monetary policy has on occasion reinforced the excesses of boom and deepened the troughs of recession (figure 7.1).

This perverse pattern was exemplified in the 1971-73 expansion. It was the strongest upswing in the world economy of the postwar period and its excesses helped produce the recession. During the 1970 recession, monetary policy moved to extreme accommodation. Short-term interest rates dropped

Figure 7.1
New high-grade corporate bond rate[1]
and 3-month Treasury bill rate, 1960-75
(percent)

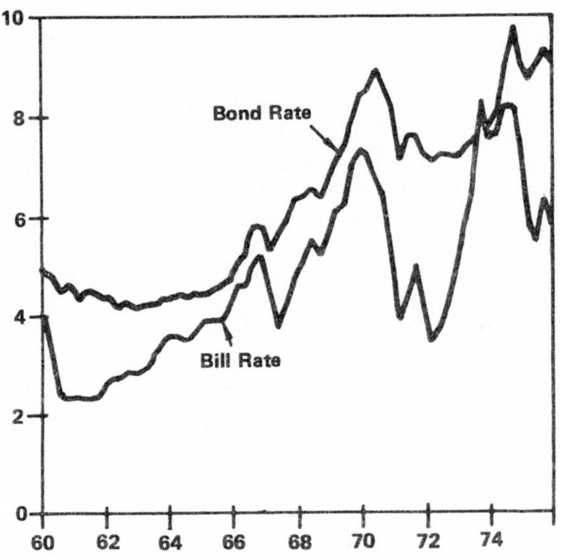

[1]Adjusted to AAA basis
Sources: Bond rate—First National City Bank of New York and, beginning in April 1972, estimates by Data Resources, Inc. Treasury bill rate—Board of Governors of the Federal Reserve System

below 4% in the first quarter of 1971 and again in early 1972. The Treasury bill rate briefly neared 3% in 1972. The maximum impact of low interest rates on the economy was felt from the spring of 1972 to early 1973, the period when real GNP surged by 8.0% over four quarters.

The 1971-73 period was also characterized by exceptionally high personal savings, as illustrated in figure 7.2. The savings rate averaged 7.6% in those years. The expansionary monetary policy in conjunction with a high personal savings rate produced an excessive flow of long-term capital. This placed financial institutions under great pressure to make long-term loans, resulting in the proliferation of real estate investment trusts, shopping centers, office buildings, and debt-financed public investments. Many of these ventures later proved to be a mistake and produced the biggest collection of bankruptcies since the early 1930's.

This experience has led to an increased desire to apply monetary policy in

Figure 7.2
Personal savings as a
percentage of disposable income, 1954-75

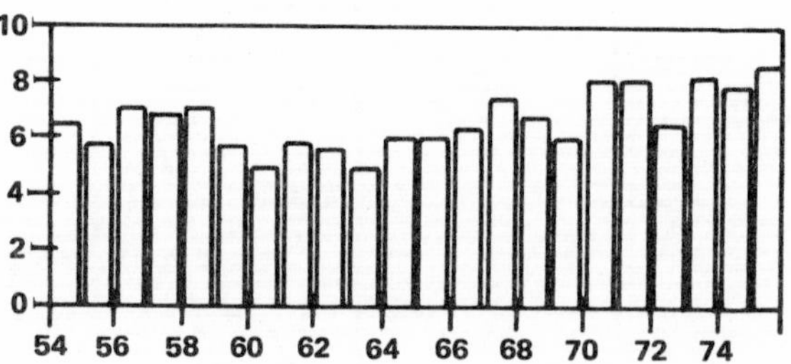

Source: Bureau of Economic Analysis, U.S. Department of Commerce

moderation, to ask it to do less in recession, and to prevent it from creating financial panics at the top of the boom. Monetarists recommend the adoption of a mechanical rule which would limit Federal Reserve policy to a steady and unvarying growth of the money supply, without the attempt at countercyclical variation. The growth of monetarism is related as much to the observation of ill-timed discretionary policies as to disagreements about economic theory.

Considerable research has been done to assess the effectiveness of alternative approaches to monetary policy. In the present context, only one particular issue is examined through model simulations: suppose that the economy did suffer from all the historical shocks of the Vietnam War, the worldwide business cycle, the food crisis, the energy crisis, the industrial capacity imbalances and price controls; but suppose that monetary policy had not attempted to respond to these events with discretionary moves, and instead had adopted a policy "rule" in 1964. A policy of steady money supply expansion has long been advocated by Professor Friedman and the monetarist school. In this study, two alternative approaches to monetary policy are tested: (1) a policy of steady expansion of nonborrowed bank reserves, and (2) a stable interest rate policy. Model simulations are used to determine how the economy would have developed over the period from 1964 to 1975 under a monetary policy rule. Would it have been more or less cyclical? And how would the situation be different today?

2. *Simulation: Smooth Growth of Bank Reserves*

To achieve a realistic outcome, one cannot assume that the Federal Reserve adhered to a single figure for its monetary rule over the entire period. The growth of potential GNP accelerated because of the entry of the postwar population group into the labor force. The Vietnam War and the food and energy crises were certain to produce some short-term increase in prices. If the Federal Reserve had made no adjustment whatsoever for any of these changes, it would have produced a condition of credit stringency so severe that a major economic crisis would have been produced several years earlier. Thus, the rule that was entered for this model solution was as follows: through its open market operations, the Federal Reserve was assumed to raise nonborrowed bank reserves at 4% in 1964, accelerating by a quarter of a percent each year until a 6% rate was reached in 1972. Thereafter, this 6% rate is retained. These rates of increases of bank reserves would have produced about the same total increase as actual policies, though in a smooth pattern. The values for reserve requirement ratios and the proportions of time and demand deposits subject to reserve requirements were assumed to follow long-range trends. Short-run fluctuations in these parameters were removed.

The results of this simulation show a more stable growth pattern over the past decade, but the overall results for economic performance are not dramatically different. In the alternative, the expansion of the Vietnam era is restrained, and the timing of business cycles is altered. But the other shocks to the economy were so drastic that there would have been dramatic changes in financial conditions even under a policy of steady bank reserve expansion.

The results for the economy in the four years 1964 to 1967 are little different from history under the alternative policy. The growth recession of 1966-67 still occurs, caused by an excessive inventory buildup as a by-product of the Vietnam War and the end of the capital goods boom (see table 7.1).

Differences between the two solutions emerge in 1968, although they are small. Financial conditions are somewhat more stable, with the short-term rates rising continuously until 1969. As figure 7.3 shows, the Federal funds rate, the most sensitive short-term interest rate reflecting Federal Reserve policy, has a very different pattern of variation from 1969 to 1973. Monetary policy is more accommodating in 1969 and 1970, a period when the Federal Reserve was exercising restraint aimed at disinflating the economy. The extreme, and erroneous, monetary accommodation of 1971 and early 1972, represented in declining short-term interest rates, is absent.

The performance of the macroeconomy, with nonborrowed reserves as the instrument of monetary control, is depicted in figures 7.4-7.7. The experiment reveals that it was the monetary factor which pushed the economy into recession in 1970. In the alternative, real GNP grows 2.3% in 1970, and over the year averages 2.5% above its historical path. The housing industry is spared from its 1969-70 contraction. Business fixed investment makes some

Table 7.1
Solution Summary, "Smooth Growth of Bank Reserves"

	Years											
	1964	1965	1966	1967	1968	1969	1970	1971	1972	1973	1974	1975
GNP and its components—billions of dollars												
Gross national product	631.9	681.4	748.4	796.0	854.8	924.3	996.7	1057.5	1120.9	1263.3	1421.5	1521.8
Real GNP (1958 dollars)	580.5	614.8	657.9	678.5	700.1	724.1	740.5	747.4	764.6	822.9	845.8	828.7
Inventory investment	5.8	9.1	14.5	9.3	6.1	7.1	8.0	6.8	5.2	11.1	18.6	-6.7
Net exports	8.4	7.2	5.4	4.7	3.0	2.5	1.4	-1.1	-1.6	8.6	-1.2	4.3
Prices and wages—annual rates of change												
Implicit price deflator	1.6	1.8	2.6	3.1	4.1	4.5	5.4	5.1	3.6	4.7	9.5	9.2
Consumer price index	1.3	1.6	2.9	2.7	4.3	5.2	5.8	4.7	3.5	5.6	10.5	9.6
Wholesale price index	0.4	1.7	3.1	0.4	2.2	3.5	4.2	3.4	4.0	12.5	19.0	10.0
Average hourly earnings index	2.7	3.7	3.9	4.9	6.2	6.3	6.7	7.4	6.6	6.1	7.8	8.7
Key economic measures												
Unemployment Rate (percent)	5.2	4.6	3.9	3.7	3.7	3.7	4.4	5.6	6.5	5.8	5.0	7.1
Industrial production (67=1)	0.814	0.880	0.974	1.011	1.035	1.096	1.126	1.074	1.068	1.196	1.314	1.221
Annual rate of change	6.6	8.1	10.7	3.8	2.4	6.0	2.7	-4.6	-0.5	12.0	9.9	-7.1
Housing starts (millions)	1.52	1.44	1.25	1.28	1.37	1.61	1.72	1.62	1.84	2.32	1.93	1.37
Unit car sales (millions)	8.5	9.5	8.9	8.4	9.2	9.7	9.2	9.9	9.3	11.3	10.5	10.0
Federal budget surplus (NIA)	-3.3	0.0	-0.3	-11.1	-9.6	7.5	-3.3	-21.8	-30.3	-13.5	3.7	-56.4
Money and interest rates												
Money supply (M1)	160.0	166.4	174.8	181.4	192.7	205.7	218.2	229.8	239.1	259.6	281.7	296.7
Annual rate of change	3.9	4.0	5.0	3.8	6.2	6.8	6.1	5.3	4.1	8.6	8.5	5.3
New high-grade corp. bond rate (percent)	4.44	4.59	5.42	5.86	6.82	7.50	8.22	7.77	7.54	7.22	8.65	9.26
Federal funds rate (percent)	3.70	4.14	4.25	4.96	5.99	6.56	6.78	7.09	6.35	7.17	8.48	5.33
Prime rate (percent)	4.60	4.63	5.12	5.86	6.58	7.17	7.27	7.44	6.92	7.05	9.10	7.33
Incomes—billions of dollars												
Personal income	497.4	537.5	585.1	629.1	684.8	745.9	815.3	870.3	932.5	1036.9	1154.0	1260.1
Real disposable income	407.9	433.6	457.6	478.1	496.2	511.4	541.6	559.1	570.7	610.6	610.2	623.3
Annual rate of change	7.0	6.3	5.5	4.5	3.8	3.1	5.9	3.2	2.1	7.0	-0.1	2.2
Saving rate (percent)	6.0	6.1	6.2	7.3	6.8	5.8	7.7	8.5	7.4	8.2	6.9	8.0
Profits after tax (percent change)	15.8	18.3	10.3	-5.0	-4.3	-1.8	0.2	0.1	5.3	44.6	39.4	-8.4
Details of real GNP—annual rates of change												
Gross national product	5.3	5.9	7.0	3.1	3.2	3.4	2.3	0.9	2.3	7.6	2.8	-2.0
Total consumption	5.7	6.0	5.4	3.3	4.3	4.1	3.8	2.5	3.2	5.9	1.4	1.2
Business fixed investment	11.3	14.0	11.7	0.3	1.6	4.9	2.2	-1.4	-1.9	13.0	10.1	-8.4
Equipment	13.7	12.9	13.7	2.8	1.2	5.5	2.6	-0.6	-1.2	16.0	11.0	-10.4
Nonresidential construction	6.7	16.3	7.6	-5.1	2.5	3.5	1.4	-3.3	-3.6	5.7	7.5	-3.0
Residential construction	-2.9	-2.9	-6.2	-2.9	0.4	12.9	10.4	-2.4	4.2	19.7	-6.3	-24.1
Federal government	-2.5	-0.3	13.1	14.1	4.6	-5.9	-12.4	-5.3	0.1	-6.0	-1.4	3.5
State and local governments	6.0	6.7	8.6	6.4	5.1	5.1	4.7	4.7	2.2	5.6	5.9	3.3

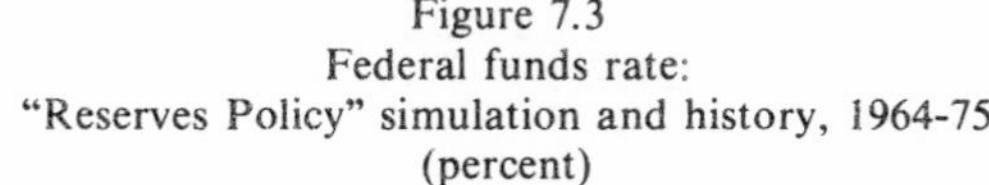

Figure 7.3
Federal funds rate:
"Reserves Policy" simulation and history, 1964-75
(percent)

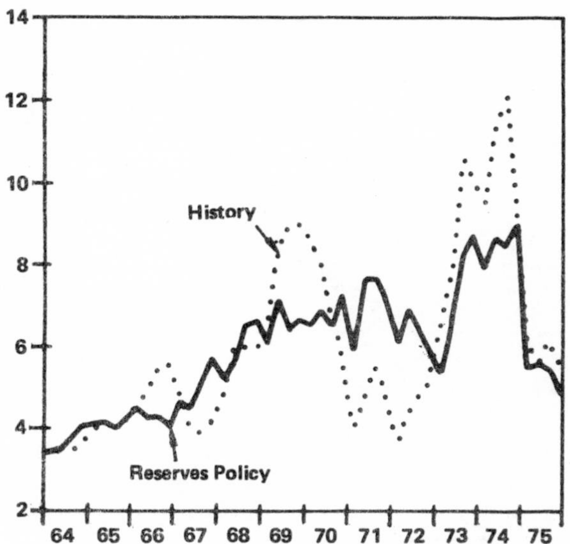

additional real gains in 1970 before levelling off. Thus, real capital formation exceeds the actual result by 4.1% in 1970 and 3.2% in 1971 in the alternative. The inflationary impact is negligible in 1970, but in 1971 the price level rises by an additional 0.6 percentage point.

In 1972, actual monetary policy shifted to a posture of extreme accommodation intended to stimulate production. The imposition of wage-price controls in August 1971 had removed the burden of controlling inflation from the Federal Reserve. The economy entered a vigorous expansion, and money (M1) growth averaged 8% during the four quarters of 1972, exceeding the targeted 6% rate.

In contrast, the alternative simulation depicts a much slower economic recovery in 1972. The maintenance of smooth growth in bank reserves leaves real GNP 3.5% below the baseline path in 1972 and the unemployment rate averages 6.5% in 1972 instead of 5.6%. But because the volume of real activity, including capital formation by businesses and households, is restrained in 1972, the economy enters a real boom in 1973, with unemployment lowered to 5.3% by the end of that year. Subsequently, the full impact of the food price increases and the energy crisis produces a severe recession. The assumed 6%

Figure 7.4
Real gross national product:
"Reserves Policy" simulation and history, 1964-75
(billions of 1958 dollars)

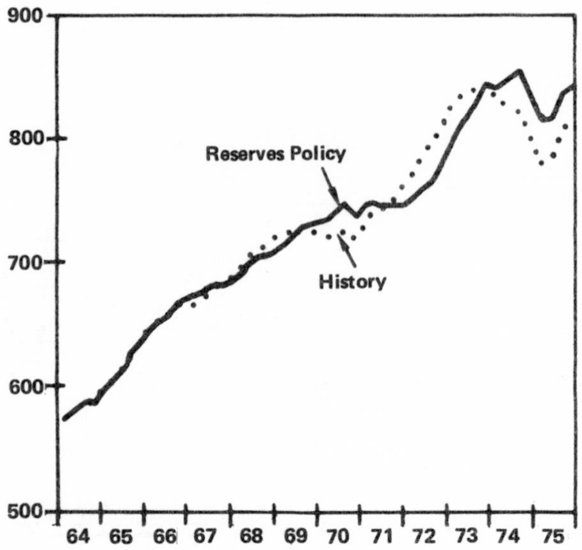

reserve growth policy is inadequate to accommodate the tremendous inflation of that period. With the Federal funds rate reaching 9% in 1974, severe damage to homebuilding, business liquidity and capital formation would have resulted eventually. By the second quarter of 1975, unemployment reaches 7.4% instead of 8.9%. Although the difference is appreciable, the economy would have been operating well below its potential.

The amount of inflation that would have occurred in these years is little different under the smooth reserve policy. Changes in the cyclical pattern of demand in product and labor markets would have had some small impact on the timing of inflation. The more stable pattern of economic growth yields some benefits, and thus the 1974 price level is 1.3% lower in the alternative simulation. But since so much of the inflation was due to the shocks of food and energy and the cumulative problems created by industrial capacity imbalances, the economy would have experienced three quarters of double-digit inflation in 1974 and the subsequent price situation would be little changed.

These findings are among the most surprising of this study. The simulation implies that the credit crunches are due more to variations in the economy

Figure 7.5
Real business fixed investment:
"Reserves Policy" simulation and history, 1964-75
(billions of 1958 dollars)

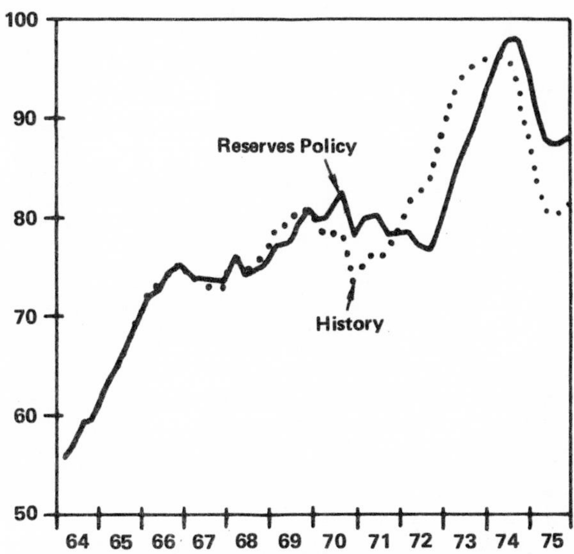

than to variations in monetary policy. Credit conditions are at least as much the product of shock and cycle-induced fluctuations in credit demands as of variations of Federal Reserve policy. Thus, even if the Federal Reserve could be forced to adopt a monetarist rule of steady aggregate expansion, the economy would still be highly unstable given the other sources of disturbance. To illustrate, the explosive 10.3% inflation of 1974 would have produced a severe credit crunch even if the money supply had grown by 5 or 6%, simply because the gap between the two magnitudes is so enormous.

A related observation is that the Federal Reserve cannot achieve a steady rate of growth in the money supply by adherence to a policy of smooth growth in nonborrowed bank reserves. As figure 7.8 illustrates, variations in money (M1) growth are as extreme in the alternative case as in history, although the time profile has shifted. Control over the money supply is indirect and uncertain, with portfolio decisions by banks and the public causing slippages in the link between reserves and money. The demand for money is influenced by a variety of factors beyond the control of monetary authorities. It is implausible to expect the Federal Reserve to precisely anticipate the level of bank reserves which will produce the targeted rate of growth in the money

Figure 7.6
Unemployment rate:
"Reserves Policy" simulation and history, 1964-75
(percent of civilian labor force)

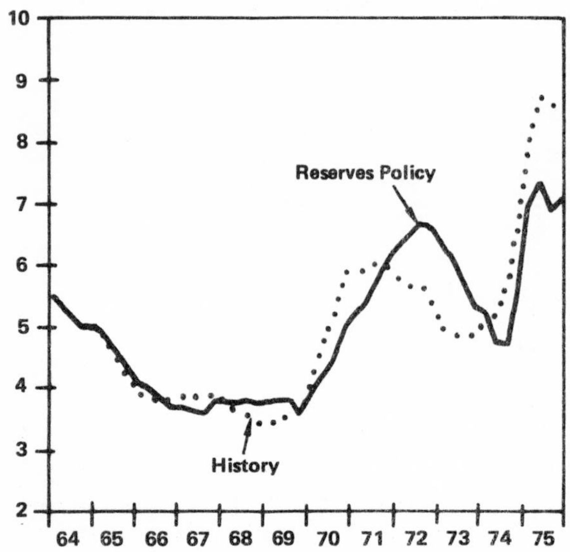

supply. Thus, for simulation purposes, the growth of nonborrowed bank reserves, rather than money, is an appropriate instrument of monetary policy.

The path of the housing industry is of special interest, since homebuilding is the principal victim of volatile credit conditions. The behavior of housing starts under a policy of steady bank reserve growth is compared to actual history in figure 7.9. From 1964 to 1967, the differences are slight; an excess supply of housing and "crowding out" of funds during the Vietnam War buildup would have produced a decline in residential construction during the initial period. The succeeding five years, 1968-72, would have been marked by much greater stability. Since the credit crunch of 1969 does not develop in the alternative, 1968 to 1970 is a period of uninterrupted growth in housing starts. Actual monetary policies induced a housing cycle in which starts dropped to a low of 1.085 million units in January 1970 and reached a peak of 2.494 million units two years later.

After early 1972, stable framework monetary policies could not have saved the housing industry from instability. The exceptional real income growth of that period, together with the extraordinarily high personal savings of 1973 would have sparked a housing boom. And once housing was overbuilt and

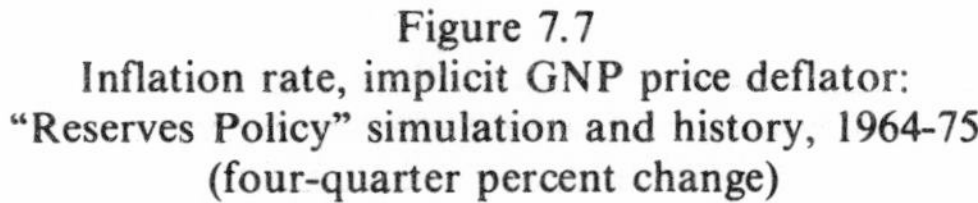
Figure 7.7
Inflation rate, implicit GNP price deflator:
"Reserves Policy" simulation and history, 1964-75
(four-quarter percent change)

double-digit inflation distorted the financial system, housing would have collapsed despite the steady expansion of bank reserves in the alternative solution. The 1975 trough would have been less severe, at 1.259 million housing starts instead of 0.955 million.

In conclusion, the housing industry, for the most part, would have fared better had the Federal Reserve followed a course of steady growth of bank reserves. The cyclical peaks and troughs would have been less extreme. A total of 19.258 million housing units would have been constructed from 1964 through 1975, compared to the historical result of 18.830 million units.

3. Interest Rate Target Policies

In order to further explore whether monetary policy could have made a larger contribution to economic stability by other methods, an alternative simulation tests the traditional interest rate approach. It was assumed that the Federal funds rate, the short-term interest rate most sensitive to monetary policy, was kept relatively stable. The growth of bank reserves to support

Figure 7.8
Money supply (M1) growth:
"Reserves Policy" simulation and history, 1964-75
(four-quarter percent change)

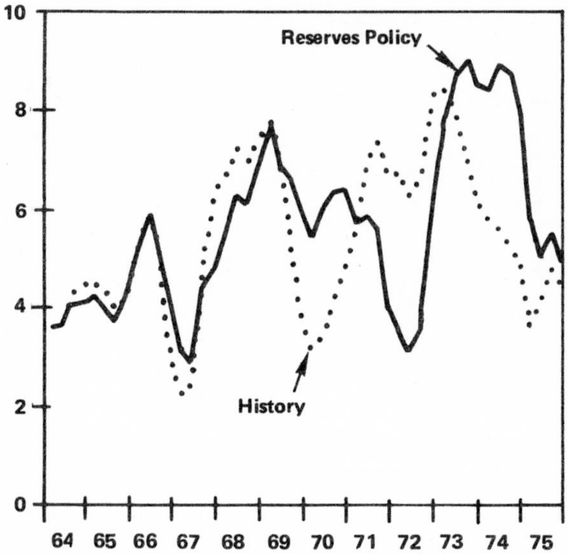

private deposits (RPD's) was manipulated to achieve a targeted Federal funds rate. The simulation target was set at 4% until the end of 1965, and then gradually increased to 6% as the War and other factors made some inflation inevitable. The rate was held at 6% from 1972 onward. Historically, the Federal funds rate has varied over a wide range, as illustrated in figure 7.3.

The interest rate target policy has been criticized heavily over the years because it appears to imply that the Federal Reserve will accommodate any and every variation in the price level or in real activity. At first blush, the policy appears to be one of making monetary policy totally accommodative to whatever else might be happening. But this interpretation was not supported by the simulation results. An invariant Federal funds rate does not leave all other interest rates frozen, and long-term interest rates would still respond to the variations in inflation, credit demands and other economic forces. Other short-term rates would show considerable independent movement, whether it be the Treasury bill rate which is more heavily affected by Federal deficits, or the prime or commercial paper rates dependent upon private short-term credit demands. Because the Federal funds rate

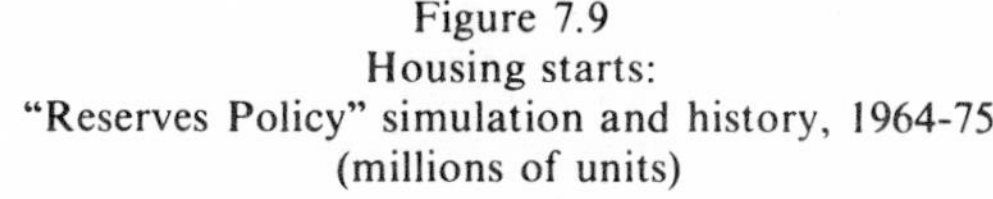

Figure 7.9
Housing starts:
"Reserves Policy" simulation and history, 1964-75
(millions of units)

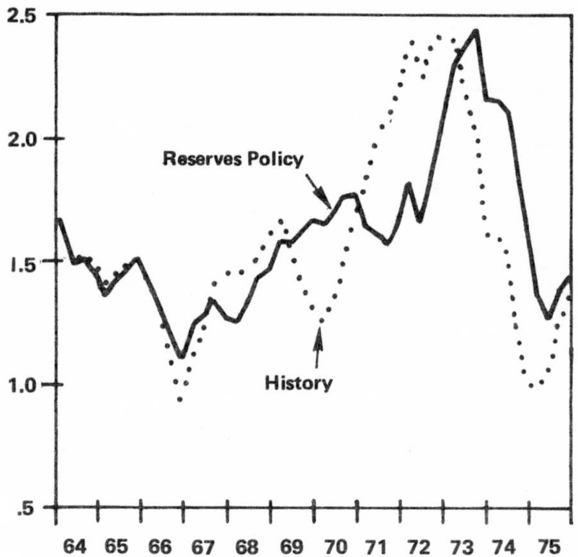

corresponds to the degree of pressure that policy is exerting on the banking system, a stable Federal funds rate means that the Federal Reserve keeps the short-term money markets in a middling state, avoiding extreme ease and credit scarcity.

The results of this simulation are remarkably good in the later parts of the period, remarkably bad in the 1960's. Comparisons with the historical outcome are presented in figures 7.10-7.14. In the late 1960's, when the stimulus of the War produced an intrinsically strong economy, the interest rate target policy creates a boom even more excessive than was actually experienced. Unemployment is pushed down an extra 0.5 percentage point to 3.0% during 1969, producing a more explosive wage-price spiral. The inflation rate by 1970 is 1 percentage point higher.

On the other hand, even in that early period, the interest rate target policy results in a healthier development for the housing industry. The money crunch of 1966-67 is milder and the disintermediation of savings flows less extensive.

In the 1970's, an interest rate target policy produces a more favorable

Figure 7.10
Real gross national product
"Interest Rate Policy" simulation and history, 1964-75
(billions of 1958 dollars)

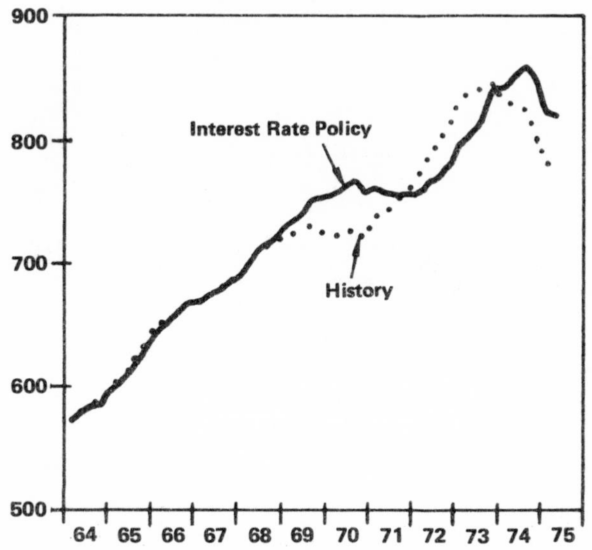

environment for sustained economic growth (table 7.2). Much of the recession of 1970 would have been avoided, with business fixed investment 11% higher in 1970 and 1971. With capital formation at a substantially higher rate, the industrial bottlenecks are less acute. Nevertheless, the impact of foreign conditions, including the overvalued dollar, would have left investment in basic industries, such as paper, steel and chemicals, below normal. Consequently, the bottlenecks are not avoided altogether. The price level is higher in the period 1971-73, but there is an offsetting benefit to inflation in later years from additional industrial capacity.

Much of the excess of the boom of 1971 to 1973 would have been avoided with an interest rate target policy. The Federal funds rate was substantially below the target rate in the period 1971 to 1972. It fell to 3½% at times, whereas the steady interest rate policy would have held it near 6%. The resultant easy credit conditions, occurring at a time of high personal saving, generated a boom in the housing and commercial construction industries which proved to be unsustainable. Under the alternative policy, housing starts would have averaged 1.83 million units in the period 1970-73, and

Table 7.2
Solution Summary, "Interest Rate Policy"

	Years											
	1964	1965	1966	1967	1968	1969	1970	1971	1972	1973	1974	1975
GNP and its components—billions of dollars												
Gross national product	630.6	679.1	744.5	792.4	862.1	949.0	1034.0	1095.0	1157.5	1293.3	1470.1	1558.9
Real GNP (1958 dollars)	579.3	613.1	655.6	677.5	708.7	743.0	760.2	757.9	767.9	816.6	850.0	826.4
Inventory investment	5.6	8.8	14.2	8.9	7.3	10.9	12.1	8.3	5.4	9.5	18.2	-5.9
Net exports	8.5	7.2	5.5	5.1	2.7	0.7	-1.4	-3.2	-3.7	8.4	-3.6	1.8
Prices and wages—annual rates of change												
Implicit price deflator	1.6	1.8	2.5	3.0	4.0	5.0	6.5	6.2	4.3	5.0	9.2	9.1
Consumer price index	1.3	1.5	2.8	2.6	4.2	5.4	6.5	5.5	4.0	5.8	10.3	9.6
Wholesale price index	0.3	1.6	3.0	0.2	2.5	4.3	5.4	4.3	4.4	12.2	18.9	9.9
Average hourly earnings index	2.7	3.7	3.8	4.8	6.2	6.9	7.9	8.4	7.5	6.7	8.1	8.8
Key economic measures												
Unemployment Rate (percent)	5.2	4.7	4.0	3.8	3.5	3.0	3.5	5.0	6.2	6.0	5.0	7.0
Industrial production (67=1)	0.810	0.874	0.967	1.005	1.061	1.167	1.198	1.110	1.083	1.179	1.325	1.220
Annual rate of change	6.1	7.9	10.6	3.9	5.6	9.9	2.7	-7.4	-2.5	8.9	12.4	-8.0
Housing starts (millions)	1.49	1.43	1.23	1.30	1.54	1.82	1.78	1.55	1.75	2.24	2.20	1.25
Unit car sales (millions)	8.4	9.5	8.9	8.4	9.8	10.6	9.8	10.0	8.9	10.6	10.8	9.9
Federal budget surplus (NIA)	-3.8	-0.6	-1.3	-11.6	-5.6	17.1	7.4	-15.6	-27.8	-14.9	8.4	-58.9
Money and interest rates												
Money supply (M1)	159.6	165.9	173.8	180.6	194.1	211.1	227.2	240.2	248.5	268.3	295.0	306.4
Annual rate of change	3.6	3.9	4.8	3.9	7.5	8.8	7.6	5.7	3.5	7.9	10.0	3.9
New high-grade corp. bond rate (percent)	4.51	4.62	5.31	5.65	6.33	6.94	8.13	8.19	8.04	7.69	8.39	9.50
Federal funds rate (percent)	3.94	4.26	4.49	4.71	4.96	5.29	5.52	5.71	5.99	6.08	6.01	5.99
Prime rate (percent)	4.76	4.71	5.31	5.82	5.86	6.21	6.24	6.42	6.58	6.45	7.23	7.48
Incomes—billions of dollars												
Personal income	497.0	536.3	583.0	626.4	686.1	756.5	836.7	896.7	961.3	1063.6	1186.6	1288.5
Real disposable income	407.6	432.8	456.5	477.1	498.9	519.4	552.9	568.2	577.5	612.9	615.6	625.1
Annual rate of change	6.9	6.2	5.5	4.5	4.6	4.1	6.4	2.8	1.6	6.1	0.4	1.6
Saving rate (percent)	6.1	6.1	6.2	7.2	6.5	5.5	7.7	8.9	8.1	9.0	7.1	8.3
Profits after tax (percent change)	14.5	18.3	9.7	-4.1	2.3	5.7	0.7	-5.1	1.8	39.0	48.6	-13.7
Details of real GNP—annual rates of change												
Gross national product	5.1	5.8	6.9	3.3	4.6	4.8	2.3	-0.3	1.3	6.3	4.1	-2.8
Total consumption	5.6	6.0	5.3	3.4	5.3	5.2	3.9	1.5	2.4	5.0	2.6	0.5
Business fixed investment	11.0	13.6	11.6	0.2	3.6	9.0	4.6	-2.1	-3.3	7.8	8.8	-8.8
Equipment	13.3	12.5	13.8	2.7	3.4	9.8	4.7	-1.9	-2.6	11.2	10.3	-10.5
Nonresidential construction	6.4	16.0	7.4	-5.2	4.1	7.2	4.4	-2.4	-4.8	-0.0	4.9	-4.1
Residential construction	-4.3	-2.3	-6.4	-2.7	9.7	18.1	5.0	-9.4	3.6	17.0	7.0	-29.8
Federal government	-2.5	-0.3	13.1	14.1	4.6	-5.9	-12.4	-5.3	0.1	-6.0	-1.4	3.5
State and local governments	6.0	6.6	7.8	7.6	6.2	5.2	5.0	4.5	1.5	5.4	6.3	2.2

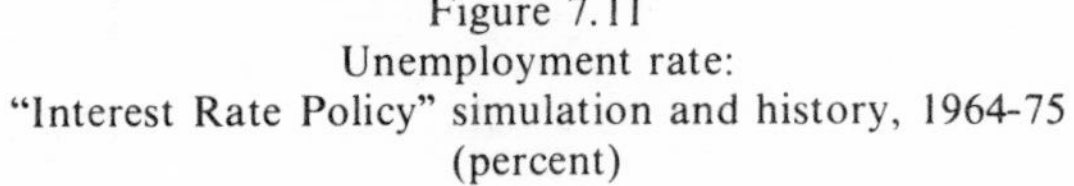
Figure 7.11
Unemployment rate:
"Interest Rate Policy" simulation and history, 1964-75
(percent)

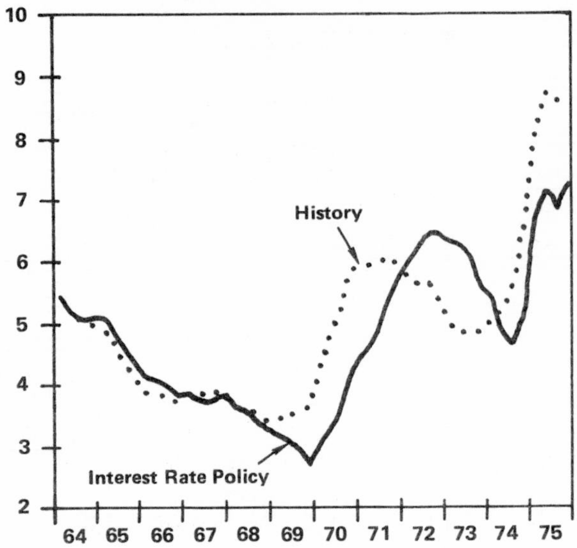

would not have reached two million until 1973. The actual boom, which carried housing starts to 2.4 million in the second half of 1972 and early 1973, produced a surplus of housing units that would have led to a considerable decline in homebuilding even if no other troubles had developed over the next two years. To a lesser extent, the same phenomenon applied to commercial construction.

With the economy held down to more sustainable growth in 1972, the 1973 expansion would have been stronger, and some of the adjustment processes of the recession would not have proved necessary.

But the most dramatic benefit of an interest rate target policy comes in the summers of 1973 and 1974, when the food and energy shocks, as well as the shock of the end of price controls, produced enormous bursts of inflation. A constant interest rate policy would have required the Federal Reserve to let the money supply grow at very high rates, by 11% from mid-1973 to mid-1974 (figure 7.14). Under ordinary circumstances, such an explosion of the money supply would have been followed by a burst of inflation one to two years later, after the stimulated real activity converted itself into tighter product and labor markets. But under the circumstances of 1974 and 1975, when there still

Figure 7.12
Real business fixed investment:
"Interest Rate Policy" simulation and history, 1964-75
(billions of 1958 dollars)

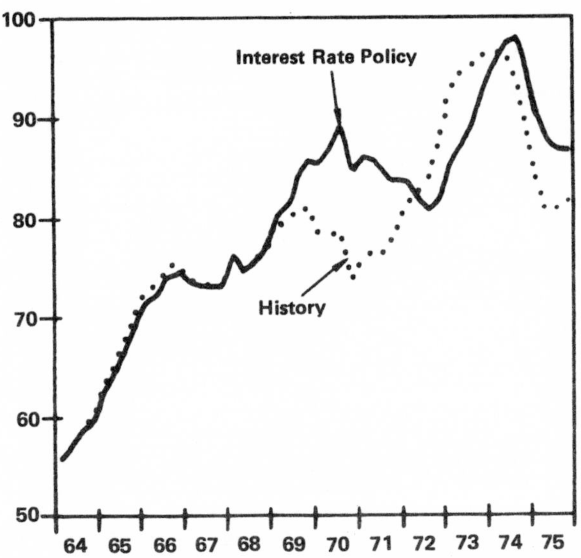

is a considerable recession caused by food and energy, these inflation effects are quite mild. A determination of whether extra inflation might develop later on in the 1970's, after the economy's return to prosperity, would require a further set of model studies going beyond the current retrospective analyses. The immediate impact of a monetary accommodation in 1974 would have been considerable. The economy would have grown at a 4% rate in 1974 rather than experiencing a 2% contraction. Real GNP is 3.5% above its historical path in 1974 and 1975.

4. Concluding Comment

The two studies of monetary policies cast up some suggestive conclusions, even though they fall far short of an exhaustive search for optimal monetary policies. First, the simulations show that there are many destabilizing forces in the economy other than monetary policy. Thus, the hopes that smooth monetary policies would achieve smooth economic performance are

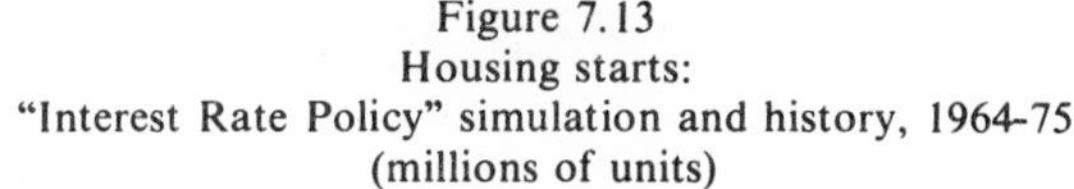
Figure 7.13
Housing starts:
"Interest Rate Policy" simulation and history, 1964-75
(millions of units)

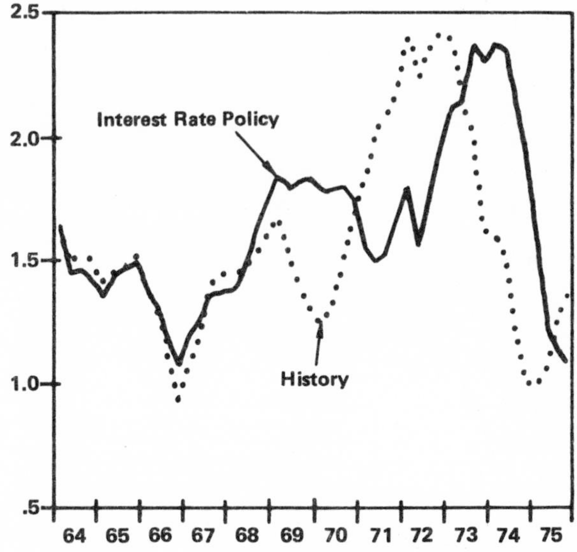

disappointed. Financial effects do have a tremendous impact on the behavior of the economy, but other sources of instability are also important.

Second, the adoption of a monetary rule seems to dampen the business cycle, but does not eliminate it by any stretch of the imagination. Third, an interest rate target policy did surprisingly well in smoothing out fluctuations in the later part of the period. Apparently the economy is spared a good deal of grief if the extremes of monetary conditions are avoided, measuring those conditions by interest rates rather than by the money supply. But here again one has to emphasize that the real problem may lie in finding the right Federal funds target on an *ex-ante* basis. After all, the simulation study selected rates which seemed reasonable in the light of actual developments of the price level, including the "shock" elements that actually occurred.

Finally, the choice of monetary policy regime must be made in the context of the longer term needs of the financial system. A well-growing economy needs a balanced increase in different components of the financial system, with different elements of debt and equity growing in ways that permit business to keep financing investment at the required rate, but which do not

Figure 7.14
Money supply (M1) growth:
"Interest Rate Policy" simulation and history, 1964-75
(four-quarter percent change)

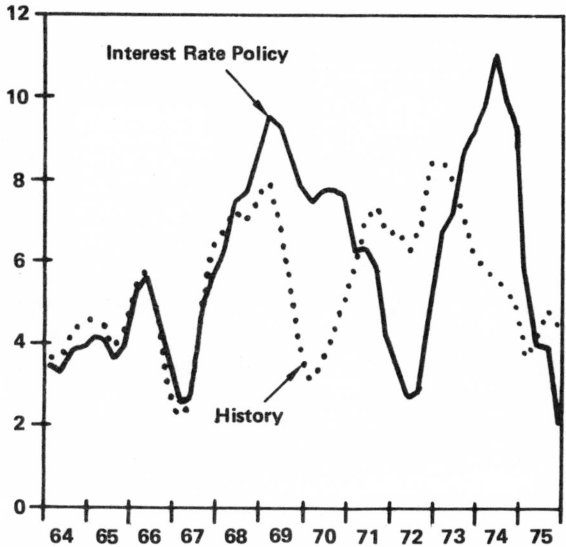

make capital so cheap that business is lured into foolish and irrational decisions. Certainly the very accommodating monetary conditions during parts of the period helped to create the unsustainable stock market booms and the merger waves which later proved injurious to economic performance.

CHAPTER 7

TECHNICAL APPENDIX

The financial sector of the 1975 DRI model consists of approximately 180 endogenous and 40 exogenous variables, encompassing the financial behavior of commercial banks, savings and loan associations (S&L's), mutual savings banks, life insurance companies, households, and nonfinancial corporations. It includes detailed submodels of the flow-of-funds of both the household and nonfinancial corporate sectors, with important linkages to consumption, housing, and business investment via portfolio adjustments. The principal instruments of monetary policy subject to Federal Reserve control are open market purchases or sales of securities and reserve requirements for demand and time deposits. The two simulations reported in this chapter employ nonborrowed reserves of member banks and the Federal funds rate as operating targets of Federal Reserve policy. The purpose of these simulations is to analyze the role of actual monetary policies as a source of real economic instability over the past decade and to compare the performance of the economy under the two alternative approaches to monetary control.

1. Simulation Notes

1.1. Smooth Growth of Nonborrowed Bank Reserves (NBR's)

In the first monetary policy simulation, it is assumed that the Federal Reserve achieves a smooth expansion of NBR's through open market operations. The growth of NBR's is constrained to a rate of 4.0% in 1964 and then accelerated by .25 percentage point in the first quarter of each year until 1972. From 1972 to 1975, the supply of NBR's is assumed to increase by 6.0% annually.

In addition, the short-term fluctuations in other policy instruments subject to Federal Reserve control have been smoothed, preserving their underlying trends. The required reserve ratio on demand deposits is held constant at .1435 from 1964 through 1972, after which it is lowered by .0015 in each quarter through 1975. The proportion of demand deposits subject to the reserve requirement is assumed to decline at a steady 1.2% rate, from .8524 in the first quarter of 1964 to .7400 at the end of 1975. Over the same period, the proportion of time deposits subject to the reserve requirement falls at a 0.7% rate from .8247 to .7466.

Taken together, the above assumptions imply a smooth growth of the supply of reserves upon which a monetary expansion can be based.

1.2. Interest Rate Target

The second monetary policy simulation assumes the Federal Reserve Board uses the Federal funds rate as its intermediate target. The Federal funds target is set at 4% in 1964 and increased by 25 basis points in each year until 1972 to accommodate the higher inflation which developed. From 1972 to 1975 the target is held at 6%. Bank reserves to support private deposits (RPD's) are adjusted continuously to produce a Federal funds rate within 10 basis points of the target.

The two monetary simulations are based on the historical tracking solution of the DRI model described in Chapter 1. The simulations contain the null errors of each behavioral equation. The variables representing real Federal government purchases of goods and services (1958 dollars) are exogenous.

1.3. Money Supply (M1) Determination

The two components of the narrowly-defined money supply—currency and demand deposits—are endogenous to the model. Both variables are part of a portfolio adjustment model which explains the expenditure and financial decisions of households, businesses and governments. For example, real demand deposits are a function of the real income flow, the price level, interest rates on close substitute assets, and a vector of beginning-of-period asset stocks.

The link between Federal Reserve open market operations and changes in the money stock is indirect, since the demand for money is strongly influenced by the real economy, and the link from reserves to money depends on the behavior of the banking system.

1.4. Channels of Monetary Influence

The DRI model contains various direct and indirect channels for monetary influence on the economy. The main direct links are the following:

Housing and the Mortgage Market: The equilibrium desired stock of housing is affected by real income, employment, the relative interest cost of financing a home purchase, and demographic factors. Disequilibrium in the housing market is measured by the number of vacancies. The supply of housing starts and mobile homes is determined by the vacancy rate, interest rates, conditions in the mortgage market and government subsidy programs.

The supply of mortgage funds depends on the mortgage market activity of commercial banks, savings and loan associations, mutual savings banks, life insurance companies, and government agencies. The mortgage sector contains equations for new mortgage commitments, outstanding commitments, acquisitions, loans outstanding and repayments of each group of mortgage market participants. The share of investable funds an institution allocates to mortgages depends on the volume of deposits, its lending and investment opportunities, the initial portfolio position in mortgages, and policies of government agencies. Federal Reserve policy, through its impact on interest rates, influences the inflow of deposits and the alternative investment returns available to each lending institution. Thus, monetary effects are channelled to the housing market through the mortgage sector, and through interest rates.

Consumption: Automobile sales are affected by total financial assets of households and interest rates. The consumer credit repayment burden provides another link between the financial sector and discretionary consumer spending.

Business Investment: Monetary policy affects business investment in plant and equipment through the neoclassical rental price of capital and flow-of-funds of nonfinancial corporations. A balance sheet measure of business liquidity enters the equations for fixed investment and inventory investment.

Government: A final channel of monetary influence is the yield on state and local government securities, which affects real government expenditures.

CHAPTER 8

THE WORLDWIDE BUSINESS CYCLE AND DEVALUATION OF THE DOLLAR

1. Introduction

One of the major contributing factors to the severity of the 1974-75 recession was the synchronization of the preceding worldwide business cycle upswing. The years 1972 and 1973 saw exceptional strength in the world economy, with all industrialized nations growing above trend. As table 8.1 and figure 8.1 indicate, the composite real GNP of eleven major industrialized nations grew 5.5% in 1972 and 6.1% in 1973. The Common Market countries increased output by 3.9% in 1972 and 5.6% in 1973, with France, Belgium, Italy and the United Kingdom leading the expansion. In the United States, real GNP rose 5.7% in 1972 and 5.3% in 1973. The Canadian business cycle coincided with that of the United States. Canada's real GNP advanced 6.1% in 1972 and 7.2% in 1973. Meanwhile, Japan was climaxing two decades of exceptional growth with gains of 8.8% in 1972 and 10.3% in 1973.

In earlier years, there tended to be a balance between expanding and slumping economies. In 1960 and 1961, the slower growth in the United States and Canada was in contrast with the booming economies of Japan and Europe. West Germany and Japan, in particular, tended to be in their weak phase while most of the rest of the industrial world was booming during the remainder of the 1960's. The years 1964-66 also saw rapid growth of the industrialized world, but there were no serious resource constraints and the oil-producing countries had not yet discovered how to use their monopoly power.

The great growth spurt of 1972-73 was associated with an extraordinary inflation, as table 8.2 and figure 8.2 show only too vividly. In North America, the inflation rate was near 6% in 1973. In the Common Market countries with a traditionally low inflationary bias—West Germany and Belgium in particular—consumer prices rose 7%. The inflation rate reached 11% in Italy, 9% in Great Britain, and 12% in Japan. When the oil crisis developed in late 1973, inflation rates moved deep into the double-digit territory in most

Table 8.1
Real gross national product
Major industrialized countries, 1960-75
(percentage change)

	1960	1961	1962	1963	1964	1965	1966	1967	1968	1969	1970	1971	1972	1973	1974	1975
Belgium	4.7	5.0	5.3	4.4	7.0	3.7	3.3	3.9	4.2	6.6	6.6	3.4	5.2	5.3	4.0	-3.0
Denmark	6.2	6.0	5.6	0.8	9.0	4.8	2.5	4.1	4.4	8.7	2.6	3.7	4.7	3.8	1.8	-2.3
France	7.1	5.4	6.7	5.8	6.6	4.7	5.6	5.0	5.0	7.6	6.0	5.4	5.4	6.1	3.6	-2.7
Germany	17.6	5.5	4.0	3.4	6.7	5.6	2.9	-0.2	7.3	8.2	5.8	3.0	3.4	5.1	0.4	-3.4
Ireland	4.3	5.1	3.2	4.6	3.7	2.6	0.6	5.8	8.5	5.4	2.7	2.9	3.4	6.8	1.2	-2.0
Italy	6.3	8.3	6.3	5.4	2.9	3.6	5.9	6.8	6.4	5.8	4.8	1.7	3.1	6.2	3.4	-3.7
Netherlands	8.5	3.6	4.0	2.9	8.6	5.2	2.6	5.6	6.4	6.8	6.6	4.2	4.4	4.6	2.0	-2.2
United Kingdom	4.5	3.4	1.3	4.1	5.4	2.2	1.8	2.4	3.2	1.4	2.1	2.2	3.0	6.0	0.8	-1.8
EEC Composite*	9.1	5.3	4.4	4.3	6.0	4.2	3.7	3.1	5.5	6.1	4.9	3.3	3.9	5.6	2.0	-2.9
United States	2.3	2.5	5.8	4.0	5.2	5.9	5.9	2.7	4.4	2.6	-0.3	3.0	5.7	5.3	-1.9	-2.0
Canada	2.9	2.8	6.8	5.2	6.7	6.7	7.0	3.3	5.8	5.3	2.5	5.7	6.1	7.2	2.3	0.0
Japan	13.3	14.5	6.6	10.7	13.2	5.1	9.8	12.9	13.4	10.8	10.9	7.3	8.8	10.3	-1.9	1.5
11-Country Composite*	5.1	4.2	5.4	4.6	6.1	5.3	5.5	3.7	5.6	4.6	2.6	3.7	5.5	6.1	-0.4	-1.8

*Based on weights at 1970 exchange rates for U.S. dollar.
Source: Organization for Economic Cooperation and Development (OECD)

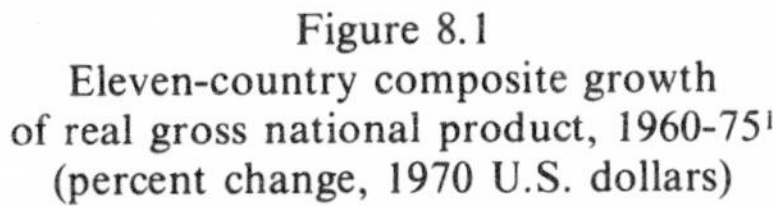

Figure 8.1
Eleven-country composite growth
of real gross national product, 1960-75[1]
(percent change, 1970 U.S. dollars)

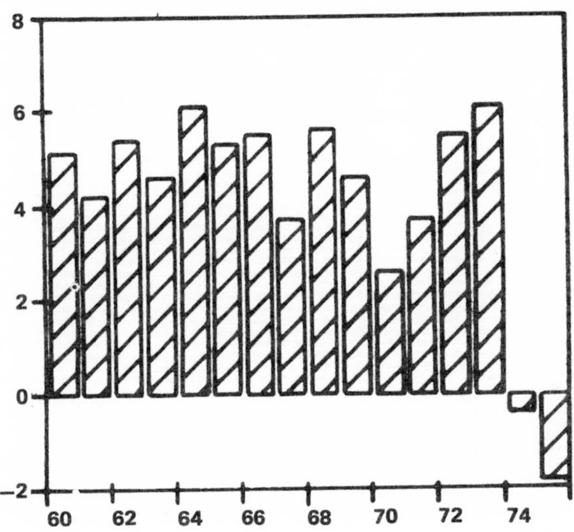

[1]See notes to table 8.1.

countries. The eleven-country composite of consumer price indexes rose 13.2% in 1974 and 11.1% in 1975. West Germany, where policy restraints were implemented early, had the best inflation record, with prices rising 7%. In Japan, Italy, Ireland, and the United Kingdom, inflation reached nearly 20%.

The coincidence of the business cycle upswings sharply accentuated the price inflation. Normally, when business cycles are not in phase, a country advancing too rapidly is likely to develop a deficit in her trade balance. Whatever shortages of materials, components, or final products might develop are at least partially met from foreign sources. But when all countries advance at the same time, this process is no longer possible. Shortages in one country lead to export demands in the other industrial countries, until the shortage becomes worldwide. At this point, an explosion of prices becomes inevitable as the market place converts shortages into inflation.

The initial price increases of 1971-73 were the result of worldwide excess demand. But once resource shortages became apparent and prices got into motion, a secondary round of speculation swept through commodity markets. The more frightened nations—particularly those traditionally dependent on external sources of supply—scrambled to hoard scarce

Table 8.2
Rates of inflation—consumer
Major industrialized countries, 1960-75
(percentage change)

	1960	1961	1962	1963	1964	1965	1966	1967	1968	1969	1970	1971	1972	1973	1974	1975
Belgium	0.3	0.9	1.5	2.1	4.2	4.0	4.3	2.8	2.8	3.7	4.0	4.3	5.5	7.0	12.7	12.8
Denmark	1.3	3.5	7.3	6.0	3.9	5.8	6.3	5.7	7.0	4.1	6.0	4.8	5.8	8.8	16.5	10.9
France	4.0	2.4	5.4	4.9	3.1	2.8	2.6	2.8	4.6	6.0	5.5	5.3	6.1	7.4	13.6	11.7
Germany	1.3	2.3	3.1	3.0	2.3	3.4	3.5	1.4	2.6	1.9	3.4	5.3	5.5	6.9	7.0	6.0
Ireland	0.3	2.9	4.2	2.5	6.9	4.4	4.4	2.9	4.5	7.7	7.9	8.9	8.4	11.9	22.3	20.7
Italy	2.2	2.1	4.7	7.4	6.0	4.5	2.3	3.3	1.3	2.6	5.0	4.8	5.7	10.8	19.1	16.9
Netherlands	5.0	1.0	1.9	3.9	5.4	4.1	5.7	3.5	3.7	7.5	3.6	7.5	7.8	8.0	9.6	10.2
United Kingdom	1.1	3.4	4.2	2.1	3.2	4.8	3.8	2.7	4.7	5.4	6.4	9.4	7.1	9.1	16.0	24.3
EEC Composite*	2.3	2.5	4.0	3.9	3.5	3.9	3.4	2.5	3.5	4.2	4.9	6.1	6.2	8.3	13.2	13.8
United States	1.5	1.1	1.2	1.2	1.3	1.6	3.0	2.8	4.2	5.4	5.9	4.2	3.3	6.2	11.1	9.2
Canada	1.3	0.9	1.2	1.7	1.8	2.4	3.8	3.6	4.1	4.5	3.4	2.8	4.8	7.6	10.9	10.9
Japan	3.5	5.3	6.7	7.7	3.8	6.6	5.1	4.0	5.4	5.3	7.7	6.1	4.5	11.8	24.4	12.0
11-Country Composite*	1.7	1.6	2.3	2.4	2.2	2.7	3.3	2.8	4.0	4.9	5.6	5.0	4.4	7.5	13.2	11.1

*Consumer price indexes of individual countries weighted by real consumption in 1970 U.S. dollars as a proportion of total

Source: OECD

Figure 8.2
Eleven-country composite rate of inflation, 1960-75[1]
(percent change)

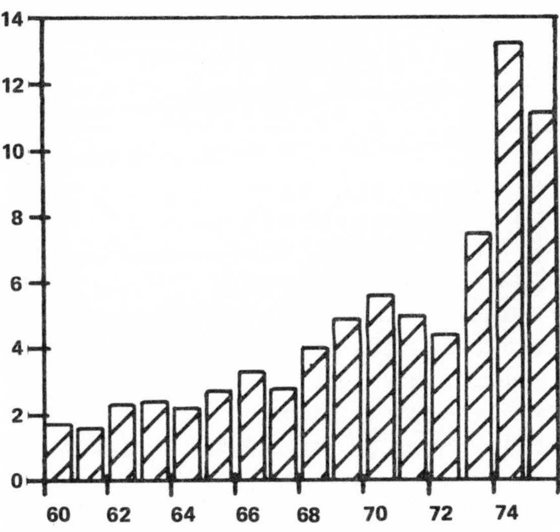

[1]See notes to table 8.2.

materials, thereby compounding the shortages. Japan rushed into the American market one month to buy up all the available wool, another month to make large purchases of copper, another month to buy suddenly scarce soybeans until the United States imposed export controls.

2. *The Collapse of the Bretton Woods System*

The synchronized worldwide boom was principally the result of the belated collapse of the fixed international exchange rate system which had been created at Bretton Woods shortly after World War II. The old system called for fixed exchange rates which could only be moved very rarely and after a considerable display of crisis. With fixed rates, if one country overheated its economy it would meet its internal shortages by imports and thereby lose international reserves. Once its reserves were at low ebb, its government would be forced to follow more stringent policies, either of its own volition or under the pressure of International Monetary Fund review. Thus, the Bretton Woods system had a conservative influence on domestic policies.

But the Bretton Woods system assumed that the United States, the principal source of international reserves under the system, would not stray too far from equilibrium in her own balance of payments. The first devaluation of the dollar in December 1971 had been delayed much too long. As a result of the Vietnam War and the overheated economy, the United States had run huge balance of payments deficits. Because the United States provided national security to the other Western industrial countries, and because of the sheer size and power of the United States, the usual discipline of the balance of payments did not apply. West Germany and Japan were willing to absorb U.S. dollars apparently without limit during the period of dollar outflows. These countries also had benefitted enormously from relatively cheap exchange rates vis-a-vis the United States, and had experienced postwar reconstruction and development on the strength of export-led growth. Thus, they not only were willing to absorb U.S. dollars for military and political reasons, but because it served their export industries. West Germany alone swallowed nearly $40 billion, knowing full well that sooner or later these dollar balances would be devalued.

The buildup of dollars in foreign hands constituted international reserves for the other countries, thereby removing the usual check on the domestic policies of the others. Thus, it appeared to the other countries that they were rich in international reserves. The United States, on the other hand, followed a policy of "benign neglect" on her balance of payments, refusing to act in the traditional fashion to bring an end to the huge deficits and reserve losses. Being the reserve currency country, the United States was able to run deficits without limit.

3. The Role of Monetary and Fiscal Policies

The abundance of international reserves made it possible for the governments in the major industrialized countries to pursue highly expansionary fiscal and monetary policies. Since World War II, fiscal policies in most countries have aimed primarily at the goals of full employment and rapid growth. Emphasis on higher rates of growth as a source of national pride and as a means of reconciling the competing income claims of powerful groups led to overzealous expansion. As an economy matures, its potential for growth becomes constrained by the availability of material and human resources. The major European countries and Japan were reaching the point at which the kind of growth exhibited over the previous two decades of recovery and "catch-up" could not be maintained. But the pressures fostered by an ever-rising standard of living remained. Skilled labor was scarce and workers continued to push for higher wages in response to the higher prices. Productivity could not keep pace with rising wages, and an inflationary bias was built into these economies. Restrictive policies were not able to slow the advance without bringing on a recession as severe as the previous boom.

The real growth of government consumption after 1960 for the major Western nations and Japan is shown in table 8.3 and figure 8.3. The massive expenditure increases occurred during the Vietnam War, but the years 1971-72 represent a second episode of rapid expansion. In Japan, real government purchases increased 7½% annually. In the European Economic Community, government consumption grew 5.0% in 1971 and 3.8% in 1972, the highest rates in a decade. While real government consumption in the United States did not change substantially, the fiscal stimulus took the form of increases in transfer payments in 1972. In summary, governments throughout the industrialized world sought to control an increasing share of resources and thereby stimulated an unsustainable worldwide expansion.

Monetary policy erred in the same direction. Beginning in 1970, policies became increasingly expansionary. The growth in nominal money supplies of the eleven countries over the 1960-75 period is presented in table 8.4.

Figure 8.3
Eleven-country composite growth of
real government consumption, 1960-75[1]
(percent change, 1970 U.S. dollars)

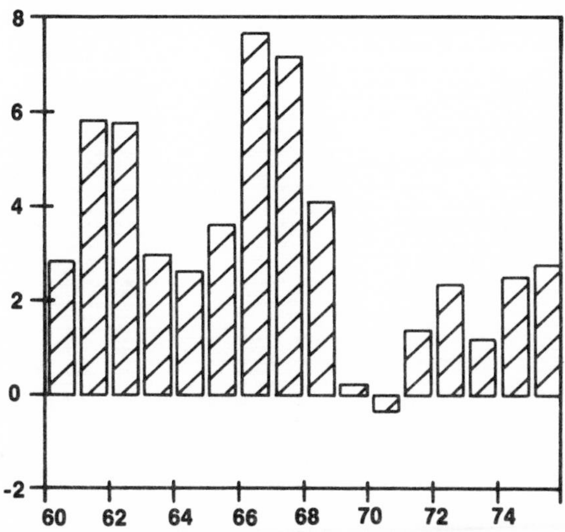

[1]See notes to table 8.3.

Table 8.3
Growth of real government consumption
Major industrialized countries, 1961-75
(percentage change)

	1961	1962	1963	1964	1965	1966	1967	1968	1969	1970	1971	1972	1973	1974	1975
Belgium	1.8	8.7	11.4	4.2	5.8	4.5	5.8	3.6	6.1	3.3	5.8	5.8	4.9	2.7	6.0
Denmark	5.3	9.9	2.9	7.3	3.4	5.8	7.5	5.9	8.3	11.2	7.9	0.7	-0.9	1.4	4.7
France	4.8	3.3	1.9	3.3	3.0	2.2	3.4	6.4	4.2	4.7	3.4	2.8	3.3	2.7	2.8
Germany	6.3	11.0	6.8	-0.5	4.7	2.3	3.2	0.0	4.8	4.9	7.2	4.0	4.2	4.6	3.8
Ireland	2.8	2.9	4.2	2.9	3.6	1.1	5.3	4.9	6.8	7.4	9.0	8.7	7.1	5.5	2.5
Italy	4.7	4.0	4.5	4.7	4.2	3.6	3.3	4.4	2.6	1.4	5.4	5.0	2.6	2.1	0.8
Netherlands	3.6	4.2	6.7	1.7	1.5	1.7	2.4	2.2	4.5	5.9	3.2	2.2	0.2	1.4	2.6
United Kingdom	3.6	3.2	1.6	1.5	2.7	2.8	5.6	0.3	-1.6	1.5	2.7	4.1	4.2	1.9	4.7
EEC Composite*	4.7	4.2	4.6	4.6	4.2	3.6	3.4	4.3	2.7	1.6	5.4	5.0	2.6	2.2	1.0
United States	5.7	5.6	2.3	2.6	3.4	9.4	8.3	4.4	-1.0	-2.5	-0.3	1.5	-0.2	2.1	2.1
Canada	13.8	4.0	1.5	5.1	5.3	9.3	7.1	7.6	3.7	10.4	4.1	3.1	4.6	4.3	4.4
Japan	6.1	8.4	8.7	5.9	6.4	4.8	4.9	5.7	4.2	5.3	7.2	7.8	7.3	4.4	7.4
11-Country Composite*	5.2	5.8	6.1	5.1	5.1	4.2	4.1	4.9	3.2	3.0	6.0	6.1	4.6	3.2	3.

*Based on 1970 exchange rates for U.S. dollar.
Central government spending for public consumption at 1970 prices.
Source: OECD

Table 8.4
Nominal money supply (M1) growth
Major industrialized countries, 1960-75
(percentage change)

	1960	1961	1962	1963	1964	1965	1966	1967	1968	1969	1970	1971	1972	1973	1974	1975
Belgium	2.0	5.6	7.3	10.0	5.7	7.3	6.6	4.7	6.8	4.5	6.1	10.0	13.6	11.8	8.6	11.4
Denmark	5.9	7.3	9.8	10.5	11.3	11.4	14.3	11.4	11.6	12.7	4.3	5.8	12.2	12.6	3.7	13.5
France	12.5	16.3	17.3	16.3	10.0	8.7	8.9	6.1	5.9	5.0	1.2	14.0	13.9	9.7	11.8	10.2
Germany	8.2	10.6	9.5	6.9	8.6	9.1	3.9	4.2	5.7	12.0	7.1	12.1	14.5	4.8	6.7	14.4
Ireland	6.7	6.1	8.3	10.4	25.8	4.8	3.5	6.2	7.6	7.7	6.5	6.2	11.8	16.7	5.5	15.8
Italy	11.8	14.5	17.5	17.1	7.0	13.7	14.9	14.3	13.0	15.1	22.8	22.7	27.4	20.0	4.5	21.7
Netherlands	5.4	8.1	5.3	9.7	8.7	10.7	7.5	7.5	9.0	8.4	11.2	16.4	18.9	6.1	4.1	17.9
United Kingdom	0.4	2.0	-5.4	14.5	3.2	3.9	-0.1	7.6	4.1	0.3	9.3	15.3	14.0	5.1	10.8	15.3
EEC Composite*	7.1	10.0	9.2	13.4	7.6	8.9	7.4	7.9	7.5	8.2	9.9	16.0	18.3	11.7	7.6	16.0
United States	-0.1	2.1	2.2	2.9	4.0	4.3	4.6	4.0	7.1	6.0	3.9	6.7	7.1	7.5	5.5	4.2
Canada	1.3	5.2	3.3	5.9	5.1	6.3	6.9	9.7	4.3	7.5	2.3	12.8	14.0	14.4	9.8	13.8
Japan	36.6	18.4	16.6	34.6	13.0	18.2	13.9	14.1	13.4	20.6	16.8	29.7	24.7	16.8	11.5	11.1
11-Country Composite*	3.3	5.3	5.1	8.3	5.9	7.0	6.5	6.5	7.9	8.5	7.5	13.2	14.0	10.8	7.5	10.1

*Based on 1970 exchange rates for U.S. dollar.
Source: International Monetary Fund (IMF)

Composite money growth averaged 6.3% from 1961 to 1965 and 7.4% from 1966 to 1970, as shown in figure 8.4. Monetary expansion in Japan became excessive in 1969. By 1971, the Japanese money supply was growing 30%, and in 1972 it grew by 25%. In Europe, composite money growth of the eight EEC nations accelerated to 10% in 1970, 16% in 1971, and 18% in 1972. The monetary stimulus was most pronounced in Italy, where money growth averaged 23% from 1970 to 1973. The composite money supply of the Common Market countries, the United States, Canada and Japan increased by 13.2% in 1971, 14.0% in 1972, and 10.8% in 1973.

Because the money supply and the price level are in a closed loop of causation, it is improper to identify the severity of monetary policy with the rate of increase of the nominal money supply. In a period of rapid inflation, an increase in the money supply that would ordinarily be considered quite normal might represent a policy of extreme tightness. On the other hand, the rate of increase of the *real* money supply—nominal money growth corrected by the inflation rate—is only a partial measure of policy because monetary policy should not fully accommodate changes in the price level. But under

Figure 8.4
Eleven-country composite
nominal money supply (M1) growth, 1960-75[1]
(percent change)

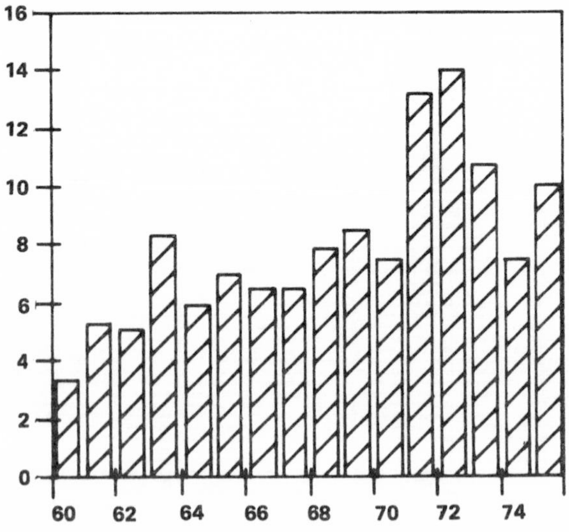

[1]See notes to table 8.4.

extreme conditions, the rate of growth of the real money supply provides a big clue to the conduct of policy.

The expansion in the real money supply demonstrates even more convincingly how policy contributed to the worldwide boom (see table 8.5 and figure 8.5). From 1961 to 1970, the growth of the real money supply of the eleven-country composite averaged 3.7%. After a slight 2.3% rate of increase in 1970, composite real money growth exploded to 7.3% in 1971 and 8.2% in 1972. These were clearly excessive rates of monetary expansion. In Japan, real money growth averaged 20% in those two years, an incredible rate even for a country riding a high growth wave. Increases in Canada and Italy were extraordinary as well. In West Germany, where policy instruments tend to be used conservatively, the average growth in the real money supply in 1971 and 1972 was an uncharacteristic 7.5%, although a 2% decline followed in 1973. For the eight Common Market countries, composite real money growth was 9.4% in 1971 and 1972. Although the results in the U.S. are modest in comparison to most countries, they must be evaluated by more stringent standards: the sheer size and central role of the U.S. in the world economy has always required it to pursue more responsible policies and to aim at a

Figure 8.5
Eleven-country composite growth of real money supply (M1), 1960-75[1]
(percent change, 1970 U.S. dollars)

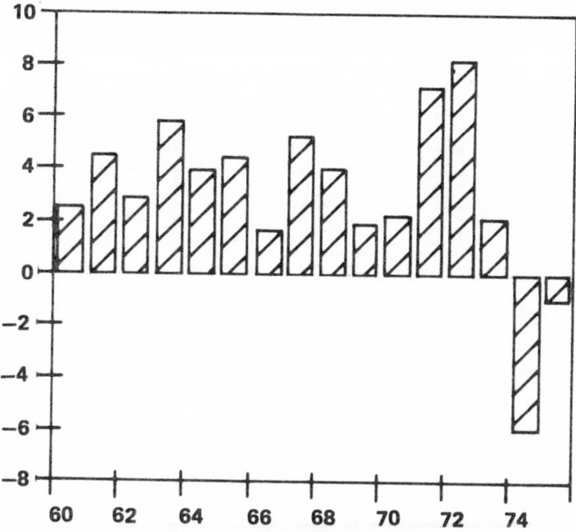

[1]See notes to table 8.4.

Table 8.5
Real money supply (M1) growth
Major industrialized countries, 1960-75
(percentage change)

	1960	1961	1962	1963	1964	1965	1966	1967	1968	1969	1970	1971	1972	1973	1974	1975
Belgium	1.7	4.6	5.8	7.7	1.4	3.2	2.3	1.8	3.9	0.8	2.0	5.5	7.7	4.5	-3.6	-1.2
Denmark	4.5	3.7	2.3	4.2	7.1	5.3	7.5	5.4	4.3	8.3	-1.6	0.9	6.1	3.5	-11.0	2.4
France	8.2	13.6	11.3	10.8	6.6	5.8	6.1	3.3	1.3	-1.0	-4.1	8.3	7.4	2.1	-1.5	-1.4
Germany	6.8	8.1	6.3	3.8	6.2	5.5	0.4	2.7	3.0	9.9	3.5	6.5	8.5	-2.0	-0.3	7.9
Ireland	6.4	3.2	3.9	7.7	17.6	0.3	-0.8	3.2	2.9	0.1	-1.3	-2.4	3.2	4.3	-13.7	-4.1
Italy	9.9	12.4	12.1	9.0	1.0	8.9	12.3	10.7	11.6	12.2	16.9	16.1	13.4	8.2	-1.9	4.4
Netherlands	0.4	7.0	3.4	5.6	3.1	6.4	1.7	3.9	5.1	0.9	7.3	8.2	10.3	-1.8	-5.0	7.0
United Kingdom	-0.6	-1.4	-9.2	12.2	-0.0	-1.0	-3.7	4.8	-0.6	-4.8	2.8	5.4	6.4	-3.7	-4.5	-7.2
EEC Composite*	4.9	7.4	4.8	8.9	3.7	4.8	4.0	5.0	3.9	3.7	4.6	9.4	9.4	2.5	-2.4	1.7
United States	-0.9	2.2	1.3	1.9	3.5	3.2	-0.8	4.6	3.6	-1.8	-0.6	1.8	4.2	1.0	-7.3	-3.4
Canada	-0.0	4.3	2.1	4.1	3.2	3.8	3.1	6.0	0.2	2.9	-1.1	9.7	8.8	6.3	-1.0	2.6
Japan	32.0	12.4	9.3	24.9	8.8	10.9	8.4	9.7	7.6	14.6	8.5	22.2	19.3	4.5	-10.4	-0.8
11-Country Composite*	2.5	4.5	2.9	5.8	4.0	4.4	1.7	5.3	4.1	1.9	2.3	7.2	8.3	2.2	-6.0	-1.0

Deflated by consumer price indexes (1970=1)
*Based on 1970 exchange rate for U.S. dollar.
Sources: IMF, OECD

relatively low inflation rate. The 4.2% real increase in the money supply in 1972 was a massive error by American standards, if not by those of most other countries.

A slowdown in real money growth in 1973 was achieved mainly because prices were leaping by this time. The real rate of growth of the eleven-country composite money supply dropped from 8.3% in 1972 to 2.2% in 1973, while the composite inflation rate went from 4.4% to 7.5%. The differences among countries can largely be explained by variations in their price experience. For example, the rate of increase of real money was higher in Canada, 6.3%, because inflation was less severe. The 1973 declines in real money recorded for West Germany, Great Britain and the Netherlands were due to substantial price increases and to a policy shift which restrained nominal money growth.

In part, the policies of excessive stimulus were created by the stubbornly high unemployment after the 1970-71 recession. In the European countries, which are accustomed to very low levels of unemployment, the unemployment rate stayed above 2%, levels considered unacceptable. The U.S. had unemployment rates of 6.0, 5.6 and 4.9% in 1971 to 1973, while the Canadian rates were 6.4, 6.3, and 5.6%, respectively.

Looking back, it is apparent that policy restraints should have been applied much sooner. But at the time, the signals were not so clear.

In Japan, Prime Minister Tanaka was firmly pursuing an expansionary course, while structural problems were developing. Recovery was proceeding fairly well in 1972, supported by large increases in government expenditure, private residential construction, and private consumption. But investment in manufacturing was declining, as there was still considerable overcapacity. The country was also running a large trade surplus. In order to solve these problems, the government stimulated investment expenditures, cut tariffs, raised import quotas, and put controls on exports. Consequently, the upswing continued until the labor market became tight and the wage-price spiral became explosive. Speculation in land, securities and commodities pushed prices higher.

West Germany made cautious attempts to curb expansion at the end of 1972. But monetary policy, aimed at restraining the expansion of domestic monetary aggregates, did not have much influence on the export-led upswing in 1973. An anti-inflationary package, including an investment tax and an income tax surcharge, was introduced in May. However, continued high levels of foreign demand and large speculative capital inflows counteracted the restrictive policy to some extent. Price mark-ups by entrepreneurs and strong demands by labor unions made control of inflation difficult. Although it is fair to say that West Germany attempted to deal with the situation sooner than most other countries, her policies were of limited effectiveness.

In France, Premier Pompidou, determined not to have a replay of the May 1968 riots of labor unions and students, vigorously pursued expansion and full employment, making little effort to keep prices down. Mildly restrictive monetary and fiscal policies were adopted in 1973, but with little effect. It was not until the oil price increase hit the French economy that real tightening became evident.

The United Kingdom attempted to eliminate the stop-go policies of the past decade and aimed for a 5% per year rate of growth with continuous fiscal stimulus. The British economy has a large foreign trade sector, and in the past, policy-making was oriented around the balance of trade. In 1972, the Heath government decided that the trade balance should not interfere with domestic growth. Therefore, it cut taxes, increased spending, and ran a large deficit. But this policy soon ran into problems. Import prices were rising because of the world boom, and when the oil price increases struck, Britain was hit with both a large trade deficit and inflation. An attempt to hold down prices and wages by statutory controls failed, lacking the cooperation of the strong British labor unions. The Heath government fell in early 1974 over a dispute with the coal miners, which culminated in a strike that forced the country into a three-day work week. The United Kingdom was the last country to adopt a policy of restraint.

In Italy, economic policy was in the hands of the Bank of Italy. The government lacked the stability to confront economic policy issues in the midst of political turmoil. With too much government money invested in enterprises that were not performing well, high taxes could not cover the deficit, and the country was forced into enormous debt. Only an emergency loan from West Germany could keep her afloat. Labor strikes and demands of workers for higher wages and shorter hours took a severe toll on productivity.

In retrospect, it is evident that recovery from the 1970-71 recession was pushed too fast in Europe. Policies were shortsighted, concern was with immediate problems of prosperity. When inflation reached the runaway stage, fiscal and monetary austerity became unavoidable. The composite real money supply of eleven major industrialized countries contracted by 6% in 1974 and 1% in 1975. By the end of 1974, every nation in the EEC, the U.S., and Japan had entered an economic decline. The long-delayed policy restraint finally helped to produce a severe worldwide recession.

4. *The Devaluation of the Dollar, 1971-73*

The long-delayed devaluations of the dollar from 1971 to 1973 contributed to the inflationary spiral in the U.S. Had the dollar's value been free to adjust on foreign exchange markets, it would have depreciated during the 1960's, thereby equilibrating the U.S. balance of payments. This process would have produced additional inflation during the 1960's. Instead, the devaluation was delayed to the 1970's, when its impact was to be magnified as a result of its interaction with other inflationary shocks.

While the dollar was overvalued in the 1960's, the competitive position of foreign goods was enhanced in U.S. markets to the detriment of American businesses. This price differential discouraged investment in manufacturing industries, particularly in primary processing industries such as textiles, chemicals, major metals, rubber, and paper. By 1972, after devaluation had occurred and competitiveness restored, these industries faced severe capacity shortages, and were poorly equipped to meet the demands of the ensuing worldwide business cycle upswing. Figure 8.6 depicts capacity utilization rates for all manufacturing and for primary processing industries, showing the imbalance that was created between primary processing and overall manufacturing capacity.

The depreciation of the dollar began in 1970 when the West German mark

Figure 8.6
Capacity utilization in manufacturing industries and in primary processing industries, 1962-75
(percent)

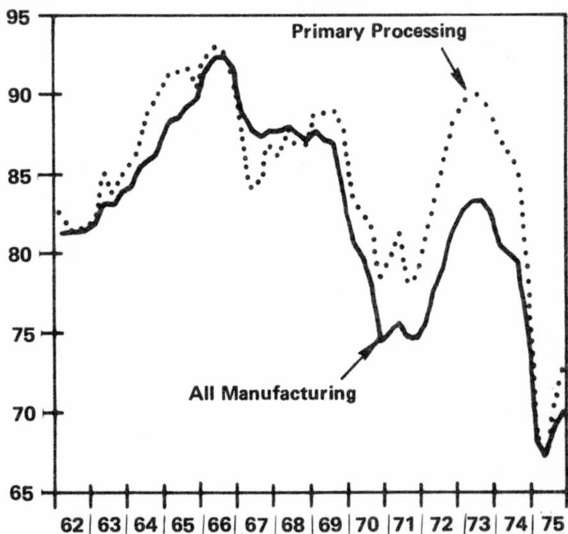

Source: Federal Reserve Board

was floated and went to a premium. In May of 1971, the Swiss franc was revalued. The first major devaluation was announced by President Nixon as part of the New Economic Policy in August 1971 and was backed up with a temporary import surcharge. It became official in December 1971 with the Smithsonian agreement, which limited the range in which foreign currencies could adjust. A second devaluation occurred in early 1973. Since that time the value of the dollar against foreign currencies has appreciated somewhat.

Some of the inflationary impact of the devaluations can be analyzed with econometric techniques. A model exercise was performed in which it was assumed that the effective exchange rate was held constant at its overvalued 1969 level. Figure 8.7 shows the historical path of the trade-weighted U.S. exchange rate. This variable affects import and export price deflators and U.S. wholesale prices in the DRI model. Relative prices are an important determinant of real trade flows, producing secondary effects on prices through demand conditions, particularly in the markets of internationally traded goods.

The initial impact of a devaluation is a rise in U.S. import prices and export prices. Higher relative import prices improve the market positions of

Figure 8.7
Trade-weighted exchange rate index for U.S. dollar
1969-75

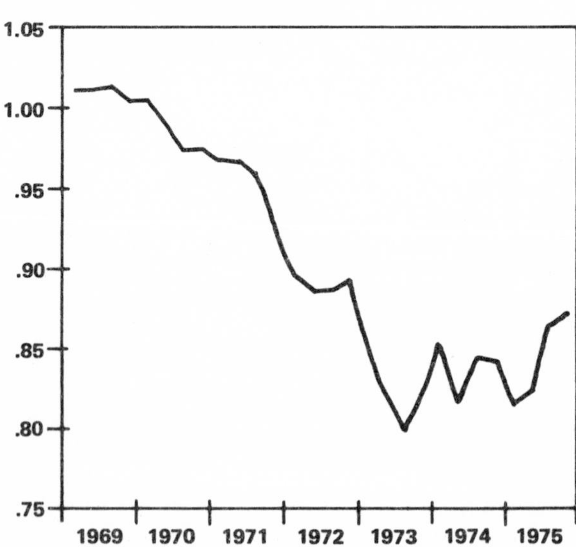

Source: Morgan Guaranty Trust

domestic producers, allowing them to raise prices. Nonetheless, real income is distributed from American to foreign transactors. Secondary effects of a devaluation include increases in the price of import-competing goods, the transmission of higher prices to wages and interest rates, wealth effects of higher prices, and a reduction in consumption.

The model simulation exercise indicates that wholesale prices would have been 7.7% below historical levels in 1972 and 11% lower from 1973 to 1975 if the devaluations had not occurred. The commodity price effects gradually filtered through to retail stages. Without the devaluation, the price level, measured by the implicit deflator, would have been lower than the actual by 0.9% in 1972, 2.3% in 1973, 3.5% in 1974, and 4.3% in 1975. The inflation rates under the alternative and historical cases are depicted in figures 8.8-8.9. The simulation clearly suggests that the devaluation was a significant contributor to the inflation of the period.[1]

The macroeconomic results of the "No Devaluation" alternative are summarized in table 8.6. The devaluation had a mild stabilizing effect on the

[1]Continuation of a fixed exchange rate would have meant huge dollar outflows, augmenting the reserves of other countries. The indirect inflationary effects are not analyzed in this exercise. In a longer perspective, there might have been less inflation if the dollar had floated much earlier.

Figure 8.8
Wholesale price index:
"No Devaluation" simulation and history, 1969-75
(four-quarter percent change)

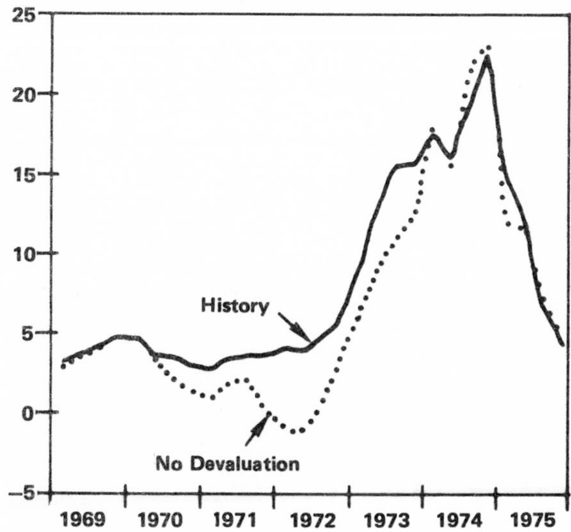

economic cycle. Had the dollar remained undervalued, the U.S. would have gained 1% in real GNP in 1973 and 1974. The 1975 recession would have been a little deeper. The real effects of the devaluation were relatively small in magnitude.

Table 8.6
Solution Summary, "No Devaluation"

	Years				
	1970	1971	1972	1973	1974
	GNP and its components—billions of dollars				
Gross national product	975.6	1053.8	1150.2	1276.9	1363.9
Real GNP (1958 dollars)	723.2	748.7	794.2	845.0	827.2
Inventory investment	5.1	7.1	9.8	16.9	15.5
Net exports	3.5	-0.9	-8.9	-5.5	-10.6
	Prices and wages—annual rates of change				
Implicit price deflator	5.5	4.3	2.9	4.3	9.2
Consumer price index	5.8	3.7	1.8	4.7	10.3
Wholesale price index	2.9	1.2	0.3	9.5	19.5
Average hourly earnings index	6.7	7.0	6.2	5.6	7.2
	Key economic measures				
Unemployment Rate (percent)	4.9	5.9	5.5	4.7	5.4
Industrial production (67=1)	1.072	1.081	1.175	1.297	1.275
Annual rate of change	-3.5	0.8	8.8	10.4	-1.7
Housing starts (millions)	1.43	2.07	2.40	2.25	1.41
Unit car sales (millions)	8.4	10.3	11.1	11.9	9.2
Federal budget surplus (NIA)	-12.1	-21.8	-17.5	-5.8	-9.5
	Money and interest rates				
Money supply (M1)	215.5	230.7	244.9	261.4	273.6
Annual rate of change	4.4	7.1	6.2	6.7	4.7
New high-grade corp. bond rate (%)	8.47	7.32	6.96	7.05	8.22
Federal funds rate (percent)	7.15	4.37	3.77	7.08	9.04
Prime rate (percent)	7.90	5.47	4.79	6.74	9.64
	Incomes—billions of dollars				
Personal income	807.0	862.0	936.5	1032.8	1113.0
Real disposable income	535.0	557.2	583.4	623.1	604.4
Annual rate of change	4.1	4.2	4.7	6.8	-3.0
Saving rate (percent)	8.1	8.2	6.7	8.2	7.7
Profits after tax (percent change)	-13.6	17.5	26.2	28.3	14.3
	Details of real GNP—annual rates of change				
Gross national product	-0.5	3.5	6.1	6.4	-2.1
Total consumption	1.7	4.2	6.3	4.9	-2.5
Business fixed investment	-3.4	-0.5	9.4	14.2	1.3
Equipment	-4.0	0.0	12.1	16.6	0.0
Nonresidential construction	-2.2	-1.8	3.0	8.1	4.8
Residential construction	-6.6	32.2	18.6	0.4	-26.7
Federal government	-12.4	-5.3	0.1	-6.0	-1.4
State and local governments	3.4	5.5	4.8	6.8	2.3

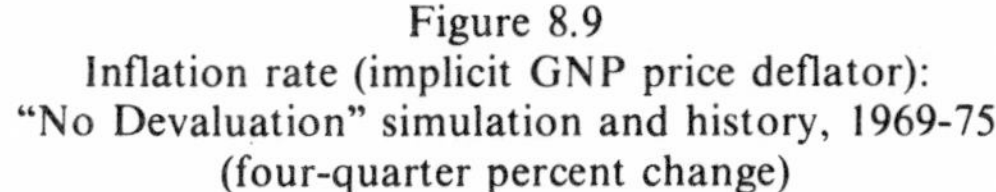
Figure 8.9
Inflation rate (implicit GNP price deflator):
"No Devaluation" simulation and history, 1969-75
(four-quarter percent change)

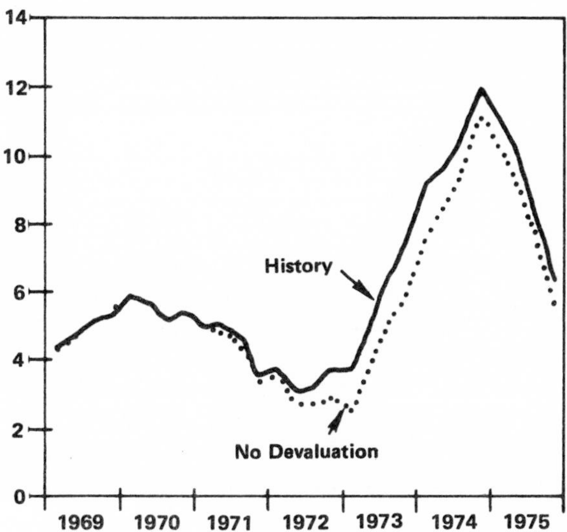

5. A Final Note

It is interesting to note that the synchronization of the world business cycle came to a rather quick end. Once the crisis had run its course and recovery began, the recovery paths diverged considerably. In the United States, dramatic above-trend growth resumed in the summer of 1975. In West Germany and Japan, recoveries resumed later in that year. Elsewhere, particularly the United Kingdom and Italy, trend growth was not seen until well into the succeeding year. Thus, while the world economy has truly become more interdependent than it was in the past, it is an exaggeration to believe that the entire industrial world will act as a unit in the future. Certainly the basic rhythm of the American business cycle, and probably the rhythm in other economies as well, continues to be determined predominantly by internal policies and internal circumstances.

CHAPTER 9

ENERGY

1. Introduction

On October 20, 1973, the Organization of Petroleum Exporting Countries (OPEC) imposed an embargo on shipments of oil to the non-Communist industrialized countries. The embargo against the United States remained in effect for five months. When it was lifted in March 1974, the refiner-acquisition cost of imported crude oil had risen to approximately $12 per barrel from a pre-embargo level of $3 per barrel (figure 9.1). The subsequent

Figure 9.1
Wholesale price index for fuels and power and consumer price index for gasoline and oil, 1957-75
(1967 = 1)

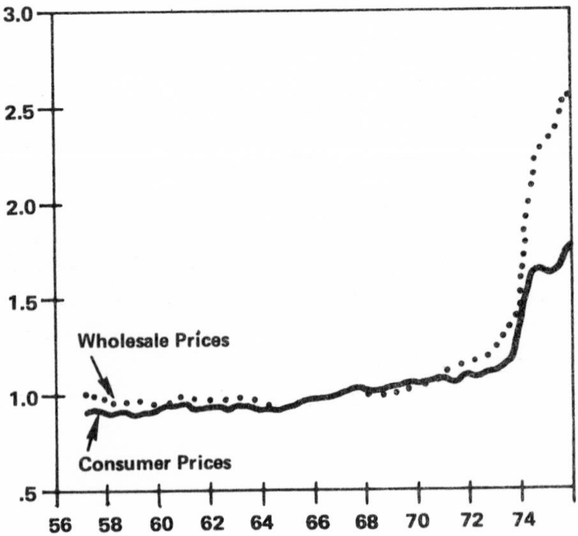

Source: Bureau of Labor Statistics, U.S. Department of Labor

quadrupling of the world price of oil set into motion inflationary forces that are still rippling through the world economy. Their effects on consumer purchasing power and attitudes helped to create the Great Recession.

The price increase was accomplished, in part, through increases in export taxes from $1.85 per barrel in October 1973 to $7 per barrel in December 1973. Tax and royalty rates have climbed steadily since then. For several decades, the oil companies had been paying taxes to the host nations. The form of taxation evolved from a system of per-barrel payments initially, to a tax on oil company profits in the early 1950's. In the ten years prior to 1957, the average per-barrel tax payment collected by Mideast governments quadrupled. However, government revenues declined over the 1958-60 period as a result of price reductions by the oil companies. This prompted the formation of OPEC in 1960. The organization was relatively ineffective before 1971, although it managed to reinstate a system of per-barrel tax payments. A 1968 OPEC resolution stated that governments may acquire participations in companies and, furthermore, may tax operator earnings that are in excess of a reasonable return.

Following the devaluation of the dollar and OPEC's Teheran Agreement of 1971, the oligopsonist relationship between the oil companies and the producing countries began to unravel. OPEC was successful in forcing price increases in 1972 and 1973 prior to the embargo. The thirteen OPEC nations controlled 85% of world oil exports.

The establishment of an effective cartel in the world petroleum market represented a turning point in economic history. Since the antitrust laws do not apply internationally nor to coalitions of foreign governments, the economic potential always exists to convert the supply of any commodity into a government-based monopoly. Because governments rarely agree for long, and because any cartel has the continuing problem of keeping all members under price discipline, such cartels are rarely formed and even more rarely continued. But in the case of oil, the economic reward for adhering to the monopoly form of supply is so enormous, initially about $70 billion a year in additional revenues, that it can serve as the unifying agent for a multi-nation alliance.

The price of oil had actually been falling through most of the postwar period, both absolutely and in relation to other world prices. Discoveries of new fields were very large, and the major oil companies possessed such a strength in distribution and marketing, exploration and production that they were able to purchase crude oil on relatively favorable terms. The wellhead cost of producing crude oil in the best fields was virtually nothing beyond the rent to be paid to the country. If the United States had not imposed an import quota program in the late 1950's, American domestic production would have reached a very sorry condition. Costs of exploring and developing new fields in the U.S. were rising and by the mid-1950's, the domestic industry had lost its competitive advantage. In 1955, a Cabinet advisory committee recommended the use of voluntary oil import restraints to maintain the 1954 ratio of imports to domestic production. The Mandatory Oil Import Program was established by presidential proclamation in March 1959. By limiting the physical volume of oil imports, it insured a return sufficient for the survival of the domestic industry. Throughout the 1960's, the cost to consumers was substantial. A Cabinet Task Force estimated the cost of the oil quota program in 1969 to be $1.17 per barrel, with the annual cost to consumers totalling $5.14 billion.[1] The resultant price of oil was not sufficiently high to deter a rapid growth in energy consumption which exceeded the growth in real GNP from 1965 to 1971. Thus, in contrast to the trend of the previous 25 years, the intensity of energy use increased. From 1947 to 1965, energy consumption grew at a 2.8% annual rate, 1.1 percentage points below the rate of real GNP growth. Over the period from 1965 to 1973, the growth of energy use accelerated to 4.2% a year.

During the 1950's and 1960's, stability of world oil prices was principally maintained by the prorationing system which limited production in the large fields in Texas, Louisiana and Oklahoma. The Texas Railroad Commission set the allowables, the number of days during which the fields could be operated in each month. While this system served as a prop to oil prices, it also provided a safety valve for the world oil economy. For example, when the Suez crisis in 1957 temporarily cut off supplies from the Persian Gulf to the western countries, the Texas Railroad Commission simply allowed the oil fields to be operated at full capacity and this source replaced the larger part of the missing short-term supply.

During the 1960's, domestic petroleum production rose slowly, and after 1970 actually declined. Drilling for new wells was reduced, with the average number of rotary rigs in operation dropping from 2400 in 1957 to a low of 975 in 1971. There were major discoveries off the coast of California and in Alaska in the latter part of the 1960's. The existence of oil resources in northern Alaska had been evident since 1923 when the U.S. government designated 35,000 square miles of territory as Naval Petroleum Reserve Number 4. Commercial drilling did not begin until 1967, and one year later oil was struck in Prudhoe Bay. In 1969, construction of the Alaskan pipeline was announced amid growing environmental concern in the United States. Construction was postponed repeatedly due to environmentalist opposition,

[1]Cabinet Task Force on Oil Import Controls, "The Oil Import Question: A Report on the Relationship of Oil Imports to the National Security," (1970), U.S. Government Printing Office, Washington, D.C., p. 260.

and while the Interior Department prepared an environmental impact statement. The pipeline project could not move forward until the energy crisis made it a national necessity.

With domestic production falling in the early 1970's and the Alaskan fields untapped, the U.S. became increasingly dependent on imported oil, as shown in figure 9.2. By 1972 the prorationing system was no longer important as production was allowed at near-capacity rates most of the time. After a long and pointless political struggle, mandatory oil import quotas were finally removed. In 1973, foreign sources supplied 6 million, or 35%, of the U.S. total petroleum requirements of 17.3 million barrels per day. The U.S. depended on Arab nations for one-third of its petroleum imports. Thus, when the political circumstances during the Arab-Israel War were ripe for the embargo, the impact on oil prices and oil supplies threatened to be devastating.

The OPEC embargo was never fully effective, and the apparent shortages that frightened consumers were unnecessary. Its potential impact was mitigated by conservation, boycott leakages and the diversion of crude oil flows by the international oil companies. The storage and sales policies adopted by the oil companies and by the Federal Government were overly cautious. Before the Mideast War erupted, Congress enacted and the

Figure 9.2
U.S. imports of petroleum and related products, 1971-75
(billions of dollars)

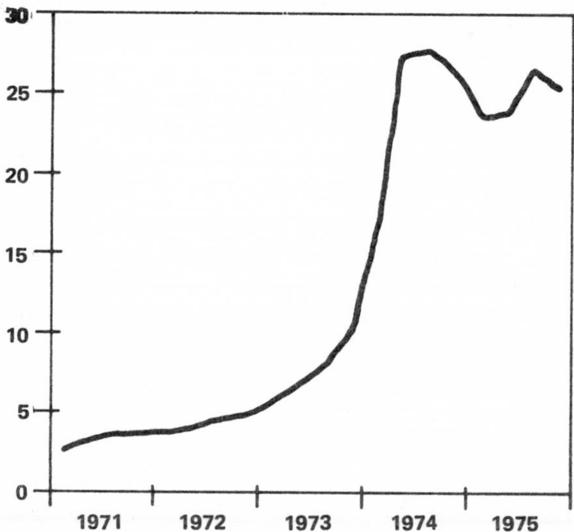

Source: U.S. Department of Commerce

Administration put into effect a mandatory fuel allocation program, designed to protect us against an exceptionally harsh winter and a prolonged embargo. Lines at gasoline stations were due to a supply policy that was based on a harsher winter and a longer embargo than actually developed.

The tax reference price of light Arabian crude oil—the benchmark upon which other oil prices are computed—was \$2.59 in January 1973 and \$3 per barrel as late as October 1, 1973. It was raised to \$5.12 on October 16, a few days before the embargo, and \$11.65 in December 1973. The price of domestic oil was left under price controls, with only the oil from new fields allowed to be sold at the market price.

The quadrupling of the price of world oil produced a drastic redistribution of world monetary reserves and of international political power. OPEC crude oil revenues rose from \$28.4 billion in 1973 to \$101.2 billion in 1974. In the same period, U.S. outlays for imported oil jumped from \$7.6 billion to \$24.2 billion annually (figure 9.2). The United States is now seeking to liberate itself from its dependence upon foreign oil sources. Project Independence, if it is to become reality, will require large physical investments in alternative sources and substantially higher prices for energy for a decade. It is an important new objective of general economic policy which will have to be weighed against the more traditional objectives of full employment, price stability, economic growth, distribution of income and equilibrium in the balance of payments.

When the oil embargo first became reality, two schools of thought developed about the impact on our economic development. The pessimistic school,which included followers of input-output economics, tended to argue that there was a relatively fixed relationship between energy use and real gross national product. This group felt that economic growth would be permanently reduced by a large amount if energy would cease to be as abundantly available as before. The neoclassical school of economists, with its firm faith in markets, believed in a high ability of businesses and individuals to adjust to relative price changes; they predicted that the price of oil could not stay at the very high rates for more than a few years. The econometricians, including the Data Resources forecasting group, ground the oil price increases through their income-expenditure models, attempting to impose energy supply limitations on the solutions. They concluded that the oil crisis would reduce real growth by perhaps 2% for a year, and raise inflation by a comparable sum.

In the actual history, this event had a sharper near-term effect on growth and inflation than the latter two schools had indicated. The energy crisis became the single largest factor in the development of the Great Recession. But the economy did manage to adjust to the new situation and near-normal growth resumed.

2. Economic Impact of the Energy Crisis

To assess the impact of the energy crisis on subsequent developments, we have constructed a model simulation based on the hypothesis that the embargo and the acute energy inflation did not occur. All other economic problems are accepted as given, including unstable fiscal and monetary policies, the history of the Vietnam War, the food crisis and the imbalances that developed in our industrial capacity. The Wholesale Price Index for fuels and power is assumed to rise at a constant 6% rate beginning in early 1973, in contrast to actual increases of 13.2% in 1973, 55.1% in 1974, and 17.7% in 1975. Imports of crude and refined petroleum were raised to their traditional levels and at the traditional prices. The assumptions about foreign economies were changed to reflect the improved economic conditions that would have prevailed abroad.

The solution without the energy crisis, summarized in table 9.1, portrays a dramatically different outcome. The economy would have reached a plateau in the second half of 1973, with real GNP growth reduced to a 1.7% rate. By the winter of 1974, a mild contraction would have occurred. Real output declines at a 3.1% rate in the first quarter of 1974, compared to the actual 7% rate of decline. The differences in the alternative growth paths becomes more pronounced in the spring and summer of 1974, as figure 9.3 illustrates. Without the energy crisis, the economy would have returned to positive real growth for two quarters before entering a brief recession. In actuality, the real GNP stayed on a downward path for five quarters, falling 7.8%. Without the energy crisis, the peak-to-trough decline would have been only 3.6%. As a result, real GNP exceeds its historical level by 3.1% in 1974 and 5.2% in 1975 under the alternative scenario.

The simulation demonstrates that the energy crisis was not the only factor pushing the economy off its equilibrium path. The expansion of 1972 and early 1973 had been excessive. Car sales ran far ahead of replacement requirements, reaching a 12.5-million-unit rate in the first quarter of 1973. Commercial construction had been excessive for several years. Housing starts were also substantially above trend during the previous boom, and had entered a downturn before the energy crisis. With credit conditions tightened in 1974, housing starts would have been brought down to levels of 1.53 million in 1974 and 1.37 million in 1975.

Interest rates would have risen sharply given the Federal Reserve's determination to moderate money supply growth beginning in the spring of 1973. The additional inflation from energy sources heightened the effects of a restrictive monetary policy. Without the energy problem, the Federal funds rate would have averaged 9.35% in 1974 instead of the actual result of 10.50%,

Figure 9.3
Real gross national product:
"No Energy Crisis" simulation and history, 1973-75
(billions of 1958 dollars)

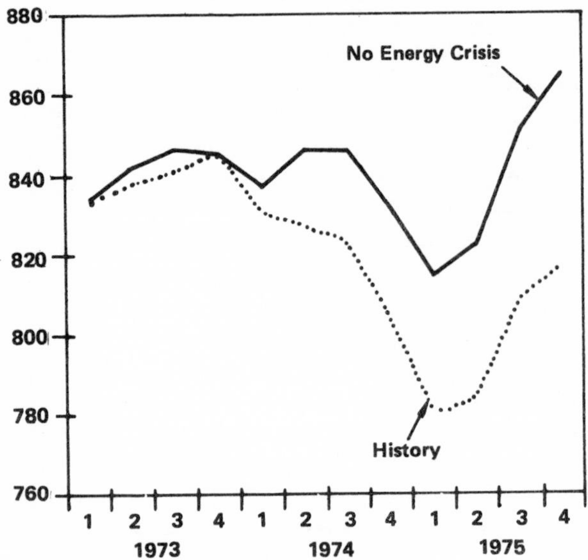

and its peak would have been 150 basis points lower. The credit crunch would have been milder.

The oil embargo produced an episode of speculative inventory accumulation. Expectations of rising materials prices and fears of shortages caused net inventory investment to surge to a record $29-billion rate in the fourth quarter of 1973. Without the energy crisis, inventory investment would have reached only $20 billion in that quarter. The shortage of productive capacity in materials industries led to further hoarding, and to excessive inventory accumulation in 1974. Thus, an inventory correction would have prompted substantial layoffs and production cutbacks in early 1975. In the alternative solution, the unemployment rate peaks at 7.2% in the second quarter of 1975 and is 6.5% at year's end (figure 9.4).

The automobile industry experienced the most dramatic impact. The energy crisis raised the cost of operating a car substantially and produced a hesitation in car purchases as the public awaited the redesign of the automobile to the new energy situation. Without the energy crisis, even given all the other problems, automobile sales including imports would have

Table 9.1
Solution Summary, "No Energy Crisis"

	Quarters									Years		
	73:4	74:1	74:2	74:3	74:4	75:1	75:2	75:3	75:4	1973	1974	1975
GNP and its components—billions of dollars												
Gross national product	1338.8	1359.2	1404.1	1440.9	1456.9	1440.0	1461.2	1524.6	1569.7	1294.7	1415.3	1498.9
Real GNP (1958 dollars)	848.5	841.9	850.7	853.2	840.6	818.2	824.0	852.2	863.2	842.0	846.6	839.4
Inventory investment	19.9	18.9	16.1	13.5	24.8	-10.9	-21.6	4.4	6.4	13.4	18.3	-5.4
Net exports	9.0	11.3	18.7	20.8	18.1	22.5	24.9	23.4	22.4	3.6	17.2	23.3
Prices and wages—annual rates of change												
Implicit price deflator	7.0	9.6	9.2	9.6	11.0	6.3	3.0	3.6	6.8	5.2	8.7	6.8
Consumer price index	8.1	8.1	7.8	10.2	10.2	6.5	4.5	7.1	6.6	5.9	8.5	7.4
Wholesale price index	3.8	12.7	3.6	20.7	14.2	-5.0	3.7	7.4	6.6	11.8	11.0	5.9
Average hourly earnings index	6.8	6.5	9.3	9.6	8.2	7.8	6.6	8.0	7.0	6.4	7.7	7.9
Key economic measures												
Unemployment Rate (percent)	4.6	4.9	4.6	4.7	5.4	6.9	7.2	6.5	6.5	4.8	4.9	6.8
Industrial production (67=1)	1.272	1.288	1.308	1.320	1.303	1.201	1.198	1.251	1.291	1.261	1.305	1.235
Annual rate of change	-2.4	5.4	6.4	3.6	-5.1	-27.7	-1.1	18.9	13.4	9.5	3.5	-5.3
Housing starts (millions)	1.68	1.69	1.71	1.47	1.26	1.20	1.26	1.47	1.54	2.10	1.53	1.37
Unit car sales (millions)	10.9	10.4	10.1	10.6	8.8	9.5	9.2	10.4	10.5	11.9	10.0	9.9
Federal budget surplus (NIA)	-3.7	-3.6	2.4	6.1	-11.8	-36.3	-84.2	-47.7	-46.2	-5.9	-1.7	-53.6
Money and interest rates												
Money supply (M1)	268.6	272.7	279.7	282.1	284.4	283.5	288.6	294.4	294.7	263.9	279.7	290.3
Annual rate of change	3.6	6.2	10.6	3.5	3.3	-1.2	7.3	8.3	0.4	7.5	6.0	3.8
New high-grade corp. bond rate (percent)	7.58	7.88	8.59	9.33	8.58	8.29	8.76	9.15	8.92	7.57	8.60	8.78
Federal funds rate (percent)	9.65	8.31	9.93	10.57	8.60	5.36	4.86	5.65	5.11	8.28	9.35	5.24
Prime rate (percent)	9.52	8.61	9.98	10.81	10.28	8.17	6.73	7.00	7.21	7.68	9.92	7.28
Incomes—billions of dollars												
Personal income	1092.0	1103.9	1136.8	1168.9	1186.6	1190.5	1211.4	1242.4	1276.3	1052.8	1149.0	1230.2
Real disposable income	624.0	616.8	620.8	622.5	617.0	613.7	643.7	635.0	643.3	620.6	619.3	633.9
Annual rate of change	0.4	-4.6	2.7	1.1	-3.5	-2.1	21.1	-5.3	5.4	6.9	-0.2	2.4
Saving rate (percent)	8.6	8.1	7.7	7.0	8.2	7.4	10.2	7.7	8.1	7.9	7.7	8.3
Profits after tax (percent change)	11.7	9.7	6.6	24.8	13.2	-10.8	-1.8	-2.1	22.5	24.8	13.6	1.9
Details of real GNP—annual rates of change												
Gross national product	1.8	-3.1	4.3	1.2	-5.8	-10.2	2.9	14.4	5.3	6.2	0.5	-0.8
Total consumption	-3.3	-2.3	4.8	4.7	-8.8	1.9	7.0	6.2	3.6	5.2	-0.0	1.9
Business fixed investment	4.7	3.0	1.2	-5.9	-15.0	-15.6	-5.4	9.2	13.8	13.1	1.2	-6.9
Equipment	3.8	0.1	2.3	-2.1	-24.1	-18.7	-1.8	7.9	11.9	15.6	0.2	-8.8
Nonresidential construction	7.0	11.1	-1.6	-15.4	14.3	-7.4	-13.8	12.5	18.6	6.6	3.9	-1.8
Residential construction	-24.2	-36.4	0.2	-16.1	-34.4	-43.3	-0.7	40.8	33.5	-2.8	-21.5	-16.7
Federal government	1.5	-0.8	-0.1	1.5	3.9	2.6	6.5	3.7	4.5	-6.1	-1.4	3.5
State and local governments	7.6	2.5	5.7	1.3	1.8	5.7	3.3	2.6	4.3	6.9	4.7	3.5

dropped from the boom peak of 12½ million to about 10 million in 1974 and 9.4 million in the first half of 1975. In actuality, after the energy crisis, automobile sales dropped to 8.7 million units in the final six months of 1974 and 8.1 million units in the first half of 1975 (figure 9.5).

The erosion of purchasing power caused by higher energy prices affected all categories of consumer spending. Real purchases of energy-using appliances and other home furnishings were reduced by 5.3% in 1974 and 10.0% in 1975 as a result of the energy crisis. Discretionary spending on goods and services was particularly sensitive to the declines in real income and real household wealth. Consumers also curtailed purchases of clothing, partly in response to the sharp price increases for energy-based synthetic fabrics. A direct impact of the energy price increases was a 7% reduction in real consumption of gasoline and motor oil in 1974 and 1975.

This econometric study identifies energy as the principal factor contributing to the 1973-75 consumer recession. Without the energy problem, total real consumption would have gained 2.8% in 1974 and 4.1% in 1975 relative to its historical levels.

Indirectly, the energy crisis had a crippling impact on business fixed

Figure 9.4
Unemployment rate:
"No Energy Crisis" simulation and history, 1973-75
(percent)

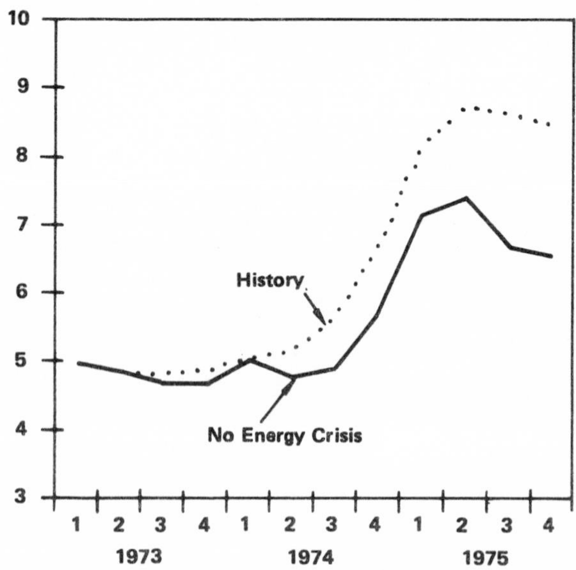

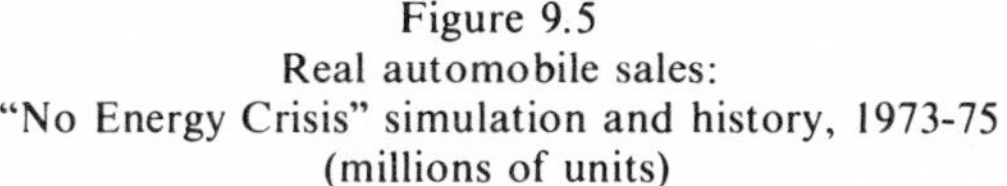
Figure 9.5
Real automobile sales:
"No Energy Crisis" simulation and history, 1973-75
(millions of units)

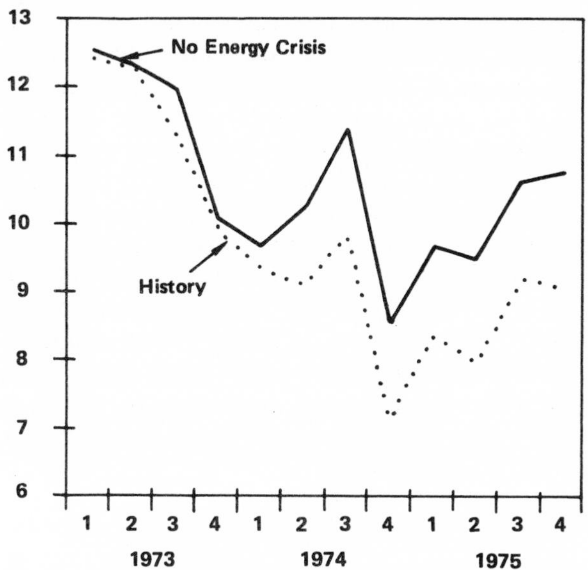

investment. In the alternative solution, "No Energy Crisis," business fixed investment in constant dollars is 12.1% above its historical path by the end of 1975. The real decline in 1975 is held to 6.9%. The energy crisis affected investment via the inflation premium in borrowing costs and the gloomy sales expectations business extrapolated from consumer behavior. These effects overwhelmed the role of the crisis as a catalyst for investment in new energy sources. Electric utilities made drastic reductions in both near-term and long-term capital programs. The automobile and airline industries also made substantial cutbacks in investment plans.

State and local governments also felt the impacts of the energy crisis. Inflation and unemployment caused a rise in expenditures not matched by the increase in tax revenues. With interest rates up, state and local governments were unable to market their securities. The distortions created by the energy crisis reduced real purchases of state and local governments by 2.5% in 1974 and 4.2% in 1975.

The inflation rate would clearly have been more moderate although still far from perfection. The average for 1974 would have been near 9.9%, compared to an actual average of nearly 12%, as measured by the implicit GNP deflator (figure 9.6). The inflationary impacts were both immediate and self-sustaining, raising the price level by 1.8% in 1974 and 3.7% in 1975. Thus, the total impact of the energy crisis on the inflation was substantially worse than the initial estimates had indicated. The reasons for total inflation effects are manifold. Increases in oil prices were rapidly transmitted to consumers due to fuel adjustment clauses in utilities' contracts and the quick turnover of gasoline and fuel oil stocks. The costs of petroleum substitutes rose in sympathy with oil. The price of coal advanced rapidly, the price of intrastate natural gas rose although the controlled interstate price changed rather slowly. The energy crisis also worked its way through the price structure through other channels. Prices of chemicals and fertilizers rose very sharply in response to the increased price of petroleum start-up materials and the scarcities created by the embargo. Capacity shortages facilitated the energy cost pass-through in industries such as primary metals, paper, cement and chemicals. As a result, wholesale industrial prices rose 22% in 1974, compared to only 12% in the "No Energy Crisis" simulation (figure 9.7). By 1975, the

Figure 9.6
Inflation rate:
"No Energy Crisis" simulation and history, 1973-75
(percent, annual rates of change)

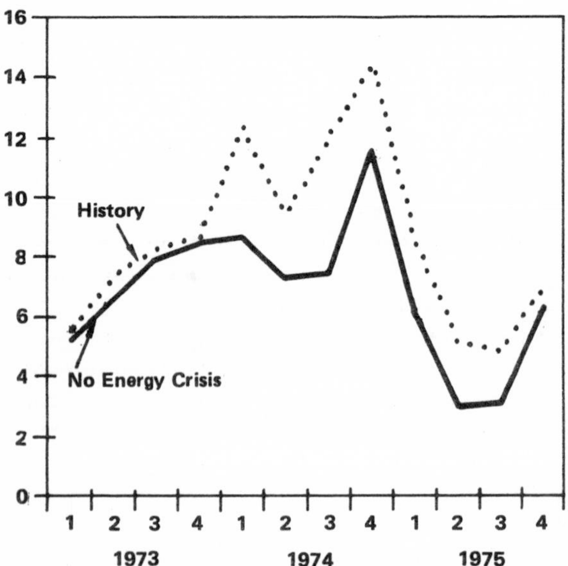

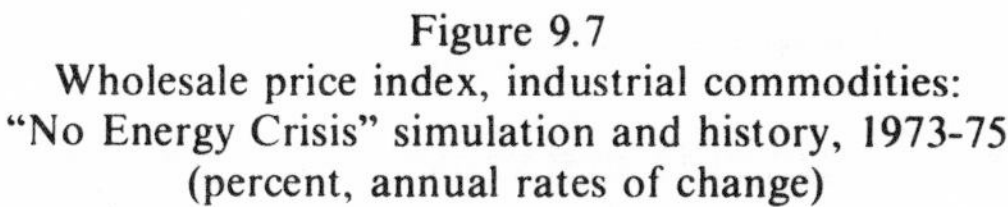

Figure 9.7
Wholesale price index, industrial commodities:
"No Energy Crisis" simulation and history, 1973-75
(percent, annual rates of change)

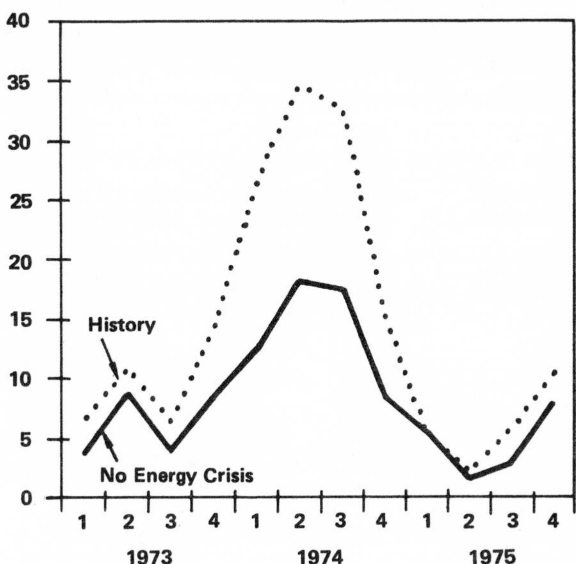

energy crisis had added 15% to the index of wholesale industrial prices and 12.5% to the WPI.

The increase in wholesale prices spread gradually through final markets. Prices of numerous consumer goods such as clothing were raised in response to the sharp increases in petroleum-based synthetic fiber prices. By the end of 1974, higher energy prices had directly or indirectly added 4.1% to consumer prices and 3.3% to the cost of producers' durable equipment. The impact on consumers' real income was especially damaging in the aftermath of the second of the food price explosions. In addition, controls on wages and prices expired with the end of Phase IV on April 30, 1974. Thus, the oil price increase interacted with all the other inflation problems to bring expectations to a fever pitch. Rising consumer prices generated additional wage demands and triggered cost-of-living pay adjustments. In collective bargaining agreements in 1974, escalator clauses became more widespread.

3. Summary and Concluding Comment

The energy crisis was the single largest cause of the Great Recession. Without it, even given all the preceding problems, the economy would have suffered no worse than a year of a small GNP decline in 1974, and would have seen 1975 as the first year of recovery. But when the energy crisis, with its gasoline lines and the quadrupling of the price of foreign oil, was superimposed upon an already highly vulnerable economic situation, it was sufficient to turn the beginnings of recovery into the sharpest decline of the postwar period.

Just as the effect of the energy crisis on inflation was about twice the estimates produced when the embargo began, so the ultimate effect on real activity was substantially worse. Without it, growth would have resumed by early 1975 as inventory stocks were partially corrected, and as the gradual increase of Federal spending and lower interest rates would have combined to produce recovery.

CHAPTER 9

TECHNICAL APPENDIX

The simulation reported in Chapter 9 was developed to isolate the impacts of the Arab oil embargo and the extraordinary increases in energy prices on the U.S. economy over the 1973-75 period. The "No Energy Crisis" simulation imposes stable growth of energy markets on the baseline solution.

1. Prices

The critical assumption in the alternative is that wholesale fuel prices increase at an annual rate of 6% from the beginning of 1973 through 1975. Thus, wholesale fuel prices average 36% below actual levels in 1974 and 42% below the actual in 1975.

Wholesale Price Index for
Fuels, Power and Related Products

	1973:1	1973:2	1973:3	1973:4	1974:1	1974:2
Alternative	1.230	1.249	1.267	1.285	1.304	1.323
History	1.252	1.312	1.358	1.450	1.763	2.042
	1974:3	1974:4	1975:1	1975:2	1975:3	1975:4
Alternative	1.343	1.363	1.383	1.403	1.423	1.444
History	2.242	2.283	2.325	2.394	2.513	2.572

A submodel of eleven wholesale commodity prices developed for the 1976 DRI model was solved to determine the linkages between fuel costs and commodity prices. (See the Technical Appendix to Chapter 5 for a description.)

The cost structures of commodity groups and final demand categories in the National Income and Product Accounts are determined from information in Table 1 of *The Input-Output Structure for the U.S. Economy: 1967,* published in the *Survey of Current Business,* February 1974. A stages-of-processing approach is used to trace the linkages from wholesale prices to the implicit price deflators (see Technical Appendix to Chapter 6).

2. Foreign Sector

Real exports *(EX58)* and real imports *(M58)* of goods and services in 1958 dollars, and their respective price deflators *(PEX* and *PM),* have been exogenized at the following values for 1974 and 1975:

	74:1	74:2	74:3	74:4	75:1	75:2	75:3	75:4
EX58	72.4	73.2	74.0	73.8	75.4	75.1	76.0	77.1
M58	64.2	62.1	62.8	64.3	63.1	61.7	63.5	65.2
PEX	1.695	1.771	1.840	1.892	1.911	1.930	1.949	1.968
PM	1.746	1.786	1.837	1.890	1.927	1.946	1.965	1.984

These values were derived from model simulations with a fully endogenous, detailed foreign sector. The assumptions underlying the solution are as follows: imports of crude oil and petroleum products in 1967 dollars rise at a 14% rate over the solution interval, 1973-75, while prices of these products increase at a 5.5% rate. Military exports grow 6% annually. Incomes from foreign investments follow trends of the previous five years. Foreign production indexes respond to the more favorable energy situation.

3. Consumption

Judgemental factors were applied to consumption variables affected by the oil embargo. Real expenditures (1958 dollars) on gasoline and motor oil were raised by $0.4 billion in 1973:4 and $1.3 billion in 1974:1. Consumption of "other nondurables" was increased by $1.0 billion in 1958 dollars in the fourth quarter of 1973. Real spending on automobiles was adjusted by $4.0 billion in 1973:4, $3.0 billion in 1974:1, -$2.0 billion in 1974:3 and $2 billion in 1974:4.

4. Dummy Variables

Dummy variables built into the model representing the Arab oil embargo were set to zero. These variables affect inventory investment, industrial production, imports and exports. Inventory investment in the fourth quarter of 1973 is significantly lower in the alternative solution as a result.

CHAPTER 10

HOW WE ESCAPED DEPRESSION

1. Introduction

In the winter months of 1974-75, the U.S. economy was on the path to depression. Between September 1974 and March 1975, production fell by 12.4%. Payroll employment was reduced by 2.36 million individuals, unemployment rose from 5.5% in August to an 8.9% peak in May. The real gross national product fell at an annual rate of 10% in the winter quarter. Consumer sentiment, as measured by the University of Michigan's index, relapsed to a level of 58%, lower than during the worst moment of the embargo in the previous winter. New housing starts, which totalled 2.361 million in 1972, plunged to a rate of 1.205 million in the third quarter of 1974, and averaged only one million in the two winter quarters. Commercial construction activity, which had fallen 19% during the preceding four quarters, fell another 13% in the two quarters ending in March of 1975. New capital appropriations of the thousand largest manufacturing companies declined 30% over the same interval. Real business fixed investment declined at an annual rate of 19%. The American economy was a vast factory that was closing down.

The economy was caught in the vicious spiral of collapsing purchasing power, employment and retail sales. Real disposable income fell 4.0% between the end of 1973 and the first quarter of 1975. The situation would have been much worse but for the strength of our unemployment insurance and other income maintenance programs. Total wages paid, corrected for inflation, fell by 5.4% over this interval.

During those six months, the rate of decline was of the same order of magnitude as the beginnings of the Great Depression of the 1930's. Back then, production was down 16.7% in the first year and real business fixed investment dropped 17.8%. Real disposable income fell 8.4%, as payroll employment was cut by 6.1%, or two million, in 1930. Unemployment rose from 3.2% to 8.9%. The sense of panic, while certainly intensified by the collapse of the stock market in late 1929, was not so different from the feelings of households and businesses in the winter of 1974-75. The food price explosion, the oil embargo, double-digit interest and inflation rates, a stock market decline of 35%, and new unemployment insurance claims of nearly one million a week represented a bundle of bad news sufficient to frighten anybody.

But whereas 1930 was only the first of three years of sharp declines, the winter of 1974-75 was followed by an early and vigorous recovery. Retail sales began to rise in April. Industrial production entered an upswing in June and housing starts picked up in July. How did the economy get off the path to depression? What brought the great postwar economic crisis to such a quick end? The DRI econometric model can as easily be used for this cliometric exercise as for the analysis of the causes of the crisis.

2. *Model Simulation: If Nothing Had Been Done*

There were five principal reasons for the end to the decline. First, there were no further external shocks to set back the economy. The crops were good and food prices showed only small changes. OPEC raised its price again, but only by 10%. Two potential policy shocks were staved off by the political process: the Congress rejected the President's proposal to deregulate domestic oil prices overnight, and the City of New York was rescued from bankruptcy through Federal loans.[1] Thus, no new horrors were added to the previously lengthening list. After a long bad run, America turned lucky again.

Second, the automatic stabilizers, which had been in place since the 1930's, did a yeoman job. Unemployment insurance benefits rose from $8.5 billion to $18.1 billion in the space of two quarters and other income maintenance programs also pumped out additional purchasing power.

Third, monetary policy shifted to an accommodating stance. The reduction in interest rates from the double-digit peak was gradual, and from both a monetarist or Keynesian point of view, too slow. Yet, the magnitude of the decline was dramatic. The Federal funds rate, the price of short-term money for banks, fell from a July 1974 peak of 12.9% to an initial trough of 5.2% in March of 1975. Long-term yields on high-grade corporate bonds declined from a peak of 10.1% in September of 1974 to 8.5% five months later.

Fourth, the availability of credit improved and the volume of private credit demands shrank as business reduced outlays for inventories, payrolls and capital expansion. The worst illiquidity on business balance sheets unwound

[1] Otto Eckstein, Eric Herr, and Yolanda Kodrzycki, "President Ford's Package for Energy and Stimulus," *Parameters and Policies in the U.S. Economy*, (1976), North Holland, pp. 352-362.

in just a few months as bond markets became an effective source of long-term industrial capital once more.

Finally, fiscal policy went through a major swing. At the "Economic Summit" convened by the new President in September 1974, virtually all outside economists urged a mixed policy of fighting inflation and recession, but the Administration emerged from its internal deliberations to recommend a tax increase. Between October and December, the economy became so impaired that even a conservative Administration was forced to propose a tax reduction. The Congress greatly enlarged the President's proposals, and beginning on May 1, 1975, the largest tax reduction in our history became reality. The combined fiscal policy measures injected $22.8 billion into the economy. Much of the stimulus was of a one-time nature, including a personal tax rebate of $8.2 billion and $1.7 billion in payments to social security recipients. The larger part of the fiscal package was enacted to be effective through the balance of the calendar year; and after some political controversy, these elements were subsequently retained. The more permanent measures included $7.8 billion in personal tax reductions accomplished with changes in the tax withholding schedules, a small negative income tax for the working poor, an increase in the business investment tax credit, and corporate tax reductions offset by the repeal of the oil depletion allowance. In addition, Federal grants to state and local governments were increased to create 320,000 new public service jobs.

While we were fortunate to escape the path to depression, it is interesting to evaluate whether the economy has the intrinsic ability to slide into depression if policy does nothing. The simulation, "No Fiscal Stimulus," contains the following assumptions:

All expenditure and tax provisions of the Tax Reduction Act of 1975 and new public service employment legislation were removed from the simulation, leaving the tax structure unchanged. The automatic fiscal stabilizers were left in place. Bank reserves against private deposits, the basic lever of monetary policy, were left at historical levels. The simulation is summarized in table 10.1.

The results of this experiment suggest that in the absence of the fiscal policy initiatives, the recession would have come to an end in the summer of 1975, but the extent of economic recovery would have been uncertain. Without the massive injection of tax rebates in the spring of 1975, the economy would have stayed on a downward course in the second quarter. Real GNP would have declined at a 6.2% annual rate compared to small positive growth under actual policies. Real GNP would have risen at an average rate of 8% in the second half of 1975; yet the level of real GNP would have fallen short of its

Table 10.1
Solution Summary, "No Fiscal Stimulus, 1975"

	Quarters				*Years*	
	1975:1	1975:2	1975:3	1975:4	1974	1975
	GNP and its components—billions of dollars					
Gross national product	1411.1	1409.6	1453.5	1504.6	1397.8	1444.7
Real GNP (1958 dollars)	776.5	764.2	777.9	794.0	820.6	778.2
Inventory investment	-19.6	-31.6	-21.8	-13.5	14.0	-21.0
Net exports	7.2	16.8	16.5	18.9	2.0	14.9
	Prices and wages—annual rates of change					
Implicit price deflator	8.2	6.2	5.3	5.8	10.4	8.9
Consumer price index	8.0	6.2	8.4	6.3	11.1	9.1
Wholesale price index	-3.1	4.1	7.9	6.6	18.8	9.0
Average hourly earnings index	8.6	7.3	8.6	7.6	8.3	8.8
	Key economic measures					
Unemployment Rate (percent)	8.5	9.3	9.4	9.6	5.6	9.2
Industrial production (67=1)	1.109	1.066	1.066	1.112	1.240	1.088
Annual rate of change	-29.5	-14.8	0.0	18.6	-1.5	-12.3
Housing starts (millions)	0.97	0.98	1.24	1.37	1.32	1.14
Unit car sales (millions)	8.2	7.5	8.6	8.8	8.9	8.3
Federal budget surplus (NIA)	-52.7	-69.8	-55.9	-59.6	-8.4	-59.5
	Money and interest rates					
Money supply (M1)	282.4	284.6	290.3	291.1	278.9	287.1
Annual rate of change	-1.0	3.1	8.3	1.1	5.5	2.9
New high-grade corp. bond rate (percent)	8.67	9.16	9.01	8.58	9.00	8.86
Federal funds rate (percent)	6.16	5.16	4.79	4.36	10.55	5.12
Prime rate (percent)	8.95	7.21	6.78	6.94	10.88	7.47
	Incomes—billions of dollars					
Personal income	1189.1	1196.4	1226.9	1261.6	1153.2	1218.5
Real disposable income	587.8	588.2	584.8	598.4	603.6	589.8
Annual rate of change	-4.4	0.2	-2.3	9.7	-3.0	-2.3
Saving rate (percent)	7.4	8.8	6.9	7.8	8.0	7.7
Profits after tax (percent change)	-26.9	-25.6	-27.7	0.5	15.2	-20.5
	Details of real GNP—annual rates of change					
Gross national product	-12.5	-6.2	7.4	8.6	-2.4	-5.2
Total consumption	1.3	-5.5	6.2	5.5	-2.5	-1.9
Business fixed investment	-23.0	-16.4	-4.9	3.9	-0.8	-14.5
Equipment	-26.5	-12.8	-6.8	1.4	-2.3	-16.9
Nonresidential construction	-13.9	-24.5	0.0	9.9	3.0	-8.3
Residential construction	-49.4	-5.9	52.5	52.0	-28.0	-22.1
Federal government	2.6	6.5	3.7	4.5	-1.4	3.5
State and local governments	3.6	1.3	-1.4	0.7	2.6	0.7

historical path by 3.8% in the third quarter and 3.0% in the final quarter (figure 10.1).

The simulation suggests a confluence of forces, independent of the tax cuts, which would have ended the recession. The end of massive inventory decumulation accounts for one-third of the rise in GNP during the second half of 1975. The abatement of inflation, the decline in interest rates and

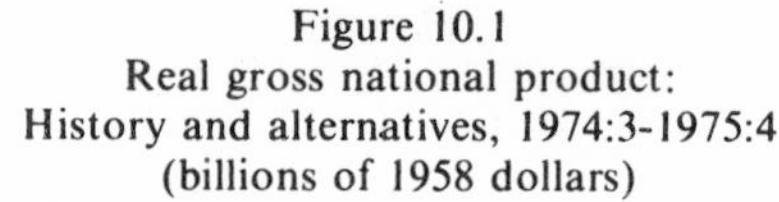
Figure 10.1
Real gross national product:
History and alternatives, 1974:3-1975:4
(billions of 1958 dollars)

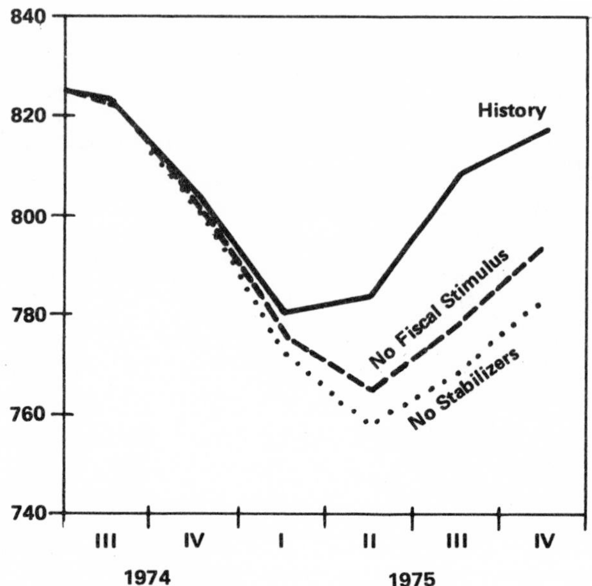

improved liquidity would have been sufficient to arrest the decline in real GNP and produce the beginnings of a recovery in the housing and automobile industries. However, business investment and spending by state and local governments would have stagnated.

A comparison of the simulation "No Fiscal Stimulus" with history serves to isolate the effects of the 1975 tax reductions and Federal spending initiatives. The full impact of the stimulus was not immediately felt. A large portion of the tax rebates and tax cuts was saved, pushing the personal savings rate to 10.6% in the second quarter of 1975, compared with 8.8% in the alternative. The proportion of incremental disposable income channelled into savings was 45% in the second quarter, 29% in the third quarter and 23% in the last quarter of 1975. Without the tax reductions, real consumption would have averaged 3.2% below the actual levels in the final three quarters of 1975. Real consumption of durables would have dropped 7.8% below its historical path. The fiscal stimulus generated an additional 400,000 car sales during 1975.

Business investment in equipment benefitted from the liberalized investment tax credit and the improvement in final sales. In the "No Fiscal

Stimulus" solution, real spending on equipment declines throughout 1975 and is 4.1% below its historical level by the end of the year. Another beneficiary of the fiscal policy initiatives was the state and local government sector, which by late 1975 was spending an additional $5 billion on goods and services as a result.

The fiscal stimulus was the pivotal factor in reversing unemployment during 1975. The unemployment rate peaked at 8.9% in the spring and dropped to 8.4% by the end of the year. Without the tax cuts and emergency public service employment programs, the unemployment rate would have climbed to 9.3% in the second quarter and peaked at 9.6% in the final quarter of 1975. At the end of the year, 8.9 million persons would have been unemployed (figure 10.2). Thus, the fiscal policy initiatives can be credited with producing, directly or indirectly, an additional 1.1 million jobs. Because capacity utilization was extraordinarily low in 1975, the immediate impact of the policy actions on inflation was small.

In a second alternative simulation, called "No Automatic Stabilizers," the automatic economic stabilizers built into the Federal budget were also shut off, beginning in the first quarter of 1974. As in the previous solution, the

Figure 10.2
Unemployment rate:
History and alternatives, 1974:3-1975:4
(percent)

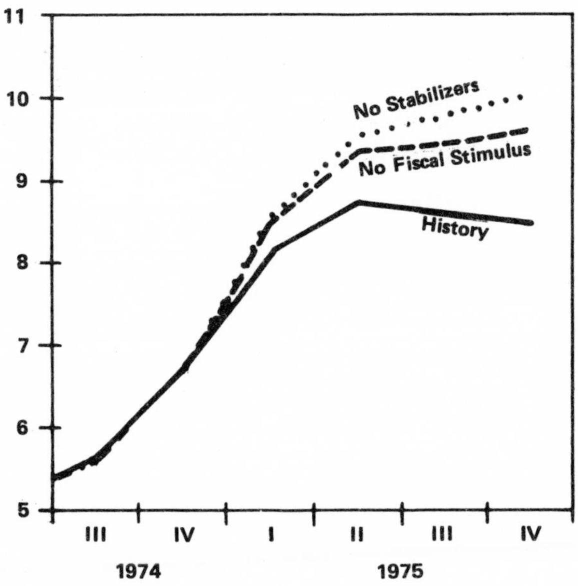

Federal tax structure was left unaltered. All government transfer payments were reduced to full-employment levels, defined by 4% unemployment. The growth of Federal grants-in-aid to state and local governments was lowered to a full-employment path. The automatic stabilizers alone injected an estimated $4.6 billion in 1974 and $17.1 billion in 1975 into the economy. The results of this simulation are presented in table 10.2.

Clearly, the recession would have been much deeper without the automatic stabilizers and the tax cuts. Real GNP in 1958 dollars would have fallen to $757.5 billion in the second quarter of 1975, 2.9% below the historical trough of $780 billion reached in the first quarter. Real GNP would have averaged 4.7% below the actual result in the second half of 1975 (figure 10.1). The economy still would have turned around in the summer of 1975, but not sufficiently to bring about a decline in unemployment. Even without the tax cuts and additional funds from government income maintenance programs, the recovery would have been led by the consumer. Real consumption, housing, and inventories would have exhibited the first signs of revival.

The unemployment rate would have been 10.0% in the fourth quarter and 9.3 million persons would have been without jobs (figure 10.2). Under this scenario, the economy would be much more vulnerable to new shocks and the risks of a prolonged depression would be commensurately greater. Also, the economic structure as we know it, and as it is built into the econometric model, might have given way to set the economy on uncharted and unpredictable paths. Nonetheless, it is an interesting finding that the economic structure is sufficiently cyclical and self-corrective that the model would produce an upturn just so long as there were no new shocks and the monetary authorities let easing of credit markets develop. A particularly critical question of structure is the persistence of long-run growth expectations for spending decisions in the face of contrary short-run evidence.

Table 10.2
Solution Summary, "No Automatic Stabilizers, 1974-75"

	Quarters				*Years*	
	1975:1	1975:2	1975:3	1975:4	1974	1975
	GNP and its components—billions of dollars					
Gross national product	1404.4	1397.9	1435.7	1484.5	1397.5	1430.6
Real GNP (1958 dollars)	772.4	757.5	768.1	783.5	820.1	770.4
Inventory investment	-19.7	-31.8	-22.1	-14.1	14.0	-21.9
Net exports	8.0	18.2	18.6	21.5	2.3	16.6
	Prices and wages—annual rates of change					
Implicit price deflator	8.3	6.1	5.3	5.6	10.4	8.9
Consumer price index	8.0	6.2	8.3	6.1	11.1	9.1
Wholesale price index	-3.2	3.9	7.7	6.3	18.8	8.9
Average hourly earnings index	8.6	7.3	8.6	7.6	8.3	8.8
	Key economic measures					
Unemployment Rate (percent)	8.6	9.5	9.8	10.0	5.7	9.5
Industrial production (67=1)	1.101	1.053	1.047	1.091	1.238	1.073
Annual rate of change	-30.9	-16.3	-2.4	17.9	-1.7	-13.4
Housing starts (millions)	0.96	0.98	1.24	1.34	1.33	1.13
Unit car sales (millions)	8.3	7.6	8.7	8.9	8.9	8.3
Federal budget surplus (NIA)	-42.4	-59.5	-42.4	-50.5	-5.0	-48.7
	Money and interest rates					
Money supply (M1)	281.4	283.1	288.1	288.9	278.8	285.4
Annual rate of change	-2.1	2.5	7.2	1.1	5.5	2.4
New high-grade corp. bond rate (percent)	8.69	9.12	8.94	8.41	9.01	8.79
Federal funds rate (percent)	6.01	4.79	4.34	3.72	10.39	4.71
Prime rate (percent)	8.83	6.97	6.49	6.53	10.76	7.21
	Incomes—billions of dollars					
Personal income	1174.0	1176.2	1198.6	1235.1	1148.5	1196.0
Real disposable income	579.3	577.1	569.7	584.9	600.8	577.8
Annual rate of change	-7.5	-1.5	-5.0	11.1	-3.4	-3.8
Saving rate (percent)	6.8	8.1	6.0	7.1	7.8	7.0
Profits after tax (percent change)	-28.4	-28.7	-31.2	-3.3	14.9	-23.5
	Details of real GNP—annual rates of change					
Gross national product	-13.9	-7.5	5.7	8.3	-2.5	-6.1
Total consumption	-0.7	-6.7	4.2	5.8	-2.8	-2.9
Business fixed investment	-23.1	-17.3	-6.1	2.4	-0.8	-14.9
Equipment	-26.7	-13.9	-8.4	-0.5	-2.3	-17.3
Nonresidential construction	-13.9	-24.7	-0.4	9.6	3.1	-8.4
Residential construction	-50.0	-7.5	51.9	47.1	-27.8	-22.6
Federal government	2.6	6.5	3.7	4.5	-1.4	3.5
State and local governments	0.6	-2.3	-4.0	-1.6	3.4	-1.3

CHAPTER 10

TECHNICAL APPENDIX

1. No Fiscal Stimulus

The simulation "No Fiscal Stimulus" removes from the tracking simulation the expenditure and tax provisions of the 1975 Tax Reduction Act signed by President Ford on March 29, 1975, and the expenditures carried out under subsequent public employment legislation. In effect, the tax system is left unchanged as a result of these assumptions.

Federal Revenue Assumptions: Federal Government personal tax receipts at annual rates are raised by $31.6 billion in 1975:2, $20.3 billion in 1975:3, and $11.9 billion in 1975:4. Three-fourths of the $8.2-billion tax rebate is assumed to be dispersed in the second quarter of 1975, the remainder in the third quarter. Reductions in withholdings account for another $7.8-billion loss in income tax revenues under the fiscal stimulus. The adjustments to personal tax receipts result from the following calculations:

Personal tax changes,
Tax Reduction Act of 1975
(billions of dollars, annual rates)

	1975:2	1975:3	1975:4	Year 1975
Rebate	24.0	8.6	0	8.2
Withholdings	7.6	11.7	11.9	7.8
Total	31.6	20.3	11.9	16.0

The effective rate of the investment tax credit is assumed to remain at its 1974 value of 5.6% during 1975. The tracking simulation assumes a 9% effective rate beginning in the first quarter of 1975. To remove the Federal corporate income tax provisions of the stimulus package, the corporate tax rate is increased by 1.05% in 1975:1, 1.65% in 1975:2, and 2.20% in 1975:3 and 1975:4. The result of these changes alone is an additional $2.1 billion in revenues. However, since corporate profits for 1975 are 9.6% lower in the simulation "No Fiscal Stimulus," the net result is a $2 billion loss in corporate profits tax revenues.

Federal Expenditures: Federal Government transfers were lowered by $2.0 billion in 1975:1, $8.8 billion in 1975:2, $2.0 billion in 1975:3, and $2.5 billion in 1975:4. These figures are annualized. The tax package included a $50-dollar payment to social security recipients in the second quarter of 1975. The total cost of this payment was $1.7 billion, or $6.8 billion at an annual rate. The additional $2 billion adjustment to transfer payments throughout 1975 cancels the 13-week extension of unemployment benefits.

Grants-in-aid to state and local governments were lowered by $0.7 billion in 1975:2, $2.5 billion in 1975:3, and $4.0 billion in 1975:4 (annual rates) to remove the public service employment grants appropriated in 1975. The unemployment rate was adjusted upward by 0.2% in the second half of the year to reflect the absence of 320,000 public service jobs. The equation for state and local government purchases captures the effect of a change in grants-in-aid.

Monetary Policy: No changes were made in the exogenous monetary policy instruments. Reserves against private deposits (RPD's) retain their historical values.

2. *No Automatic Stabilizers*

The simulation "No Automatic Stabilizers" differs from the "No Fiscal Stimulus" alternative by the assumption that all automatic stabilizers built into the U.S. fiscal system are turned off. The tax policy changes are identical in the two simulations. They differ with respect to Federal Government expenditures and state and local government transfer payments.

Federal Expenditures: Federal transfer payments are reduced to the level which would prevail at 4% unemployment. The transfer provisions of the Tax Reduction Act of 1975 and the extension of unemployment benefits are removed. The assumed volume of transfer payments is $3.2 billion below the historical level in 1974 and $11.4 billion below the actual in 1975.

Federal transfer payments
(billions of dollars)

	1974:1	1974:2	1974:3	1974:4
Alternative	101.9	107.9	115.0	120.3
History	104.0	110.8	118.4	124.5
Difference	-2.1	-2.9	-3.4	-4.2

	1975:1	1975:2	1975:3	1975:4
Alternative	126.5	131.1	136.6	142.4
History	135.8	147.2	148.4	150.9
Difference	-9.3	-16.1	-11.8	-8.5

Grants-in-aid to state and local governments are reduced by $0.5 billion in the fourth quarter of 1974 and increase at an 8% rate thereafter.

Grants-in-aid
(billions of dollars)

	1974:4	1975:1	1975:2	1975:3	1975:4
Alternative	45.0	45.9	46.8	47.7	48.6
History	45.5	50.2	52.2	55.9	58.0
Difference	-0.5	-4.3	-5.4	-8.2	-9.4

State and Local Government Expenditures: The equation for transfer payments of state and local governments was solved with the unemployment rate set at 4%. Transfer payments were then lowered to full-employment values. The assumed expenditures are $1.3 billion less than the actual in 1974 and $4.5 billion less in 1975.

CHAPTER 11

LESSONS FROM THE GREAT RECESSION

1. Introduction

Adversity is a great teacher. What should we learn from the ten years of extraordinary troubles which culminated in the Great Recession? In this chapter, the broader conclusions are drawn from our detailed econometric examination.

2. The Causes of the Great Recession: A Summary

In the preceding chapters, each of the six principal causes of the Great Recession is examined in isolation. Table 11.1 summarizes these separate exercises by showing how each cause contributed to the inflation rate in the peak year of 1974, while figure 11.1 graphically shows the impact of each factor on the inflation rate over the entire period. Similarly, table 11.2 shows the impact of the principal factors in creating unemployment in its peak year

Table 11.1
Impact of shocks on the inflation rate in 1974
(percentage points)

Contributing factor	Contribution to inflation rate*
(1) Energy Crisis	1.7
(2) Agricultural Price Explosion	1.5
(3) Devaluation of Dollar	1.2
(4) Monetary Policies, 1964-74	0.9
(5) Price Decontrol	0.8
(6) Fiscal Policies, 1969-74	0.3
Sum of (1)-(6)	6.4
Rate of Inflation, 1974	10.3

*Inflation rate is historical tracking solution of the Data Resources Model minus inflation rate in the alternative solution with the respective shock removed.

Table 11.2
Impact of shocks on unemployment in 1975
(percentage points)

Contributing Factor	*Contribution to unemployment rate**
(1) Energy Crisis	1.9
(2) Monetary Policies, 1964-75	1.6
(3) Agricultural Price Explosion	0.9
(4) Price Controls	0.2
(5) Fiscal Policies, 1969-74	0.1
(6) Devaluation	-0.2
Sum of (1)-(6)	4.5
Unemployment Rate, 1975	8.5

*Unemployment rate in historical tracking solution minus unemployment rate in the alternative solution with the respective shock removed.

of 1975, while figure 11.1 summarizes their contributions over the entire period.

The *energy crisis* created by OPEC's quadrupling of the world price of oil was the single most important contributing factor to the inflation. As the price of oil worked its way through the economy, it raised the inflation rate by 1.7 percentage points beyond what it would otherwise have been. The inflation rate would have been even higher if the energy crisis had not also contributed to the destruction of prosperity. By adding 1.9 percentage points to the unemployment rate and reducing real GNP by over 5%, the energy crisis weakened demand in the economy generally and thereby partially offset a portion of the direct inflationary impact of energy. If prosperity had been left unchanged, the total contribution of energy to the inflation rate would have exceeded 3 percentage points in 1974.

The shock of almost equal dimensions was the *food crop disaster* which produced the worldwide explosion of agricultural prices. The 20% rate of increase in consumer food prices which began early in 1973 had already begun to work itself into the wage demands of 1974, and thus worsened the wage-price behavior of the economy. The higher food prices added 0.9 percentage point to the unemployment rate, principally through the destruction of confidence in the minds of consumers. The demand for consumer durable goods, particularly automobiles, began to decline within three months of the beginnings of the food price explosion.

Monetary policies were the third factor serving to create both the inflation and the recession. If monetary policies had pursued "a stable framework rule," limiting the growth of the money supply in the 1960's and keeping real interest rates reasonably stable in the middle 1970's, the economy would have been spared a considerable portion of its instability in prices and employment. The extremes of ease, followed by the repeated credit crunches, were important contributing factors to the business cycle, and particularly intensified the cycle which culminated in the Great Recession. Unstable monetary policy produced severe instability in business finance. The years of ease led to overextensions of credit, the formation of excessively optimistic expectations for long-term investments in various fields, inflated stock prices, and waves of corporate mergers and acquisitions. When easy money was followed by money stringency, expectations were bitterly disappointed. Businesses dependent upon external finance scrambled to restore their liquidity and defend their balance sheets against the risks of bankruptcy by slashing employment, inventories and long-term investment plans.

Devaluation of the dollar, which began in August 1971, also contributed to the inflation rate, adding 1.2 percentage points in the year 1974. But the devaluation has to be interpreted rather gingerly. The dollar had been kept at a rigid value that did not reflect economic conditions for two decades. American goods became too expensive, competitive trade position was lost, and U.S. employment suffered. Thus, the large devaluation, nearly 20% at its peak, telescoped into a few years a sinking of the value of the dollar which should have taken place over two decades. Consequently, the devaluation contributed to employment rather than unemployment during the recession. Even after allowing for the negative effects of the inflation on real activity, the net result of the devaluation was to reduce the unemployment rate by 0.2 percentage point.

Figure 11.1
Consumer sentiment index and discomfort index*

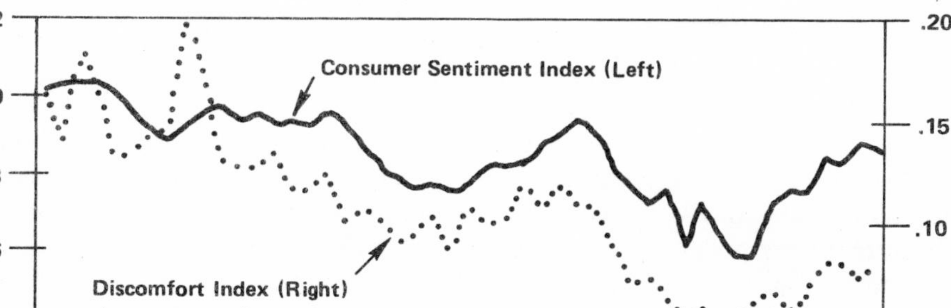

*Discomfort index=1/(unemployment rate + inflation rate (CPI))

The *end of price controls* added 0.8 percentage point to the inflation of 1974, and thereby indirectly raised the unemployment of the recession. The net effect of price controls over the entire period was very small, but their termination came at a most inopportune moment, in May 1974, worsening an already disastrous inflation situation. In consequence, unemployment was worsened by 0.2 percentage point in the following year.

The *impact of fiscal policies* of the 1960's on inflation was too small to be measured in the year 1974. But fiscal policy was a significant factor in getting the inflation going in the mid-1960's. The massive error of fiscal policy was the underfinancing of the Vietnam War in 1965-66. By 1974 the impact of that error would have disappeared, since a recession and price controls intervened. Later errors, including the restrictive budgets of the gradualism of 1969 and the excessive budget increases prior to the 1972 election, were relatively minor in relation to the size of the economy. Since fiscal policy erred in both directions at different times, the net effect on the inflation rate was only 0.3 percentage point in 1974.

The sum of the effects of the particular factors listed do not add up precisely to the entire inflation or unemployment. The unexplained residual inflation rate represents 3.9%. A rate of this order of magnitude would have developed even if none of the particular factors had gone wrong. The reason is quite fundamental. The American economy does not possess a Phillips curve which reconciles reasonable full employment with reasonable price stability. Even if unemployment had been kept above 4% during the Vietnam War years, a wage-price spiral would gradually have gotten into motion and the short-term Phillips curves would have deteriorated. Further, world material prices stopped falling in the mid-1960's and began to increase. With fixed exchange rates, these materials price increases were converted into a higher domestic price level and accelerated the wage-price spiral.

In the case of the unemployment rate, the six contributing factors that have been analyzed account for 4.5 percentage points of the 8.5% unemployment rate in the trough year of 1975. Thus, only 4% remains to be accounted for. This is a rate near the frictional level.

In summary, then, the double-digit inflation of 1974 and the Great Recession of 1975 were caused by the unhappy coincidence of the energy and food shocks, and by extreme and unstable monetary policies. Excessive ease of monetary policy in 1971-72 helped create the excessive investment boom and overoptimistic expectations. When monetary policy sought to freeze the money supply during the worst of the price shocks, a financial crisis was created which was the worst since the Great Depression. The end of price controls and the devaluation of the dollar contributed to the inflation, and thereby to the economic crisis. Thus, the economy became the victim of external misfortunes and a bunching of errors in policy.

While the Great Recession can be explained by piecemeal analysis, this study would not be complete without looking for underlying themes which might provide a unifying thread to this series of "accidents." Perhaps the much-sought, new paradigm for economic theory to suit the new historical situation will turn up in the search.

3. *Has the System Survived?*

In several critical dimensions, the American economy has put itself back together and is functioning very much as it has for many decades. First, the increase in output per manhour, a measure of productivity, shows little sign of slowdown further after the Great Recession. The long-term productivity trend remains at 2% or higher. Productivity did suffer extraordinarily during the recession, but this is largely accounted for by the cyclical adjustment mechanism. By mid-1976, productivity had recovered very substantially and was near its historical formula. On the other hand, the productivity slowdown that began in the late 1960's persists.

Personal saving has also remained high through the episode. Indeed, during the worst moments for the economy, the personal saving rate was at a peace-time peak. Consumers reacted to uncertainty by increasing their saving. As the economy recovered, the saving rate dropped to the neighborhood of 7%, still slightly above the long-run historical average. This personal saving is an important element in the nation's capital formation. Business saving was held down by a decline in retained earnings and the inadequacy of historical cost-depreciation accounting, but the sharp profit upswing of 1976 brought it closer to its usual levels.

The growth in capital and labor productivity, in turn, combined to produce a continued high rate of increase of the economy's overall potential. The economy did not return to the 4% potential growth rate that prevailed rather briefly from 1966 to 1973. But those years saw exceptionally rapid growth of the labor force. The recent reduction in the growth of potential to 3.3% is attributable mainly to the decline in labor force growth and to the diversion of a fraction of the capital formation to pollution abatement and development of new energy sources, and leaves potential near its long-term trend.

Finally, and perhaps most importantly, the Great Recession did not produce social tension or an increased struggle over income distribution. Indeed, more than anything else it appears to have been a sobering experience that helped bring to an end the strife created in the years of affluence in the Vietnam War in the mid- and late 1960's.

4. Hangover Effects from the Great Recession

Productivity, saving, potential growth and social harmony are the roots of economic progress and ample proof that our economic system has a considerable resilience. Nonetheless, one must recognize that there are important hangover effects from the Great Recession. Foremost among these is a continued high rate of inflation. The increase in the price level remains far above the rates to which we were accustomed. Consumer confidence does not recover fully while inflation proceeds and the economy suffers from an increased vulnerability to external shocks.

The Great Recession and the preceding boom are also reducing the forward momentum of several critical sectors in the economy. State and local governments were hurt very badly by the financial squeeze and by the loss of tax revenue. This large segment of the economy, accounting for one-sixth of all employment, had been one of the main props of economic growth. But in recent years this stimulus had disappeared. A decline in the school-age population and lowered expectations for the quality of public services were occurring even before the Great Recession. The financial disaster that struck New York City and that threatened other communities took the dynamism out of this sector.

There also are major components of the capital stock which were grossly overdeveloped during the preceding boom. Office buildings, shopping centers, world shipping, jumbo airliners, airports are available in overabundance. Thus, the rate of capital formation is unlikely to return to normal until the economy has grown to absorb these excessive stocks of capital. The financial system cannot fully recover from the extreme conditions reached several times in this difficult decade. Business liquidity as a whole was fully restored by the reliquefication of 1975-76, but the balance sheets of secondary companies are more difficult to bring into equilibrium so long as lenders remain nervous about potential loan losses.

The stock market has been nearly destroyed as a source of equity capital. The volume of new security issues outside of routine public utility issues has been small and confined to the choicest of companies. The stock market's traditional function as a source of risk capital has virtually disappeared in the last ten years. It has become a card game in old securities, played by large financial institutions, staked with the public's savings.

5. Permanent Changes in the Economy

While the system remains intact—still a market economy producing economic growth with a slowly improving distribution of income and wealth—the ten difficult years produced some permanent changes. They lie principally in the international sphere. First and most important, the rise of OPEC has shifted power and is redistributing the flows of income and wealth among nations. The high cost and the vulnerability of supplies create a major new uncertainty for the operation of industrial economies. Structural adjustments to improve the efficiency of energy use in response to the high prices will take years to accomplish. There will be no escape from the energy problem until major new technological sources reach the point of competitiveness.

The rise of OPEC has also accelerated the changing relationship among less developed countries and the industrial nations. While the power of oil is unique and the need of raw materials suppliers for markets and technology should help assure supplies, the industrial nations will be forced increasingly to negotiate with foreign governments. Thus, the world material picture has become politicized.

On the other hand, the flow of trade and investment among the advanced industrial countries survived the Great Recession well, and quickly resumed extraordinary rates of growth. The industrial economies are increasingly linked, allowing greater specialization and competition, and helping to accelerate economic progress. Several new countries are also approaching a degree of development that makes them join the ranks of the advanced industrial state. These countries in transition include Brazil, South Korea, Taiwan, Israel, and Mexico. These changes are of immense benefit, but they do intensify the worldwide business cycle of industrial activity. They will require a reduction in the national autonomy in the pursuit of domestic economic policies as well as an anti-protectionist attitude.

On the domestic scene, the involvement of government in the economy has been expanding since the New Deal, but the last ten years have seen large and qualitatively significant increases. Business is regulated in greater detail in such matters as environmental controls, occupational safety, consumer protection and equality of job opportunity. While these changes were long overdue, they shift the focus of business management from the traditional goals of expansion and profitability toward success in the governmental arena.

These permanent changes have increased the uncertainty of economic decisions for households, businesses, nonprofit organizations and governments. Institutional arrangements have not yet adjusted to this new circumstance. The major groups in the society, such as labor, government, business, and universities, have not yet learned to develop common approaches against the onslaught of new problems. The United States lacks the analytical machinery to develop solutions, and our political process has not yet shown itself capable of developing and applying policies that would assure the success of the economy under the new circumstances.

6. Discoveries and Rediscoveries

The history of instability of the last ten years has also shed light on questions of economic behavior traditionally examined through economic theory and econometrics. There are many questions for which the historical record develops analyzable data only in times of violence. A period of stable growth of output and slowly drifting prices sheds rather limited light on any of the questions. Thus, the static version of Keynesian economics found in the basic textbooks was readily suitable for the calmer of the postwar years. The monetarism which rose as the rival to the Keynesian school revived and sharpened many useful notions from the classical tradition, and was useful for forecasting in the years that sharp variations in monetary policy were a major cause of the business cycle.

Without claiming the full underpinning of econometric testing, let me summarize some broad hypotheses which can be derived from the historical record of the last ten years and from the econometric modeling exercises of this volume. These assertions are largely rediscoveries of propositions that had been generally understood at earlier times but had been forgotten in the period of placid economic progress.

1. The economy is vulnerable to shocks and they are an important source of business cycle fluctuations. The period of relatively stable growth between the Korean War and Vietnam was exceptionally free of exogenous events that could affect the economy. There is little to mention besides the extended 1959 steel strike and the Kennedy-steel confrontation on prices in 1962.

Since 1965, the shocks have come thick and fast, and have been the decisive movers of the economy. The Vietnam War created the boom and the beginnings of inflation in the late 1960's. The world food disaster of 1972-73 put us on the road to double-digit inflation and marked the end of the period of consumer optimism. The OPEC world oil price increase pushed us into double-digit inflation, and the embargo finished the job of demolishing consumer confidence. The end of price controls in the midst of all this helped create the inflation climax.

During the period of relatively mild inflation, there were buffers to take care of what might have been more severe shocks. When the Suez Canal was closed in 1956-57, the excess capacity of United States crude oil production quickly filled the gap and kept the world industrial economy advancing without disruption. When world crops fluctuated in those years, the huge surpluses of crops in government hands easily filled the gap and helped keep prices stable.

2. *There are various mechanisms in the private economy which amplify the impacts of shocks and convert them into business cycles.* At least three mechanisms must be singled out: the financial system, consumer behavior, and errors in expectations of business.

3. *The financial condition of the country has deteriorated because of the history of instability.* "Credit crunches" have become more severe and have characterized the end of every business cycle upswing. Interest rates and stock market yields have discounted worsening inflation and increased risk premia. The ability to raise external capital by business and the housing industry has gradually become impaired as financial markets have responded to the new conditions by increasingly penalizing the smaller companies, new enterprises, and even state and local governments.

The shocks have accentuated this deterioration and increasing cyclicality of the financial system. Surging prices multiply the financing needs of business, particularly because the worst of the inflation inevitably comes as a surprise and therefore is not provided for in business or personal financial planning. The resultant need for credit comes at the very moment that the high inflation frightens the central bank. The supply of credit therefore is constricted at just the wrong moment, helping to produce severe recession. This, in essence, was the nature of the business cycle collapse of the winter of 1974-75.

4. *Consumer expectations are volatile and inflation-sensitive.* The behavior of consumption during a period of instability shows that households react promptly and strongly to changes in the economic environment. In periods of good economic performance, with high income growth and little inflation, consumer commitments for automobiles, other durable goods, and housing were extraordinarily high, higher than the consumption functions propounded by Keynes, Duesenberry, Friedman or Modigliani-Ando would have suggested. Consumers reacted to more than estimates of their temporary or permanent income or wealth; they also reacted strongly to the degree of uncertainty in their environment. In the years of worsening inflation, they quickly and sharply curtailed their commitments for these big-ticket items. The Michigan Consumer Sentiment Index is a crude but meaningful measure of consumer confidence, and as figure 11.1 shows, the strength of consumer

sentiment follows rather closely the behavior of consumer prices and of national unemployment.

This responsiveness of the consumption function to short-term changes in economic conditions poses new challenges to macro policies designed to manage aggregate demand. Any disturbance to prices and employment, whether created by the business cycle, food or energy shocks, policy surprises, or other causes, has a quick and powerful impact, greatly magnifying the full impact of the initial impulse.

5. *Business expectations can be wrong, and occasional periods of massive error are a major factor in the business cycle.* Business has been operating in an unstable environment, with the years of high growth followed by credit crunches and recessions. It was probably impossible for business to correctly anticipate the timing and magnitude of these fluctuations. Indeed, the record of economic forecasting by the professionals, both econometricians and judgemental forecasters, shows that they are unable to anticipate more than a fraction of such variations. Nonetheless, the record shows some tendency to systematic error, even after the fallibility of forecasting is recognized. The boom of the early 1970's saw numerous excesses of investment, which cannot be entirely blamed on too low a real cost of capital. Expectations became overexuberant. Financial pressures to achieve rising earnings-per-share, building on inadequacies of accounting principles rather than real business success, reinforced these tendencies. When the Great Recession began to set in in the first quarter of 1973, business was extremely slow to moderate its plans. Whereas households staged a quick retreat at early signs of increased food prices, business investment and inventory policies operated on a grossly false set of future expectations for the succeeding eighteen months.

It is possible that the experiences of these years have made business more sensitive to changing external economic conditions and that it will respond more promptly to market variations in the future. The use of econometric models and national economic information systems provides some of the tools for such an improvement.

6. *The stability of governmental institutions does matter to the economy.* The United States is not accustomed to instability in its central government. Normally, in economic policy matters, the Congress follows the lead of the President. While the President and his advisers are also fallible, at least there is a cohesion and direction.

But presidential leadership in economic policy deteriorated during the last ten years, and during some crucial moments it collapsed. In the Vietnam War, the presidency declined; Lyndon Johnson was unable to lead the Congress or the country into the kind of fiscal policy that would have minimized the inflationary impact from the War. The tax increase to finance defense spending could not be instituted, thereby helping to set the stage for the subsequent worsening troubles. The Watergate crisis similarly produced a period of eclipse for the presidency which hurt the economy. The price-wage control program, whatever its original merits may have been, was allowed to dissolve into disorder, creating an industrial price explosion. The usual check on the monetary authorities was lost while Nixon was removed from office, giving them the freedom to follow their instincts without rein, creating an old-fashioned financial panic.

7. *Extreme fluctuations in monetary policy have accentuated the economy's instability.* Monetary policy must take part of the blame for the increasing frequency and severity of credit crunches, and for overstimulating investment and the stock market during upswings. The credit crunch is a critical part of the business cycle. During most business cycle upswings, monetary policy was too easy, leaving interest rates low too long, and increasing the money supply at too high a rate. As a result, over-expansionary tendencies by business were reinforced, and the stock market briefly inflated, triggering waves of mergers and the formation of conglomerates. Late in each business cycle, monetary policy has turned very restrictive, creating extreme credit stringencies and making it impossible for business to complete its investment plans. The four credit crunches of the decade were at the heart of the business cycle mechanism and did much to impair the smooth functioning of the economy. A steadier approach to monetary policy would have avoided the mistakes of both extremes of ease and tightness.

8. *But no single simple rule is sufficient to guide monetary policy.* The simulation experiments in Chapter 7 show that a monetarist rule, setting policy to assure a smooth and proper rate of growth of the narrow money supply, would have out-performed actual policy during the Vietnam War and the initial years of the 1970's. But that rule would have been no significant improvement over actual policy during the years of the food and energy shocks, and to the extent that policy was monetarist just prior to the Great Recession, it was a major cause of it.

A rule of steady nominal or real interest rates would have allowed the economy to sail more smoothly through the periods of food and energy shocks. But it would have been a disaster during the Vietnam War years. It is evident that if there is a set of principles to conduct a rational monetary policy, it must contain elements of monetarism, elements of interest rate policy, and some explicit consideration of the particular causes of each business cycle.

9. *The Keynesian theory of fiscal policy received strong support during the Great Recession.* The tax cut of 1975, which was imposed under trying conditions, was spent promptly and fully, with the extra retail spending fully matching the tax cut in just five months. On the other hand, when the tax cut

was allowed to shrink prematurely in 1976, purchasing power began to stagnate.

10. Government expenditures proved a far less effective instrument than tax reduction. In the particular circumstances, the tax cut multiplier clearly exceeded the spending multiplier. Government expenditures proved a weak tool of stabilization policy. The expenditure programs, admittedly limited in nature and partly delayed by the disagreements between the Congress and the President, came much too late, lagging the trough of the recession by an average of about eighteen months. Further, the bulk of the increase in discretionary spending was in grants-in-aid to local governments. It is difficult to trace their economic impact since these governments have the ability to devote some of the grants for tax relief or repayment of past debts.

11. Price and wage controls produce little benefit in peacetime, cannot survive for long, and can do considerable harm. While the controls imposed in 1971 definitely reduced the rate of price inflation for several years, they began to erode within weeks of their announcement. The succeeding phases reflected more than the lack of ideological support from the President and his economic advisers. The political system made inroads into the controls rather quickly. More fundamentally, the controls clearly worsened the sense of shortage in industrial markets, diverted some scarce materials into exports, created new uncertainties for investment plans for expansion, and when the controls finally could not be held any longer, they produced a price explosion at the very worst possible moment, which lost whatever price gains had been accumulated. The controls were a contributing factor to the Great Recession.

12. The nature of the world economic system matters keenly to the United States, and the changes it is now undergoing are of great importance to our own prosperity. The worldwide shortage of materials and the resultant inflation were by-products of the conversion of a fixed exchange rate system into one of greater flexibility. Had the change come earlier, the years of dollar glut would have been averted. Further, the formation of OPEC and the politicization of other raw material supplies are creating new uncertainties for industrial economies as well as new inflationary pressures. Finally, the advanced countries are just beginning to learn what the principles of exchange rate policy must be in the new situation. In a world of huge amounts of nervous liquid capital, uncoordinated domestic monetary and fiscal policies, and unilateral interventions in the markets for their own currencies, there is little chance that exchange rates will find their "proper" value. Yet, the fate of each country's industries and internationally traded goods depends critically upon the exchange rates. The reconstruction of the international economic order will require that these matters be sorted out and that suitable agreements be reached.

7. *Will the Future Be Any Better?*

Any answer to this question is more a reflection of the personality of the writer than a hard assessment of the facts. The last ten years have taught us the importance of surprises and the true impenetrability of the future. Econometric methods and elaborate information systems can reduce the uncertainty about the future to a modest degree. But these methods are useful principally for modeling those aspects of the economy which are known, those characteristics of structure that can be found in the historical record. Double-digit inflation and the Great Recession were the results of new elements: an unpopular war, the first explosion of food prices in twenty years, and the organization of OPEC. The surprising character of these events follows a pattern that can be found through all of human history: major surprises are never anticipated except by a few lonely prophets whose credibility cannot be assessed.

The proper response of economic institutions, both private and public, is to devise policies and to make decisions which have a reasonable prospect of success even in the face of adversity. They must be examined for their vulnerability to changing economic, political and financial circumstance. This is a far cry from the kind of long-range uni-valued planning that is occasionally advanced as an answer to our problems. We live in a world of surprises, and we might as well organize ourselves accordingly.

POSTSCRIPT

STAGFLATION: IS THERE A WAY OUT?

1. Introduction

The persistence of inflation in combination with high unemployment is the central economic phenomenon of the late 1970's. Stagflation—inflation in combination with growth inadequate to fully employ the labor force—was generally recognized in 1970, when recession did not bring relief from the Vietnam War inflation. Subsequent efforts through price controls, stimulating fiscal and monetary policies, manpower programs and other approaches have not succeeded in bringing it to an end. According to current forecasts, stagflation is expected to persist as far as the trained eye can see.

Stagflation is a self-perpetuating condition. Inflation creates high interest rates, undermines business and consumer confidence, and keeps government from boosting demand through budget policies. Unemployment and low capital utilization, on the other hand, weaken the incentive to invest, thereby holding back private spending and the increase of the economy's potential.

The persistence of stagflation over the past eight years has unloosed a wave of criticism of economists. After the heady days of the early and mid-1960's, when economists seemed able to tell government how to achieve prosperity with reasonably stable prices, it has been a disappointment to the public, and most especially to editorial writers, that macroeconomics appears to have been a light that failed.

This study is advanced in the spirit that there is little mystery to the process of stagflation. It is not some deep intellectual conundrum requiring a new paradigm: the historical process and the characteristics of the economy which have produced the current stagflation are easily understood. The study also identifies the cures. What remains to be settled is whether the cures are better or worse than the disease.

The study employs various econometric techniques to reach its conclusions.[1] The DRI Model of the U.S. Economy is the principal analytical device, both to analyze the history and to explore the policy choices. At

[1] I am grateful to Douglas Rice for performing the model simulations and generally coordinating the study, to Robin Siegel for the econometric work on wages and to Stephen Brooks for the work on taxes.

certain critical points, hypotheses had to be redefined by additional studies of matters on which the stagflation issues pivot.

It is generally recognized that stagflation is a product of the past. The Vietnam War, food and oil price explosions, and financial instability combined to create the current impasse. The scientific task is to sort out the elements that make stagflation persist, to measure the role of the principal causes, to estimate the dynamic responses that determine the time profile of wage-price behavior, and to identify structural weaknesses of the economy.

2. *Stagflation in Historical Perspective*

Stagflation can be measured by the "discomfort" index, the sum of the unemployment and inflation rates. Figure 1 shows the record for this index for this century. Greater discomfort could be found in previous periods: in World War I a much higher rate of inflation pushed the discomfort index to a peak of 28 points. The Great Depression produced the century's peak with a score of 30 in 1934, when unemployment was 22% and inflation over 7%. The price explosion at the end of the controls of World War II produced another pair of high discomfort years in 1946 and 1947. But for the succeeding three decades, 1974 and 1975 stand out as the worst. Indeed, the figure shows that

Figure 1
Consumer well-being:
"Discomfort" index, 1900-90
(percent)

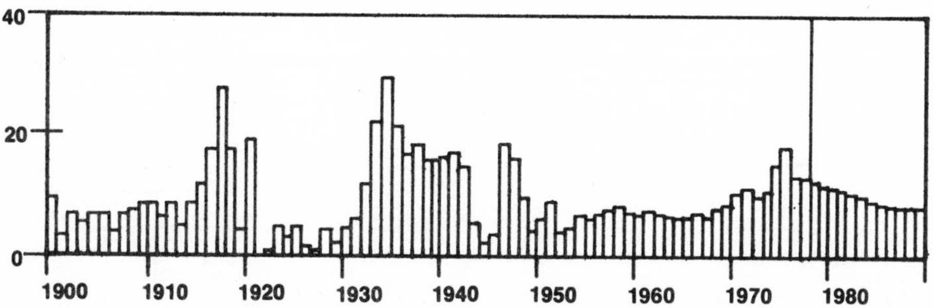

The "discomfort" index, a measure of consumer well-being, is calculated as sum of unemployment rate and inflation rate (implicit price deflator), but not less than zero.
1978-1990 based on DRI December 1977 long-term forecast.
Source: History—NBER, BLS, BEA.

the experience since 1974 is the worst since the 1930's, with both unemployment and inflation contributing to the persistently high index. Figure 2 shows the deterioration since 1960. In the early years of that decade, the discomfort index averaged about 7%, with unemployment near 5% and the rate of price inflation near 2%. The coming of the Vietnam War in 1966 made the index get worse, but it did not begin to take on double-digit values until 1970. In that year, a mild recession raised unemployment but did not improve inflation as the wage round contained a catch-up element to compensate for the previous guidepost policies. The index accelerated in 1971 in a recovering economy, frightening the government into the imposition of wage and price controls. After a brief respite, the explosion of food and oil prices and the onset of the Great Recession produced the modern peak figures for the discomfort index, and ushered in the new period of persisting stagflation.

Seen in this historical perspective, the current episode is more notable for its persistence than the violence of economic performance. Recent trauma were not the match of the three previous periods of extreme economic instability. But the problem is bad enough to deserve top intellectual and policy priority, and it runs counter to the traditional American belief in the perfectability of institutions.

3. The Role of Energy

The OPEC oil embargo and the subsequent quadrupling of the world price of oil were among the principal causes of the 1974 price explosion and of the

Figure 2
Consumer well-being:
"Discomfort" index, 1960-1977
(percent)

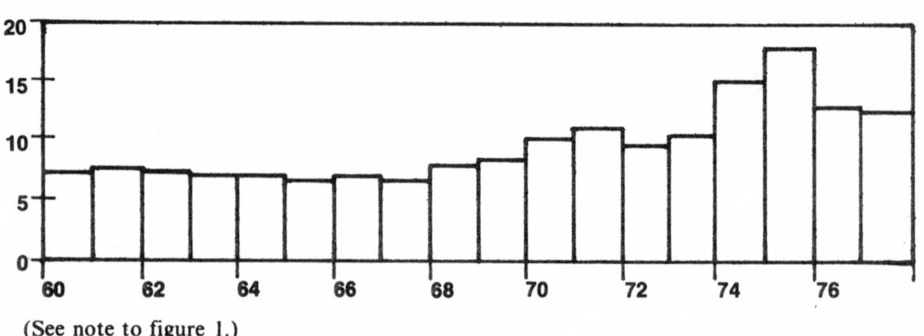

(See note to figure 1.)

1974-75 recession. To what extent can the subsequent stagflation be directly blamed on energy problems? Since 1975, the price of OPEC oil has risen no faster than other prices. However, the United States has controlled the price of domestic oil and gas, and so U.S. energy prices are in the midst of a seven-year adjustment period in which they move to equality with world prices. As a result, energy adds a fraction of a point to the inflation rate. It also raises unemployment because of the indirect effects of inflation on prosperity.

Table 1 summarizes the impact of energy prices on the U.S. economy, as portrayed by DRI model simulations. In the base case, the increase for the wholesale prices for fuel and related products and of fuel import prices is held to a 5% annual rate. In the alternative, the actual path of this index is imposed. The total effect of the higher energy prices on the discomfort index peaked in 1975 when they had their biggest impact on finished goods prices and on unemployment. Thus, energy accounted for 3 out of the 18 points of the discomfort index of that year. In 1976 and 1977, the discomfort index was boosted by 1.6 points by energy. The effect will be similar for 1978-80, under the compromise energy program. Gradually the impact is being converted from an increase in unemployment to an increase in inflation as the economy recovers over this business cycle.

Table 1
The energy crisis and stagflation in the U.S. economy, 1975-80[1]

	1975	1976	1977	1978-1980F
Energy impacts on				
Inflation	1.1	0.0	0.4	0.9
Unemployment	1.9	1.6	1.2	0.8
Discomfort index	3.0	1.6	1.6	1.7

F is the forecast with compromise energy program.

[1]The effects of lower energy price inflation as estimated through the DRI Model of the U.S. Economy. Wholesale prices for fuel and related products, and import prices for fuel were held to 5% annual inflation rates from 1973 to 1982. Estimates differ somewhat from those of Chapter 9 because the simulation starts at a later date.

By 1984, oil and gas price decontrol will be complete, and oil prices will be rising only moderately faster than general inflation, at least until there is another major change in the energy situation. There are fears that there will be a second energy crisis in the mid- or late 1980's, when Saudi Arabia may find it rational to begin to bring down her enormous exports. But that is a matter to pursue on some future occasion.

4. Could the United States Have Followed the German Strategy?

West Germany experienced the same OPEC price increases, and, because of the lack of domestic oil sources, the price shock to the energy situation in Germany was worse than in the United States. However, the inflation rate in West Germany has been lower than in the U.S. by several percentage points ever since 1974 (figure 3). While unemployment is up as much in Germany as in the United States (figure 4), the reduction of inflation to a 3½% rate suggests that this economy is escaping stagflation more effectively.

The policy approach in West Germany was different. No attempt was made to control domestic energy prices and so German businesses and households were required to pay the full increases charged by OPEC. Not surprisingly, West Germany has shown more progress in encouraging conservation. Environmental considerations have also been waived more extensively, permitting a quicker substitution of coal for imported oil. The West German government also avoided strong policies of stimulus, preferring to keep pressure on West German industry to accentuate the traditional policy of growth through exports.

While it is encouraging to see that an industrial country was able to escape

Figure 3
Inflation rate,
United States and West Germany
(percent)

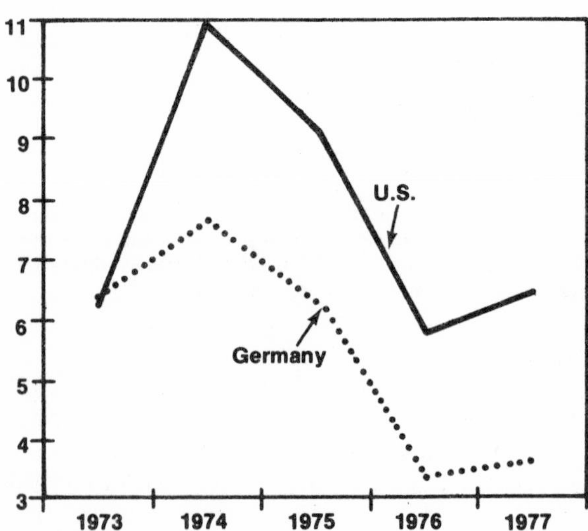

Inflation rate is the consumer price index for U.S. and retail price index for West Germany.

Figure 4
Unemployment rate,
United States and West Germany
(percent)

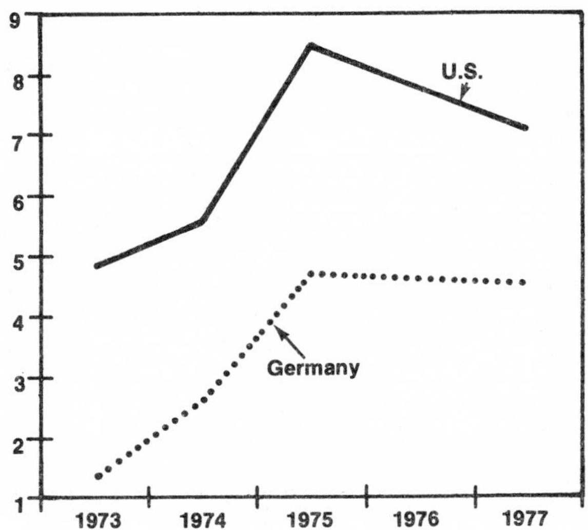

inflation, the lessons to be drawn from the German experience are limited. There are important differences between the West German and our own situation. First, because Germany has always been dependent on imported oil, energy consumption by business and consumers is more frugal. The ratio of energy consumption to GNP in West Germany, as in other European countries, is only about 60% as large as our own.[2] Automobile design emphasizes fuel efficiency because gasoline has long been heavily taxed. The average dwelling is of smaller size and the stand-alone single-family home is less common. Commuting distances are smaller, reducing the energy consumption for transportation. As a result, the energy crisis has had a lesser direct impact on West Germany and required a lesser adjustment in lifestyles.

The difference in overall economic performance between West Germany and the United States is actually quite small, and policies are probably not the heart of the matter. In the years 1973 to 1976, real GNP growth in the two countries followed a nearly identical pattern. It was only in 1977 that the divergence developed. While U.S. GNP (figure 5) advanced at a 4.9% rate with the help of stimulating policies, West German growth slipped to 2.5%. This slowdown was as much the result of accident as of design. The growth of

[2] E.R. Fried and C.L. Schultze, *Higher Oil Prices and the World Economy*, Brookings, 1975, p. 18.

Figure 5
Real gross national product growth,
United States and West Germany
(percent)

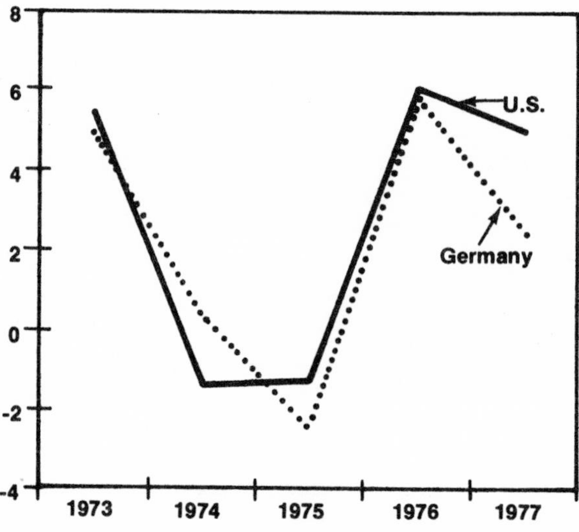

Figure 6
Real government spending growth,
United States and West Germany
(percent)

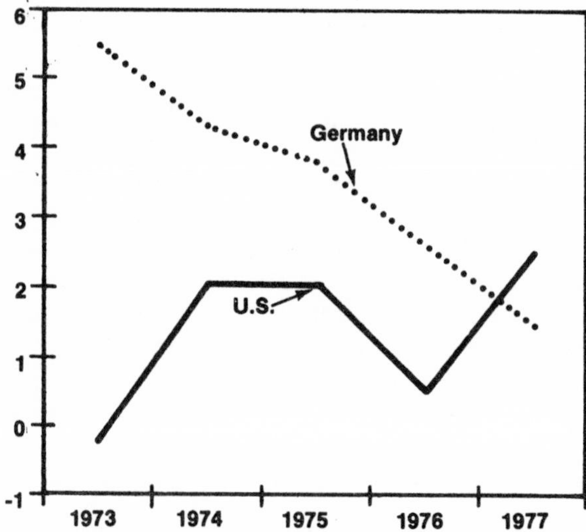

real government spending, which had been much higher in West Germany than in the United States, kept coming down in 1977 because of various obstacles to nuclear power and other public investments. In the U.S., on the other hand, spending accelerated after the Democratic Party gained full control of the government (figure 6). The tax side of German fiscal policy was probably more restrictive than the government had intended: corporate tax reform produced more revenue than expected. Personal tax collections were also quite strong as the government minimized the standard stimulating strategy of personal tax reduction.

The rate of wage increase in Germany was 7%, about a point lower than in the U.S. Since the 1930's, the German labor movement has been weaker than our own, and there are useful elements of incomes policy.

The biggest difference in economic performance is in exports (figure 7). West Germany developed a huge export surplus as oil imports were kept stable and industry struggled to substitute new foreign for fading domestic markets. Export performance was particularly high in the Socialist bloc and

Figure 7
Real net exports as a
percent of real GNP

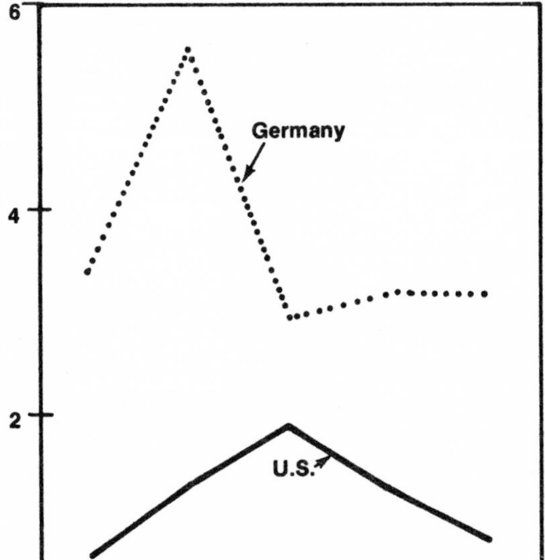

the oil producing nations. In the United States, in contrast, oil imports surged in 1977, and exports were hurt by an over-valued currency. Had the United States followed the German strategy of paying her oil bill with exports, an impossible international financial situation would have been created because the world oil payments deficit would have had to be carried by weak countries of limited credit worthiness.

There are some lessons in the successful German effort to bring the inflation rate down. A stronger energy policy has reduced the inflationary impact of OPEC and has avoided the rising volume of oil imports. The German version of incomes policy produces a somewhat lower rate of wage increase. The strength of the D-mark has reduced the cost of imported industrial materials and foodstuffs in West Germany, whereas the decline of the dollar has added to inflation in the U.S. On the other hand, slack in the West German economy is holding back business investment, while the export strategy has made industry dependent on foreign markets to an unsustainable degree, ultimately requiring large structural adjustments.

5. *Price Expectations: The Burden of History*

The biggest single cause of the stagflation is the poor history of inflation of the preceding years. The consumer price index rose an average of 8.1% in the years 1974-77, and had been gradually accelerating for a decade. As a result, inflation expectations of consumers, workers and investors were quite inflamed and decisions geared accordingly.

The impact of expectations is most visible in the rate of wage increase. A large body of research[3] has shown that actual wage settlements fully discount price inflation, with the inflation expectations based on the inflation record of the preceding several years. The equation in the 1978 DRI model assumes that long-term price expectations are formed over a period of four years, short-term expectations on about one year. Table 2 shows the results of thorough retesting with the most recent data, designed to identify the periods over which price expectations are formed. The best equation shows a six-year long-term price factor. While it is not possible to define the interval at a level

[3]O. Eckstein and R. Brinner, "The Inflation Process in the United States," a study prepared for the Joint Economic Committee, U.S. Congress, February 1972, reprinted in *Parameters and Policies in the U.S. Economy*, North Holland, 1976; R.J. Gordon, "Wage-Price Controls and the Shifting Phillips Curve," Brookings Economic Papers, 1972, No. 2, pp. 385-421; S.J. Turnovsky and M.L. Wachter, "A Test of the 'Expectations Hypothesis' Using Directly Observed Wage and Price Expectations," *Review of Economics and Statistics*, 1972, pp. 47-54, and J.L. Carlson and M. Parkin, "Inflation Expectations," *Economica*, May 1975, pp. 123-138.

Table 2
Regression results comparing alternative specifications for Long-term price factor in wage equation

Lag on Long-Term Price Factor	Short-term Price Factor	Long-term Price Factor	Actual Relative to Potential GNP	Change in Actual Relative to Potential GNP	Guidepost Dummy	Control Dummy	$\bar{R}^2$	DW
7-year lag	.54	.40	23.02	14.12	.94	2.21	.8576	1.248
	(7.88)	(3.37)	(7.58)	(1.60)	(4.49)	(3.38)		
6-year lag	.52	.43	23.15	11.88	.88	2.23	.8655	1.828
	(7.86)	(4.08)	(7.99)	(1.38)	(4.25)	(3.51)		
5-year lag	.53	.35	22.50	12.42	.87	2.24	.8595	1.767
	(7.79)	(3.55)	(7.64)	(1.40)	(4.13)	(3.46)		
4-year lag	.56	2.8	22.07	13.48	.89	2.26	.8551	1.719
	(8.08)	(3.14)	(7.40)	(1.48)	(4.15)	(3.44)		
3-year lag	.54	.26	22.33	13.10	.91	2.25	.8527	1.687
	(7.17)	(2.90)	(7.29)	(1.40)	(4.21)	(3.39)		
2-year lag	.53	.23	21.56	17.25	.98	2.22	.8430	1.590
	(4.42)	(1.72)	(6.53)	(1.73)	(4.39)	(3.24)		
No long-term factor	.73	--	18.94	26.30	1.06	2.24	.8391	1.560
	(16.84)		(6.40)	(3.08)	(4.84)	(3.23)		

Equation estimated was

$$400 * \log(WAGE_t/WAGE_{t-1}) = a_0 + a_1 * 100 * \log(P_{t-1}/P_{t-5}) + a_2 * 100/x * \log(P_{t-1}/P_{t-1-4\times x}) + a_3 * \log(GNP_t/GNPK72_t)$$
$$+ a_4 * \log(GNP_t/GNPK72_t)/(GNP72_{t-1}/GNPK72_{t-1}) + a_5 * GUIDEPOST + a_6 * CONTROL$$

where WAGE is the wage index, P is the implicit price deflator for consumption expenditures, GNP72 is real gross national product, GNPK72 is potential gross national product, GUIDEPOST is a dummy variable to account for the effect of wage-price guideposts during the Kennedy and Johnson administrations, CONTROL is a dummy to capture the effect of price-wage controls during the Nixon administration, and x is the number of years of lag on the long-term price factor. Estimated from quarterly data, 1956 to 1977:3. Numbers in parentheses are t-statistics.

of high significance very precisely, it is evident that the lags are long, with the statistical quality of the equations deteriorating as the lags are shortened.

To identify the contribution of price expectations to stagflation, a model simulation was run from 1977 to 1983 in which it was arbitrarily assumed that the actual price expectations were replaced by a 4% inflation rate (figure 8). The assumed improvement in inflation expectations ranges between 2 and 3%. The result is dramatic. Lower price expectations are converted into lower wage increases, lower unit labor costs and, therefore, into lower actual inflation. Real demands and activity initially improve, although later on a part of the inflation gains is lost as a result. The discomfort index, which is

Figure 8
Effect of price expectations:
rates of inflation, with expectations of 4% inflation
versus the current 6 to 7%,
1977:4-1983

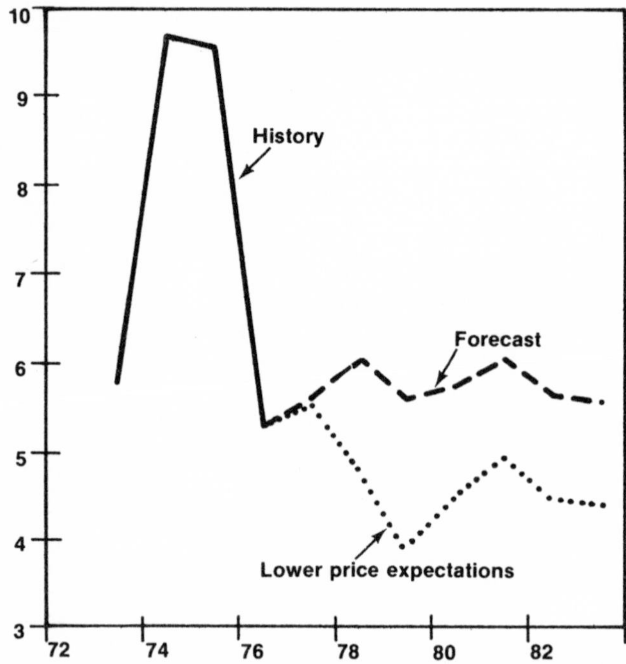

Calculated by model simulation, with 4% price expectations substituted for actual historical experience in the calculation of wage demands. The inflation rate shown is for the implicit price deflator.

Source: History—BEA; Forecast—DRI TRENDLONG1277 forecast.

projected near 12 in the base case, improves to about 10 in the "better expectations" case.

Can the public be "brainwashed" of these price expectations? In a sense, this was the theory of the price and wage controls imposed by President Nixon: if expectations could be improved dramatically by a wage-price freeze, the economy might emerge from the episode on a different wage-price track. The experiment did not work, but the test was a very limited one. The freeze lasted only ninety days and excluded agricultural prices. The subsequent control phases were generally interpreted as retreats. Further, the controls were imposed just after a major wage round was concluded. By the time the next wage round began in 1973, the control program was already weak. The food price explosion, which began in early 1973, and the oil price explosion in late 1973 were so massive that whatever benefits of better expectations may have existed were swept away.

Nonetheless, the brief period of effective controls provides some material for econometric analysis to see if inflation expectations can be changed through strong government action. The equations fitted to the price and wage data of those years do show that the prices of several major categories of industries were held down by the controls, and even the wage equation shows a small reduction. The bigger question, however, is the longer range effect on expectations: were they improved beyond the actual price record developed during the controls? Or, conversely, did the public discount that improvement as an aberration?

The statistical record on which to test this proposition is rather slight. But what evidence there is suggests that the public accepted the improvement in the price record at its face value, no more and no less. The rate of wage increase after the controls were over was estimated with about the same standard error and without bias as in earlier or later years. There was no carryover effect, as table 3 makes clear. On the other hand, the public did not ignore the better price record: the few good quarters enter the wage equation as fully as any other quarters, even though the performance was achieved by controls rather than market forces.

Table 3
Residuals of wage equation,
Post-control period

	1974	1975	1976
I		.000	-.002
II	.005	-.005	-.002
III	.003	-.001	.000
IV	.000	.002	.001

In summary, the inflamed price expectations created by the history of inflation are the single biggest factor in creating the current condition of stagflation. With price expectations in the 6-to-7% range, wages will increase between 8 and 9% in periods of reasonably normal unemployment. The resultant 6-to-7% increase in unit labor cost, which in turn represents 60% of all costs in the economy, makes it very difficult to achieve a decelerating price pattern.

6. Does Collective Bargaining Make a Difference?

Unions are commonly assigned at least part of the blame for inflation and therefore also of stagflation. Yet, when viewed in a longer historical perspective, there is little evidence that organized workers receive particularly large nominal wage increases.

Recently, a sizable disparity has developed between the rate of increase of unionized and nonunionized workers. Figure 9 shows the annual rates of increase for unionized and nonunionized workers in manufacturing since 1972. Until 1974, the pattern for the two groups was quite similar, reaching a peak of 8½% for both groups. But in the recession year of 1975, the rate of wage increase for unionized workers benefited from a further increase to near 9%. In 1976, this extraordinary gap shrank slightly, but the difference remained 1.8%. In 1977, the gap persisted.

Why are unionized workers obtaining larger wage gains in recent years? Econometrics can shed some light on this question. The basic wage equation in the DRI model, containing variables for short- and long-term price expectations and unemployment, has been applied to wage series for the heavily unionized and less unionized industries in manufacturing. Because the series of figure 9 are only available since 1972, other series were compiled from the standard, overtime-corrected average hourly earnings data, using the "key group" defined in an earlier paper[4] as measures. These data do not show dramatic differences between the two groups, raising a question about the extent of disparity shown in the recently developed series plotted in figure 9. But the statistical tests do show that there are important differences in the wage behavior of the two groups. The statistical conclusions are summarized in table 4. First, the higher correlation coefficients for two equations that split the manufacturing labor force into two groups show that a different wage equation applies, i.e., that unionization changes behavior. Second, the reaction of wages to prices is nearly the same in the two sectors; the sum of the

[4]O. Eckstein and T.A. Wilson, "The Determination of Money Wages in American Industry," *The Quarterly Journal of Economics*, August 1962, pp. 379-414.

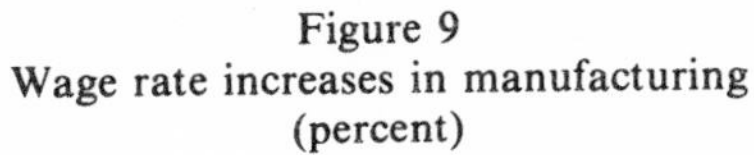

Figure 9
Wage rate increases in manufacturing
(percent)

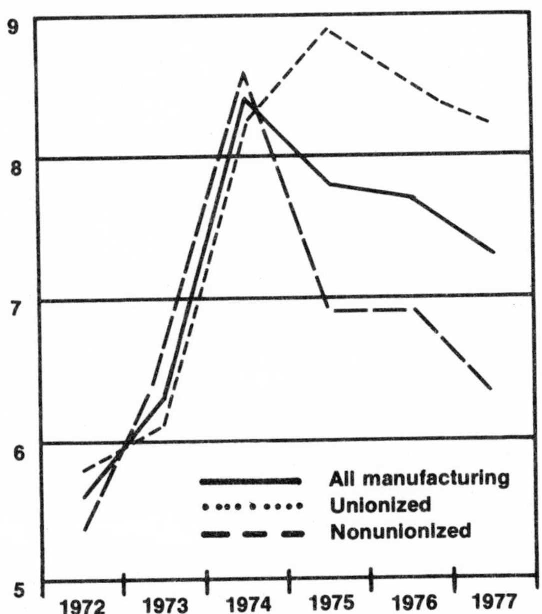

price coefficients is not statistically different from unity in either case. The unionized industries seem to attach a greater part of the weight to the short-term as opposed to the long-term price factor, which may be a reflection of the prevalence of cost-of-living clauses in their contracts. It is also not surprising that the guidepost variable is highly significant for the heavily unionized and is insignificant for the rest. The control variable for Phase I of the price-wage controls is significant in both sectors, reflecting the universality of that program.

The important difference between the behavior of unionized and nonunionized industries lies in the reaction to unemployment. In the more competitive labor markets, high unemployment has a large and quick effect on the rate of wage increase. But in the unionized industries the effect is much smaller and less significant. This factor explains the disparity in wage results after 1974. High unemployment has done little to bring down the wage increases in the big collective bargaining situations, but it has severely

Table 4
Estimated price and unemployment elasticities for
Heavily unionized versus less heavily unionized
Manufacturing industries

	Short-term Price Factor	Long-term Price Factor	Unemployment Rate	Guidepost Dummy	Control Dummy	$\bar{R}^2$
All manufacturing	.48	.60	-3.01	.68	3.40	
	(3.42)	(2.84)	(-3.36)	(1.43)	(2.30)	.6044
Heavily unionized industries	.69	2.8	-1.55	1.21	3.34	
	(6.54)	(1.80)	(-2.31)	(3.39)	(3.02)	.7645
Less unionized industries	.41	.64	-3.27	.50	2.72	
	(3.81)	(4.02)	(-4.79)	(1.39)	(2.41)	.6981

Equation estimated was

$$\log(WAGE_t / WAGE_{t-1}) = a_0 + a_1 * \log(P_{t-1}/P_{t-5}) + a_2 * \log(P_{t-1}/P_{t-17}) + a_3 * \log(U) + a_4 * GUIDEPOST + a_5 * CONTROL$$

where WAGE is the wage rate, P is the implicit price deflator for consumption expenditures, U is the unemployment rate, GUIDEPOST is a dummy variable to account for the effect of wage-price guideposts during the Kennedy and Johnson administrations, CONTROL is a dummy variable to capture the effect of price-wage controls during the Nixon administration.

$\bar{R}^2$ is the adjusted multiple correlation coefficient, a measure of the explanatory power of the equation.

affected the ability of nonunionized or weakly unionized workers to obtain wage gains.

The insensitivity of highly unionized industries to unemployment is not surprising. Wage determination in these industries is not a market solution but a bilateral negotiation in which quite different preferences are expressed. The high-seniority workers who presumably have a larger influence in the political decisions of unions are less threatened by unemployment than the younger workers with less seniority. They are interested in continued gains in wages and fringe benefits and place less weight on the resultant loss of jobs. In the competitive labor markets, on the other hand, an excess supply of labor converts itself into a lesser wage increase through market forces.

In some of the highly unionized industries, price behavior matches the insensitivity of wages. Elaborate cost calculations determine normal prices, and companies consider it a major shortcoming if actual prices fall short of the cost calculations. Both prices and wages reflect the market structure of large units, and interact to reinforce the rigid wage-price patterns.[5]

7. *Other Labor Market Factors*

A part of the stagflation of recent years has been attributed to the changing age and sex structure of the labor force. Because of the big increases in teenage workers after 1965, the national unemployment rate associated with any particular degree of tightness in the labor market is now somewhat higher. Women also have suffered high unemployment rates. However, more women now wish permanent full-time positions and should be considered a part of the primary labor force.

Teenagers will constitute a shrinking proportion of workers over the next ten years. This factor should reduce the degree of stagflation because it will mean somewhat lower unemployment rates for any given level of economy operation. Figure 10 shows the results of a calculation of unemployment for the next six years if there were no improvement in the mix of the labor force. The gap between actual and potential GNP is held constant in the two calculations, and thus it is entirely the improvement in the composition of the labor force that produces the change in unemployment. The gain growing out of this factor is 0.2 percentage points, a measurable but minor improvement in stagflation.

[5]See O. Eckstein and D. Wyss, "Industry Price Equations," in *The Econometrics of Price Determination, Conference*, Federal Reserve Board, 1971, pp. 133-165, and O. Eckstein, "A Theory of the Wage-Price Process in Modern Industry," *Review of Economic Studies*, October 1964, pp. 167-186.

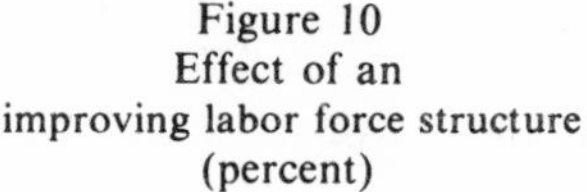

Figure 10
Effect of an
improving labor force structure
(percent)

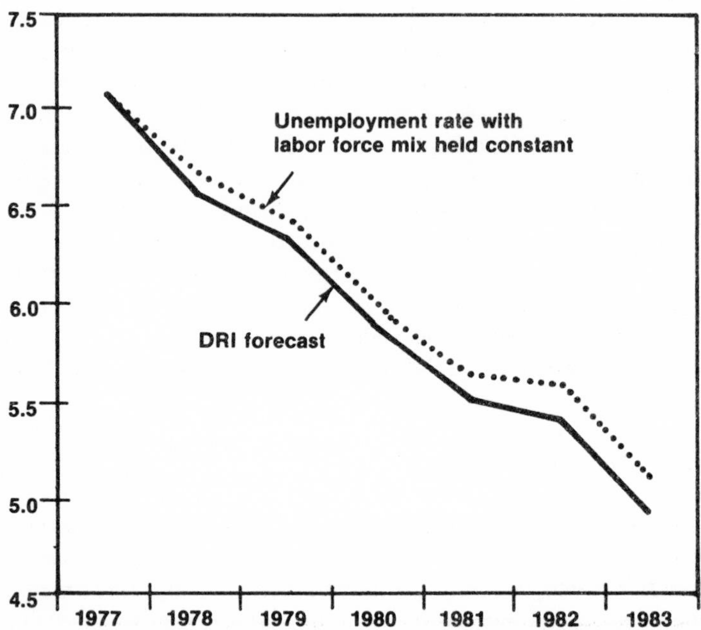

Calculated from an equation modeling the unemployment rate on the GNP gap (potential GNP less actual GNP) and an age-sex weighted labor force concept. This equation was then solved using a projection of the weighted labor force in which the labor force shares of the age-sex cohorts were held constant. The weighting scheme was based on average wage levels provided by the Bureau of Labor Statistics.

Another factor frequently cited in explaining stagflation is government policy to raise minimum wages. While the minimum wage is among the causes of high youth unemployment, it is not a measurable factor in the creation of stagflation. Figure 11 shows the results of a statistical test using standard equation for straight-time earnings, in which the minimum wage was one of the independent variables. While the variable was significant, its impact was slight and infrequent. The solid line in the figure shows how wages would have moved, according to the equation, if the minimum wage were never changed.

8. The Rising Tax Burden and Stagflation

An increasing tax burden can contribute to stagflation in various ways. The

Figure 11
Effect of minimum wage legislation on overall inflationary experience (percent)

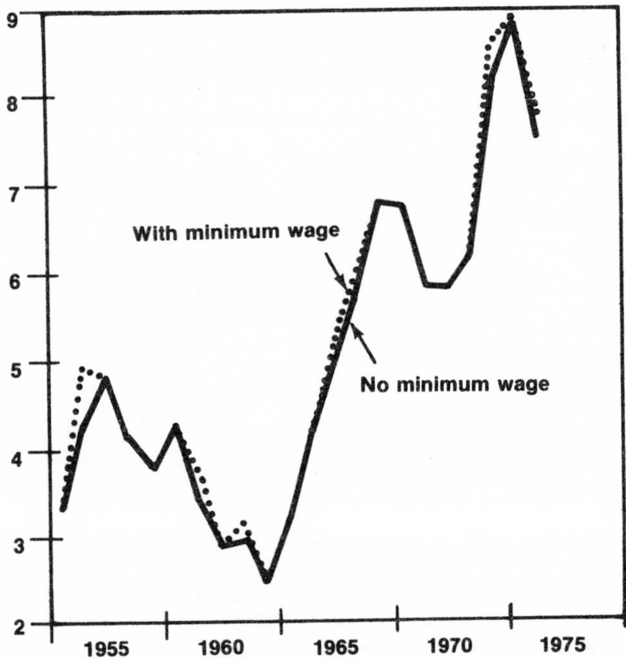

The inflation rates plotted are derived from an equation modeling wage rates of production workers in the private economy (excluding overtime and mix effects) using the minimum wage rate as an explanatory variable. The equation was then solved with (dot) and without (line) the minimum wage term to measure the effects of the minimum wage.

extra cost to business and households, particularly of sales, excise and payroll taxes, adds to inflation, both directly and indirectly. The supply of labor and capital can be curtailed to reduce the potential and worsen inflation. Efficiency of resource use can be reduced by induced attempts to escape the rising tax burden. The advance of productivity can be hurt by discouragement of innovation. Government support of public capital formation and research and development can be crowded out by other claims on the budget.

Figures 12 to 16 show, in summary form, the changing tax burden. Figure 12 shows that taxes are taking a rising share of the gross national product. Like most previous wars, the Vietnam War led to an increase in the government share of resource use, in this case from 28% to about 31% of GNP. When the war was over, the burden did not return to the previous share,

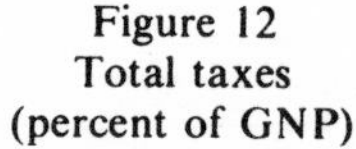

Figure 12
Total taxes
(percent of GNP)

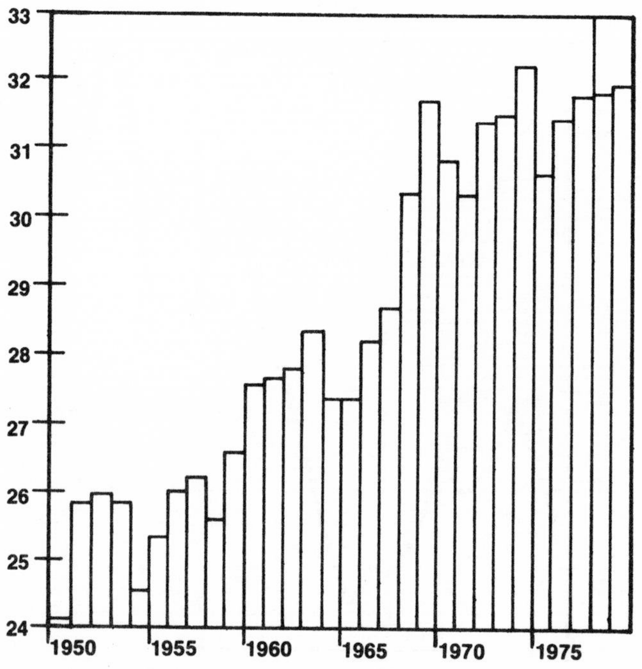

but instead continued to creep upward. The Federal budget has experienced enormous growth for income payments to individuals, including health benefits, and has also become a major source of financing for state and local governments through bigger grant-in-aid programs. Indeed, the purposes of federal expenditures have shifted away from public capital formation, education and research support toward income and grant programs which are used almost entirely for current public and private consumption purposes.

While the total tax burden has risen sharply, the distribution among major tax sources is quite diverse. Corporate income taxes have fallen sharply as a percent of GNP, from an average of 5½% in the years 1950-57, to an average of 3.5% in the years 1975-80 (figure 13). Since the share of profits in GNP has drifted downward as well, the decline in the average effective rate of corporate taxes on profits is not as sharp, but very substantial nonetheless. As figure 14 shows, the average effective tax rate has declined from 47% in the former period to 39% in the latter. The decline in corporate taxes is principally due to

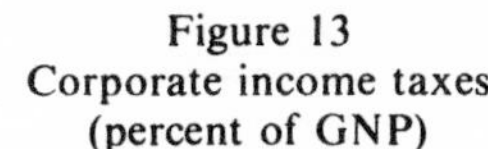
Figure 13
Corporate income taxes
(percent of GNP)

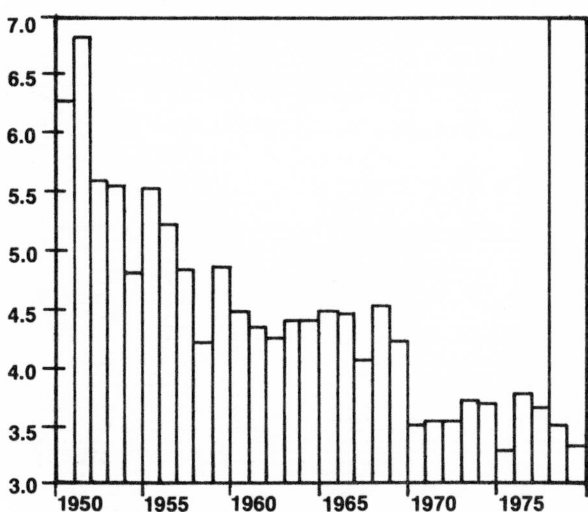

the introduction and broadening of a variety of investment incentives, and to foreign tax credits and incentives to export. In the next few years, the proposed reduction of rates will also be important in lowering this tax burden.

The personal income tax burden, which most directly affects the willingness to work, has been about stable since the increases of the Vietnam War (figure 15). The effects of inflation on revenues through the progressive rate structure have been roughly offset by the series of reductions. The structure of the personal income tax has an important effect on the supply of labor, but the changes of recent years are a mixed bag and it would be rash to claim that the structure has either been improved or deteriorated in this regard. On the one hand, inflation has raised the marginal tax rates very substantially, and the toughened treatment on capital gains has raised the obstacles to innovational activity, entrepreneurship and new business formation. On the other hand, the introduction of a 50% ceiling on earned incomes has left an increased incentive for high-income professionals and business executives. The personal tax has been restructured (and will be restructured further under the President's 1978 proposals) by terminating the tax for low income workers, largely undoing the effects of inflation. For the typical family of four, the President's proposals would impose no tax on a

Figure 14
Effective corporate tax rate
(percent)

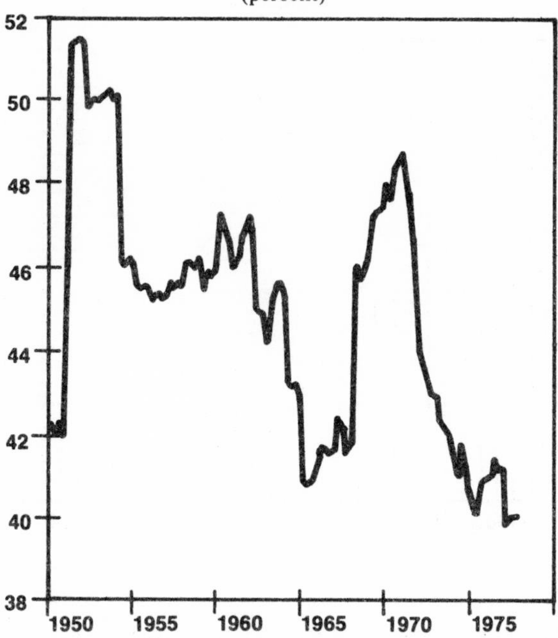

Figure 15
Personal income taxes
(percent of GNP)

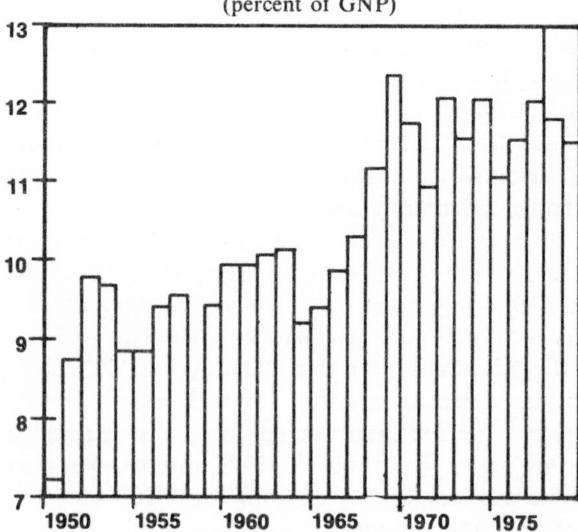

worker with income of $5,400; twenty years ago, a family with an income of $2,800 would have been paying no tax, which would correspond to an income level of $5,900 at 1978 prices.

The structure of the personal income tax also affects the ability of individuals to provide investable capital. On the whole, the tax system has become less and less favorable in this regard. Various policies to promote equity, particularly tougher capital gains taxation, the imposition of the minimum tax, the partial reforms of tax shelters, and the reform of estate and gift taxes, make it more difficult to form individually owned capital. This is in sharp contrast to the ever more generous tax incentives for corporate capital formation through the retained earnings route. These disparate strategies are reflected in the dramatic decline of the stock market.

While it is impossible to reach any strong conclusions about the effects of increases of corporate and personal taxes on stagflation, the effects of indirect and payroll taxes are less ambiguous. As figure 16 shows, these taxes have increased from less than 11% of GNP to nearly 17%, an increase of 6% since

Figure 16
Indirect business and payroll taxes
(percent of GNP)

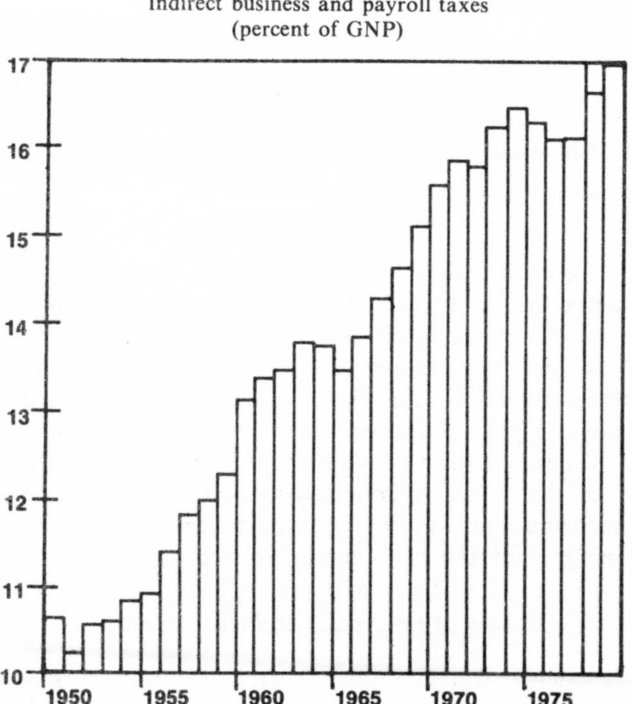

the mid-1950's. The direct impact of this tax increase on the price level is at least 6%, which, when spread over 22 years, is still a small amount, 0.3% a year. However, this is an underestimate of the effects. Higher excise and payroll taxes initially raise the inflation rate by these percentages, but the extra inflation becomes part of the wage-price spiral through price expectations. Consequently, there are further feedbacks which multiply the initial impact. In addition, large increases in payroll tax burdens, the largest of which lie ahead, raise the cost of labor to business and lead to the substitution of capital and materials for labor. Thus, they reduce the volume of employment for any given volume of production. Further, to the extent that inflation affects the level of activity, production itself is curtailed. Thus, the increase in indirect business and payroll taxes is a significant contributor to stagflation.

The total net tax burden on work has risen sharply as a result of higher payroll taxes and more generous unemployment insurance benefits. Figure 17 shows the net tax burden of a worker receiving average gross wages compared to his receiving average unemployment insurance benefits. The net tax burden—or effective tax rate on employment—is defined as equal to the average effective personal tax plus his half of the social security tax, plus the loss of unemployment insurance benefits. The figure is only illustrative, since the effect will vary according to income class, state of residence, family circumstance, and other factors. The calculation ignores the rising employer burden of payroll taxes. The figure does show, beyond a reasonable shadow of a doubt, that working is being taxed more and more heavily.

9. *The Cures for Stagflation: Drastic Approaches*

The above analysis provides a realistic setting for considering the possible cures for stagflation. To repeat, the principal cause of stagflation is the deep-seated set of price expectations created by the last ten years of inflation, particularly the last four years of rapid inflation. Secondary causes are the continuing need to move domestic energy prices to world price levels, the sharp increases in payroll and energy taxes, the insensitivity of collective bargaining in major industries to unemployment, cost-oriented pricing by some industries that seems impervious to market forces, and the decline of the dollar's purchasing power in buying foreign materials, goods and services. With this background, the cures can be defined.

9.1. *Three to four years of rigid price and wage controls*

If we really mean to end stagflation, a strict, effective and complete system of

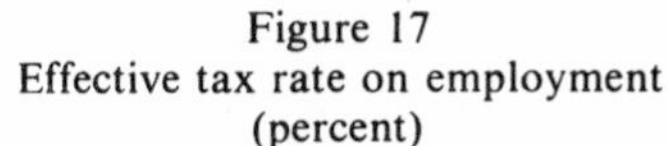

Figure 17
Effective tax rate on employment
(percent)

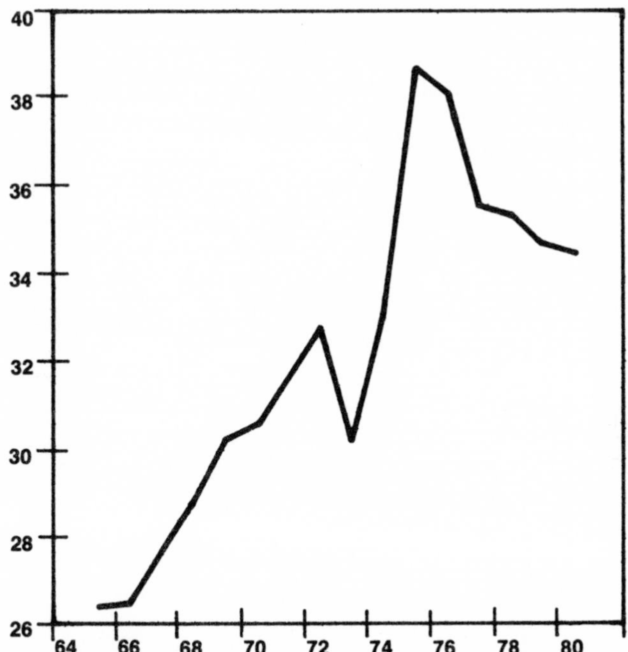

An individual moving off unemployment rolls loses untaxed unemployment benefits and gains wages and salaries net of personal and social security taxes. His disposable income increases by much less than the increase in his gross wages. This difference between gross wages and disposable income is the effective tax on employment.

The analysis assumes the individual receives average unemployment benefits or has a job paying average gross wages. The tax rates applied to this income are (a) the average personal tax rate that applied in each period and (b) one-half of the effective social insurance tax rate.

Projections are based on DRI forecast of December 1977, and do not include President Carter's proposal to tax unemployment benefits. The rate also falls in the later years because extraordinary unemployment benefits of the 1975 recession have expired.

wage and price controls, kept in place for a full three to four years, will accomplish the change in price expectations that is necessary. If the system could remain intact through such an episode, and no new disasters such as a renewed world oil crisis would befall us, an era of high employment with reasonable price stability would be entered.

Except for the rare moments when we impose cost-price controls, virtually all informed opinion considers them an economic and political impossibility. John Kenneth Galbraith[6] has been virtually their only serious supporter.

Nonetheless, stagflation is the central economic ailment of our day, and we had better take one more look at this cure before we dismiss it once more from polite conversation. The arguments fall into two kinds, economic and political. A period of controls suspends the use of relative prices and markets to assure the efficient, decentralized working of the economy. But relative prices change only modestly in a routine three-year period, and if, by sacrificing the market mechanism for a few years, stagflation could be ended, controls would be a debatable proposition. More practically, a period of price controls is one in which business decisions and management are almost exclusively focussed on the relations between business and government, on coping with the price controls, on retaining employees despite inability to adjust compensation, on selling in uncontrolled markets abroad, on obtaining needed production materials and other such controls-created difficulties. Price and wage controls also may have a very significant effect on investment. If prices are controlled, they cannot rise for those products for which there is a need to attract above-average quantities of capital. Consequently, there may be less capital formation in industries with potential bottlenecks. It should be kept in mind, however, that the years of the Nixon price controls were years of heavy investment. But on that occasion, their peculiar termination and the events that followed washed away whatever benefit they had created in lowering inflation.

The political objections to price and wage controls are more persuasive. A rigid system of controls presupposes that there is a strong government able to carry out an elaborate plan designed to promote the national purpose, immune to pressures and corruption. Perhaps the United States possessed such a government for the first two or three years of World War II, and perhaps during the first hundred days of the Roosevelt administration in 1933. But this has not been our method of government at any other time in this century. The United States is a pluralistic democracy. The president must maintain a coalition of interest groups if he is to stay in office or to assure retention by his own party. The Congress is directly elected to represent the constituents in its states and districts and these include various producer and consumer groups. Big business, particular industries, the AFL-CIO and a few individual unions, farm organizations, environmental organizations, consumer groups, older citizens, minority groups, professional associations and numerous other groups all act directly in the political process through the presidency, the agencies of the executive branch, the Congress, and state and local governments.

[6]J.K. Galbraith, *The New Industrial State,* (1967), Houghton-Mifflin, Boston, pp. 247-261.

Price and wage controls are inconsistent with pluralistic democracy. The political forces will not line up on the side of controls, indeed will be against them. If controls are attempted anyway, the President soon has the choice of abandoning them, the model followed by Nixon, or of keeping them partially intact even after the brief moment of enthusiasm has passed, thereby assuring his own early retirement. This clearly was the fate of President Truman when he could not be a serious candidate for renomination in 1952. When the Democractic Congress overstayed the World War II controls in 1946, it suffered a similar fate and was turned out of office.

9.2. Five to seven years of unemployment

The other economically feasible strategy for ending stagflation is to raise unemployment to 8% or more and to keep it at that level until inflation has been brought to a low rate, and stagflation brought to an end. According to the model simulations, it will take five to seven years to bring the inflation rate below 3% by this method (figure 18). This strategy will work because labor markets will be so slack that unorganized workers will suffer rapidly diminishing wage increases. Product markets also will be very slack and so competitive forces will hold prices down. As the price record improves, the rate of wage increase in the highly unionized sector will also fade because of better price expectations.

Like price and wage controls, a five-to-seven-year strategy of 8% unemployment is probably impossible both on economic and political grounds. It is dubious that the economy would still be functioning in recognizable fashion when the years were over, even apart from the political reactions. The rate of investment would decline because there would be so little need for capacity expansion, and the profit share of income would fall substantially because of underutilization of capital. The rate of productivity advance would be seriously damaged in a variety of ways: through collective bargaining and legislative remedy, labor would bring about increased work-spreading through restrictive work rules, shorter workweeks, and rising obstacles to layoffs. Tax burdens would increase on those who work to maintain the incomes of the unemployed and those who have been driven out of the labor force. The cost of government would also be increased by the new need to cope with rising social unrest. One would not wish to contemplate the impact on the world economy.

The political implications of the high unemployment strategy are equally damaging. The principal rewards of the capitalist system are freedom of choice and economic progress. High unemployment increases distributional injustice. The United States was very patient during the Great Depression,

Figure 18
Reducing inflation through unemployment
(percent)

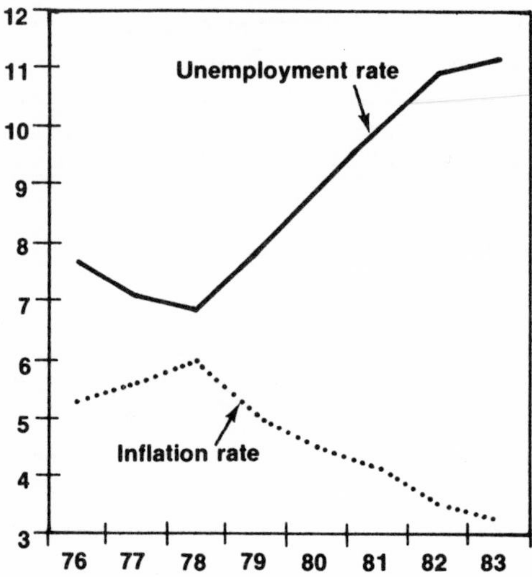

This model simulation, with policies to raise unemployment about 1 percentage point per year, would cut the inflation rate (implicit price deflator) to about 3% by 1983.

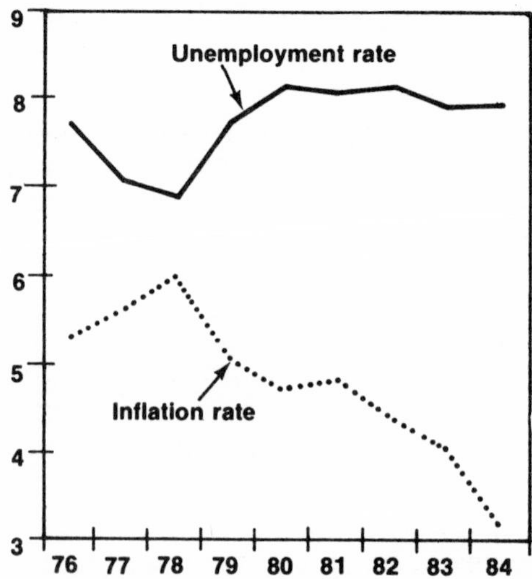

Simulation with policy to raise unemployment to 8% and keep it at that level. Inflation reaches the 3% level in 1984.

and anti-democratic movements were only beginning to germinate. But at that time, the public was convinced that the government was attempting to escape the depression, whereas in the present circumstance the strategy of high employment would be a deliberate policy choice. It should also be noted that the mild choice offered in the presidential election of 1976 evoked a pro-employment response at the ballot box. For all these reasons, the high unemployment strategy can be dismissed.

10. The Cures for Stagflation: Nibbling approaches

Once long periods of full price-wage controls or high unemployment are dismissed from consideration, smaller measures remain on the table which do not really offer the possibility of ending stagflation. If applied judiciously, and if new inflationary impulses from domestic policies or foreign developments are avoided, the severity of stagflation can gradually improve. Over a five-to-ten-year time frame, and with a little luck, they may even suffice to escape stagflation.

The measures usually advanced fall into five categories. They are: (1) improving government policies so they create less inflation; (2) making markets more competitive; (3) encouraging big business and big labor to be less inflationary within their range of discretion on prices and wages; (4) stimulating investment to promote productivity and avoid inflationary bottlenecks; and (5) developing new manpower or wage subsidy policies to reduce the level of unemployment at any given operating level of the economy. The approach also assumes that aggregate demand management through fiscal and monetary policies succeeds in avoiding a reduction in the unemployment rate below the natural rate and keeping sufficient slack in product markets to avoid demand-pull inflation.

It is not the purpose of this paper to explore the full range of such measures. But it should be recognized that, even under the best of circumstances, their impact is very limited. There are flaws in the wage and price setting mechanisms of the more concentrated industries. Government actions often are inflationary, and indeed, 1977 was one of the worst years for government-created inflation including the increase in payroll taxes, the return to stronger agricultural price support and stockpiling policies, the increase in the minimum wage, the reassertion of a stronger environmentalist viewpoint in various policies, the adoption of the steel trigger price system. The fact is that a pluralistic democracy is an inflation-creating machine. A strong President has an exceptional ability to resist these inflationary pressures as Lyndon Johnson demonstrated during his years of high popularity in 1964-66. But there have been mighty few years in which post-war presidents could point to much accomplishment along these lines. It should also be stressed that the total amount of inflation created by this entire process is not all that great. The American economy did have years of inflation rates below 2% with moderate unemployment when policies were little better. Perhaps the first point of excess unemployment and a point and a half of inflation can be attributed to the collection of flaws of the private sector and of government policies. To keep the volume of government inflationary actions—including the granting of protection to industry—requires constant vigilance and must be part of any anti-stagflation strategy. But it cannot solve the problem.

10.1 Incomes Policies

Since stagflation is partly attributable to noncompetitive elements in labor and product markets, some progress can be achieved through voluntary private actions. The guidepost policies of the mid-1960's had a modest, beneficial effect, though they required an excessive use of presidential energy, but would not work in a situation of rapid inflation.

A stronger policy would use the tax system to influence price and wage actions. The TIPS concept, a tax-based incomes policy as advanced by S. Weintraub, H. Wallich and A. Okun, would either penalize businesses by charging them extra income tax if their wage or price increases exceed particular guidelines, or would reward business and labor by reducing their income or payroll taxes if they comply. Whether such a system is ultimately distinguishable from a full system of price and wage controls remains to be seen. If it is much less, it will not make a significant dent in stagflation.

10.2 Investment Policies

Improved productivity and adequate plant capacity can contribute to the reduction of stagflation. Indeed, this is one of the ingredients of President Carter's strategy, as reflected in his proposals for $7 billion of corporate tax relief including an expanded investment tax credit.

The effect of investment on stagflation is indicated in figure 19, which shows the results of two model simulations. The first shows a very large increase in the investment tax credit which substantially boosts investment for four years through its impact both on the incentive to invest and the available internal cash flow. This strategy ultimately proves effective in reducing stagflation, but it takes patience. For the first four years, increased

Figure 19
Investment policies and inflation

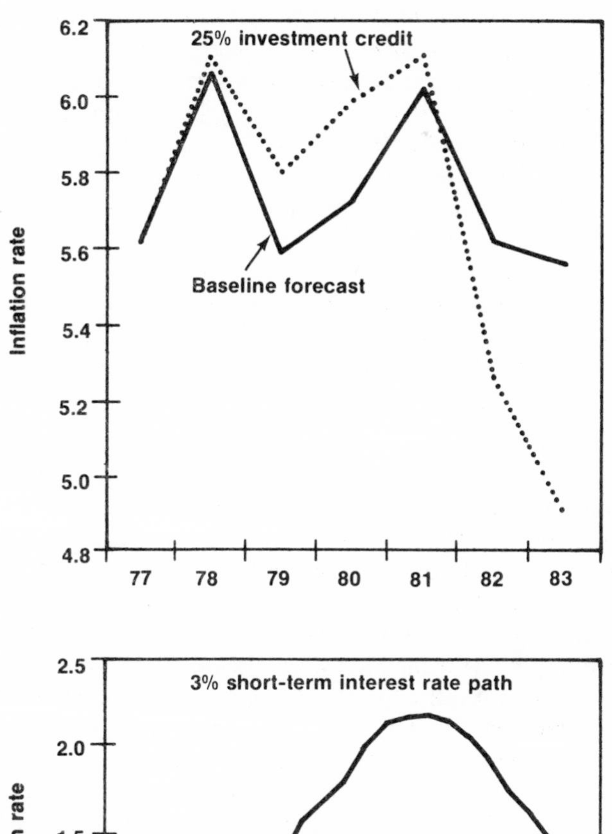

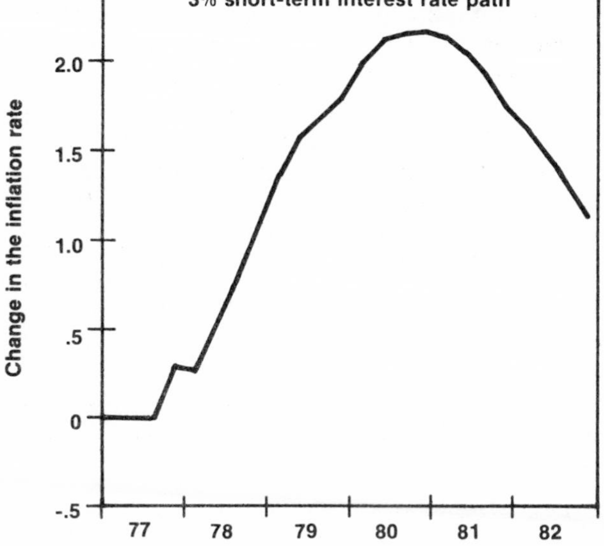

investment principally adds to the total level of activity and thereby makes inflation worse. The peak worsening of inflation occurs in years two and three, when it is boosted by about three-tenths of a percentage point. But by years five and six, the extra capacity is completed and substantially eases the pressure on industrial utilization rates. As a result, these markets remain in equilibrium rather than showing deteriorating delivery conditions and rising prices, and inflation of industrial prices is reduced. Potential GNP grows more rapidly and productivity is higher, affecting unit labor costs. By year six, the inflation rate is reduced by 0.7 percentage points for the economy as a whole.

The second simulation aims at more investment through easy money policies. The result is poor. Demand is higher, boosting inflation. There is more capital formation, but much of it is housing. Industrial capital is boosted only modestly, so the price and productivity benefits are small.

10.3 Employment Policies

Public employment and incentives to encourage private hiring are another policy area of promise. If unemployment of disadvantaged and inexperienced workers can be reduced by public service jobs or by incentives to business that subsidize wage costs, the unemployment component of stagflation can be ameliorated directly. The drop in unemployment in 1977 and 1978 shows that public service employment can have a significant effect. During the period in which public service jobs rose by 400,000 people, unemployment dropped an extra half a point beyond estimates calculated by Okun's law, the historical relation between unemployment and real GNP growth.

There is a factual question whether this kind of reduction in the national unemployment rate affects wages. The direct approaches to unemployment reduction must assume that the labor markets in which wages are set are not affected by measures that reduce unemployment of the disadvantaged.[7] On that assumption, employment policies seem able to cut the Discomfort Index by a visible amount, perhaps as much as a full point.

11. Conclusion

Stagflation is a deep-seated phenomenon of the U.S. economy of the second half of the 1970's. It is the result of some interactions of the public and private

[7]An earlier DRI study sketched the requisite dimensions of policies aimed at current unemployment without pumping up the GNP. See O. Eckstein, R. Gough and F.L. Cooper, "Strategies for High Employment," *Data Resources Review*, September 1976, pp. 65-84.

sectors and of outside disturbances. Stagflation began with the Vietnam War which caused the economy to operate in the territory of demand-pull inflation. Food and oil, a world boom, shocks and inflationary policies of government aborted the cure that was under way in 1970-73.

These governmental and external disturbances to balanced, noninflationary growth were greatly magnified by inflationary biases in the private economy. By far the most important is the persistence of inflationary price expectations. Wage claims fully discount inflation expectations which are formed from the consumer price behavior of the preceding four to six years. Thus, once inflation is going, wage pressures make it extremely difficult to let the wage-price spiral slow down. Pricing in many industries follows a similar pattern: the history of costs determines current target prices, further prolonging the wage-price spiral. Interest rates are also determined by inflation expectations: they remain high, thereby discouraging the productive investments that could augment capacity and improve productivity.

The outside world—excluding OPEC—has been a minor factor in U.S. stagflation. The big decline of the dollar in 1971 was a long-overdue correction. The further drop in 1977-78 mainly reflected the continuing energy situation and the relative cyclical phases in the United States, West Germany and Japan. Weaker foreign recoveries have added to U.S. unemployment.

What, then, can be done? It is totally alien to American attitudes to accept the idea that a problem is insoluble. Recognizing that the drastic cures must be ruled out and that the "nibbling" approaches work slowly, the following program is the inevitable conclusion to be reached.

11.1 Public Sector Inflation

Since much of the responsibility for the current stagflation must rest on past government policies, policy recommendations must begin with improvements in the public sector. Fiscal and monetary policies must aim to manage aggregate demand so it does not return to the demand-pull inflation territory. Given the difficulties on the cost and expectations side, the effects of excess demand would be far worse in the next episode than in the years 1965-75.

Fiscal policy should aim at an orderly reduction in the full-employment budget deficit during periods of recovery. If the full-employment budget is allowed to sink into deeper deficit in good times, the task assigned to monetary policy becomes so great that credit crunch and recession are the inevitable outcome.

The other areas of public inflation are the tax, expenditure and regulatory decisions which push up costs and reduce the incentives to work, innovate and invest. The Administration and the Congress must give a greater weight to price stability in reaching these decisions. So long as inflation is a separate subject to be ignored when serious matters of agriculture, business taxation, social security financing, industrial relations, and energy are considered, there is no prospect of escaping inflation or stagflation. Whatever gains are scored by other methods will be lost to renewed inflationary impulses from government.

11.2 Private Sector Inflation

The private sector suffers from inflationary bias which magnifies the impulses which may originate abroad or in government policies. It is no easy task to reduce this inflationary bias. Private voluntary actions require a sense of national purpose and responsibility which can only be evoked by strong presidential leadership or national emergency. Every president has an obligation to use the powers of his office to seek some cooperation from the largest economic units in business and labor. Whether general principles of incomes policy are a help or a hindrance in such efforts depends upon the specific circumstances at the time.

Inflationary bias in the private economy is also partly determined by government policies on such matters as antitrust, regulation and protection against foreign competition. In the long run, the most effective policies are those which strengthen competition. The government should resist the numerous pressures originating in the private sector which aim at diminishing competition.

It is easy to draw up lists of desirable government actions. It is harder to convert such lists into reality in a pluralistic democracy in which attention spans are short and narrow political goals have inflationary side effects. With good leadership, some luck, and high public awareness, there is a reasonable prospect to escape stagflation over a 5-to-10-year period. To allow the U.S. economy to reach its full potential to raise living standards, solve social problems, assure our national security, and improve the quality of life, the effort is necessary.

APPENDIX

THE DATA RESOURCES MODEL: HISTORICAL PERSPECTIVE AND AN OVERVIEW

1. Introduction

The historical study, *The Great Recession,* was conducted with the use of the Data Resources Model of the U.S. Economy. This appendix describes the model and puts it in a historical perspective.

The initial version of the model was built in 1968-70, with its first forecasts produced in 1969. Each year, the model is reestimated to keep it up-to-date with the government's data revisions. This provides the opportunity to make improvements drawn from new theoretical developments, simulation and forecasting experience, and user needs.

Beginning in 1974, the violence of economic events required major innovations in model building. This produced the third generation of macro models, of which the Data Resources (DRI) model is the prototype. This appendix describes this kind of model and relates it to its predecessors. The simulations in this book were largely run on the 1975 version. The descriptions here also incorporate the developments in the 1976 and 1977 editions.

2. Historical Perspective: The First Generation

Econometric models for advanced industrial economies have gone through three generations. The first generation began with Tinbergen's pre-war models of the Dutch and U.S. economies.[1] After the hiatus of World War II, when even the U.S. economy was controlled and planned, Lawrence Klein

[1]Jan Tinbergen, *Selected Papers,* (1959), North Holland, Amsterdam, pp. 36-84, and *Statistical Testing of Business Cycle Theories,* Volume 2; *Business Cycles in the United States of America: 1919-1932,* (1939), League of Nations, Geneva.

began the American tradition of model building.[2] The early Klein models of the late 1940's and of the 1950's were very much in the Keynesian tradition, modeling the circular flow of income and expenditure. The principal equations explained the major components of final demand, including consumption, fixed investment, inventories and housing. Government demands and exports were exogenous. The income side accounted for the gross national product in terms of the total wage bill, taxes, profits, and the other components of national income. The models were typically built in real terms, with the price-wage mechanisms superimposed in nearly recursive fashion and in highly aggregated terms.

Other investigators built models with some significant variations. Colin Clark[3] developed a quarterly business cycle model in the late 1940's which emphasized the inventories mechanism as the principal source of short-run variation, basing it on sales expectations and cash balances. Duesenberry, Eckstein and Fromm[4] built a simulation model designed to analyze anti-recession policies in more detail, including the use of decision rules for particular instruments and stochastic simulation experiments. The OBE (later BEA)[5] and Michigan models[6] were other models built by Klein and his students.

By today's standards, the first-generation models were small, beginning with Klein's original 12-equation model, expanding to 32 equations in the Michigan model. Dynamic structures were much simpler and the equations were limited to the larger aggregates of the national income accounts because of computational constraints.

3. The Second Generation

The second generation began in the early 1960's with the development of the large-scale Brookings model,[7] and continued with the early versions of the

[2]Lawrence R. Klein, *Economic Fluctuations in the United States: 1921-1944,* (1950), Cowles Commission Monograph No. 11, Wiley, New York; and L.R. Klein and A.S. Goldberger, *An Econometric Model of the United States, 1929-1952,* (1955), North Holland, Amsterdam.

[3]Colin Clark, "A System of Equations Explaining the United States Trade Cycle, 1921-1944," *Econometrica,* June 1949, pp. 93-124.

[4]James S. Duesenberry, Otto Eckstein and Gary Fromm, "A Simulation of the U.S. Economy in Recession," *Econometrica,* October 1960, pp. 749-809.

[5]Maurice Liebenberg, Albert A. Hirsch and Joel Popkin, "A Quarterly Economic Model of the United States: A Progress Report," *Survey of Current Business,* May 1966, pp. 13-39.

[6]Daniel B. Suits, "Forecasting and Analysis with an Econometric Model," *American Economic Review,* March 1962, pp. 104-132.

[7]James S. Duesenberry, Gary Fromm, Lawrence R. Klein and Edwin Kuh, *The Brookings Quarterly Econometric Model of the United States,* (1965), Rand McNally, Chicago.

Wharton model[8] and of the Federal Reserve-MIT[9] (now called MPS) model. The Data Resources models up to 1974 also fall in this general category. Each represented a sizable team effort spanning several years, and consequently contained considerably more disaggregated and elaborate equations for the final demands, incomes, labor markets, and wages and prices. The Brookings and Fed-MIT models were primarily testing grounds for new theories and the technology of larger-scale model-building. The Wharton model, going beyond the earlier pioneer forecasting of the Michigan and even earlier Klein models, was the first intensive quarterly forecasting effort which began to replace previous informal methods. The DRI model was part of the development of the first national economic information system.[10] These models were larger than their antecedents. The initial version of the Brookings model contained 150 equations, the 1976 Wharton model about 200 equations. The original Fed-MIT model had 66 equations, but later versions (MPS) grew to 175 equations. Early versions of the DRI model (e.g., 1971) were about 300 equations. Faster computers and better programs allowed the more efficient development of equations, and made solutions of larger models practical. The increased size was due to the desire to model the economic processes more fully as inputs to institutional decision-making.

The principal advances sprang out of the general econometric work of the field as a whole, indeed, the Brookings model project energized many scholars to make their results usable in the large-model context. The Almon and Koyck methods for estimating distributed lags made more precise dynamic structures possible. Jorgenson's neoclassical theory of investment had become available. The lifetime consumption theories of Modigliani, Ando and Brumberg opened up new possibilities for the consumer sector. The wage and price equations developed by Phillips, Eckstein, Wilson, Fromm, Perry, Schultze and others allowed better, if still inadequate, wage-price sectors. And, particularly in the MPS model, the Jorgenson technique of defining synthetic time series variables derived from profit maximization assumptions was carried over into other demand equations, including housing and the consumption of durable goods.

[8]Michael K. Evans and Lawrence L. Klein, *The Wharton Econometric Forecasting Model,* (1967), Economic Research Unit, University of Pennsylvania, Philadelphia.

[9]Frank F. De Leeuw and Edward M. Gramlich, "The Federal Reserve-MIT Model," *Federal Reserve Bulletin,* June 1969, and Albert Ando, Franco Modigliani and Robert Rasche, "Equations and Definitions of Variables for the FRB-MIT-Penn Econometric Model, November 1969," in Bert Hickman, ed., *Econometric Models of Cyclical Behavior,* (1972), National Bureau of Economic Research, Cambridge, pp. 543-598.

[10]Otto Eckstein, *The Data Resources Econometric Forecasting System, A Preliminary Account,* April 1970; also "The Organization and Retrieval of Economic Knowledge," Kiel Symposium of the International Economic Association, July 1975, and "Information Processing and Econometric Model Forecasting," paper presented to the Ottawa Meeting of the Econometric Society, June 1977.

Besides this general progress in macro-econometrics, the second generation of models was characterized by five major innovations: (1) the use of input-output analysis to calculate production in a time series framework; (2) the development of financial sectors; (3) the introduction of endogenous, behavioral equations for state and local government taxes and expenditures; (4) the use of explicit demographic elements, thereby blurring the previous distinctions between short- and long-run models; and (5) social indicator equations.

3.1 Input-Output Analysis

Input-output analysis was introduced into time series-oriented econometrics by Arrow and Hoffenberg,[11] who developed a technique for combining the fixed-coefficient, Leontief-matrix estimates of industry production with technologically based time trends that shift the relationships, and with systematic cyclical variables. The initial attempts to apply the technique empirically were not successful. The Brookings model[12] used a simpler approach to incorporate input-output into a full-scale econometric model, a technique which combines the fixed coefficient estimate with an autocorrelative adjustment that automatically corrected the observed errors by extrapolation. The DRI model[13] applied the Arrow-Hoffenberg technique, explicitly modeling the trend and cycle influences on production coefficients, and including other systematic influences, such as detailed changes in the mix of final demand. The current DRI model uses an 84-industry input-output matrix to calculate the Leontief estimates of production, which are then aggregated and applied in 56 quarterly industry production equations.

3.2 Financial Sectors

The introduction of financial sectors into large-scale models must be credited to Frank De Leeuw who did the initial work for the Brookings model.[14] This financial sector consisted of 19 equations for the demand and supply of

[11]Kenneth J. Arrow and Marvin Hoffenberg, *A Time Series Analysis of Interindustry Demands,* (1959), North Holland, Amsterdam.

[12]Franklin M. Fisher, Lawrence R. Klein and Y. Shinkai, "Price and Output Aggregation in the Brookings Econometric Model," *The Brookings Quarterly Econometric Model,* op.cit., pp. 653-679; and Gary Fromm and L.R. Klein, "Solution of the Complete System," J.S. Duesenberry, et. al., eds., *The Brookings Model: Some Further Results,* (1969), Rand McNally, Chicago.

[13]See V. Sundararajan, "A Flexible Coefficient Bridge Model: Trend-Cycle Adjustments in Input-Output Analysis," (1971), unpublished.

[14]Frank F. De Leeuw, "A Model of Financial Behavior," *The Brookings Quarterly Econometric Model,* op. cit., pp. 465-530.

money, time deposits of commercial banks, U.S. Government securities, household and business debt, savings accounts, and several interest rates. The short-term 90-day Treasury bill rate was estimated from the relationships among loan demands, commercial bank deposits and the bank reserves provided by monetary policy. The resultant short-term rate then became the principal device for estimating the long-term interest rate through the long-established term-structure theory, modified by the supply of government securities. Interest rates were determinants for several kinds of spending, including investment through the cost of capital, housing principally through the relationship between short- and long-term interest rates, and public construction for schools through the long-term rate.

The early DRI models modified this approach by assuming a two-sector capital market. The long-term interest rate was determined independently of the short rates, principally from inflation expectations, the supply of liquidity provided by monetary policy, and the net cash needs of several sectors. This approach was developed by Martin Feldstein and Otto Eckstein.[15] Later editions of the model contained expanded financial sectors of this type, adding 24 interest rates, with particularly elaborate modeling of the mortgage sector and the behavior of the various financial intermediaries.[16]

The Federal Reserve-MIT (MPS) model substantially expanded its financial sector, and integrated it increasingly with the real sectors. In particular, it added a model of the mortgage market, which showed how major financial intermediary institutions allocated the savings account inflows to their various portfolio purposes, including mortgages. The model also strengthened the importance of financial effects in some spending equations. The mortgage market conditions became prime determinants of housing activity.[17] The stock market became a prime mover of household wealth, which in turn was a determinant of consumer spending.

3.3 Endogenous Local Government Sector

The treatment of the state and local sector as an endogenous behavioral component of the economy was pioneered by Henderson[18] and Gramlich,[19]

[15]Martin Feldstein and Otto Eckstein, "The Fundamental Determinants of the Interest Rate," *Review of Economics and Statistics*, November 1970, pp. 363-375.

[16]Otto Eckstein, Edward W. Green and Allen Sinai, "The Data Resources Model: Uses, Structure and Analysis of the U.S. Economy," *International Economic Review*, October, 1974, pp. 595-615.

[17]Edward M. Gramlich and Dwight M. Jaffee, *Savings Deposits, Mortgages and Housing, Studies for the Federal Reserve-MIT-Penn Economic Models*, (1972), D.C. Heath & Co., Lexington.

[18]James M. Henderson, "Local Government Expenditures: A Social Welfare Analysis," *Review of Economics and Statistics*, May 1968, pp. 156-163.

[19]Edward M. Gramlich, "State and Local Governments and their Budget Constraints," *International Economic Review*, June 1969, pp. 163-182.

and was first introduced into large-scale models in the Federal Reserve-MIT model. In these studies, local fiscal behavior was endogenously determined from the sector's revenue needs. Eckstein and Halvorsen,[20] in work for the initial DRI model, extended this approach, making outlays dependent upon the financial position of state and local governments and their normal growth of revenues, along with demographic factors, and introducing preferences for balance among tax sources into the revenue equations.

3.4 Demographic Influences

Demographic factors received a major emphasis in the initial DRI models. The shift in age structure created by postwar population changes began to be a significant determinant of macroeconomic matters in the mid-1960's. Further, improvements in computer technology made it possible to use quarterly models for medium-term analysis and even the short-run forecasting horizon shifted beyond the traditional single year. Therefore, short-run models needed to incorporate major features previously limited to long-term analyses, many of which depended on changing demographics. These included the endogenous determination of aggregate supply (potential GNP). Equations for the demand for housing incorporated the growth in the age groups that represent new demand for housing. Automobile demand was linked to the growth of the driving age population. The health-related consumer services were related to the growing older population. The demand for state and local government spending was related to the changes in the school-age population.

3.5 Social Indicator Equations

By the early 1970's, it was recognized that successful macroeconomic performance would not automatically alleviate all dimensions of the poverty problem. While the successful employment performance of the 1960's had been of enormous benefit to all groups in the labor force, the benefit had not been uniform, and for some groups unemployment remained high even when the national rate was below 3½%. These differences were due to various legacies of the past, such as low human investment, poor work attitudes, and

[20]Otto Eckstein and Robert F. Halvorsen, "A Behavioral Model of the Public Finances of the State and Local Sector," Smith and Culbertson, eds., *Public Finance and Stabilization Policy,* Essays in Honor of Richard A. Musgrave, (1974), North Holland, Amsterdam, pp. 309-332.

job discrimination, as well as the demographic shifts of the mid-1960's when the number of young workers rose sharply. Because economic policy increasingly focussed on attempts to reduce unemployment for specific groups and began to be evaluated in terms of its impact on them, the initial DRI models embodied equations which calculated the detailed structure of unemployment by age, sex and race. These equations also permitted the analysis of labor market policies in a large model context.

3.6 Shrinking Multipliers

Many of the innovations of the second generation of models made them less "keynesian" compared to their predecessors. The introduction of financial sectors, of interest rates, and of wealth effects in spending equations gave a greater recognition to the importance of money. Fiscal policy simulations run without accommodating monetary policies showed reduced multiplier effects. In addition, the renewed emphasis on demographic factors reduced the income elasticities in various spending equations, partially shifting the burden of explanation from income growth to population growth. This also served to reduce multipliers.

Finally, the introduction of wage equations embodying a near-accelerationist point of view began to build a greater sensitivity to inflation into the models. When combined with long-term interest rate equations embodying inflation expectations, new links were built into the model which automatically caused extra inflation to reduce real activity. Thus, the second generation of models, which held the stage from 1963 to 1974, had moved a long distance toward a centrist position in the controversy between fiscalists and monetarists.

4. The Third Generation

The third generation of models began after the economic crisis of 1973-75 demonstrated several major shortcomings. None of the models was able to portray the full violence of the events of those years. The relatively smooth growth of the historical period 1953 to 1973, which was the data sample on which they were fitted, did not reveal the full cyclical vulnerability of the economy, nor did their design offer sufficient points of contact with external matters such as raw material prices, oil prices, worldwide booms and recession, and other features such as supply bottlenecks which only became evident during that period. The third generation of models was designed to remedy these identifiable shortcomings. The DRI models after 1975 have probably gone furthest in providing a framework for analyzing such events, growing to a size and complexity made possible by the increased scale and speed of third-generation computers. In particular, the later machines made it unnecessary to design the model with a recursive block structure, and most of the equations in the model were made simultaneous.

The later DRI model contains seven major innovations compared to its 1969-74 predecessors.

4.1 Modeling Sector Flows-of-Funds, Balance Sheets, and Financial Real Interactions

Since 1974, the DRI model has contained specifications for nonfinancial corporate uses and sources of funds and the balance sheet. The uses and sources of funds behavior is explicitly modeled simultaneously with the changes in the corporate balance sheet. Outlays for physical or financial assets (uses of funds), derived from the model's spending equations, determine the corresponding financing. Sources of financing include cash flow, proceeds from the sale of financial assets, accumulation of short- and long-term debt, and new equity issues. The need for external financing is estimated from the gap between internal sources and projected uses of funds. The profile of financing that closes this gap depends upon the costs of the various financial instruments and the existing balance sheet position. Given the determination of the various sources and uses of funds for each period, the resulting changes in the balance sheet are calculated, and the balance sheet itself, by a set of identities. Hence, the flows-of-funds behavior determines the nature and composition of the corporate balance sheet.[21]

The balance sheet conditions produced by the corporate flow-of-funds model become significant inputs into the business spending equations. Some of the traditional balance sheet liquidity ratios and the composite interest burden relative to cash flow are variables which help to explain business outlays on fixed investment, inventories and employment. These variables provide an important new set of links from financial conditions to real spending, and raise the power of monetary policy. These liquidity effects substantially enhance the impact of monetary policy on business spending

[21]This work has been directed by Allen Sinai, and aided by Terry Glomski and Roberta Gerson. The framework underlying the flow-of-funds equations builds on the portfolio theoretic-approach in James S. Tobin, "A General Equilibrium Approach to Monetary Theory," *Journal of Money, Credit and Banking*, May 1969, pp. 15-29; and William Brainard and J.S. Tobin, "Pitfalls in Financial Model Building," *American Economic Review Proceedings*, May 1968, pp. 98-122. See W.H.L. Anderson, *Corporate Finance and Fixed Investment*, (1964), Harvard University Press, Cambridge, for an early model of the corporate flow of funds.

beyond what had previously been identified through interest rate and cost of capital measures.

This innovation increases the cyclicality of the model's representation of the economy. Near the upper turning point of the cycle, the business balance sheet typically deteriorates sharply: internal cash flows slow their growth while spending commitments are still rising strongly. Debt is accumulated rapidly, and too little of this increase is long-term debt. Belated turns in monetary policy typically raise the cost of capital sharply, dramatically deteriorating the balance sheet ratios, thereby reducing business spending on fixed investment, inventories and employment. Conversely, near the lower business cycle turning point, business has completed the reduction of its commitments, monetary policy has eased the cost of capital, and business balance sheets have been reliquefied. This helps to set the stage for the upswing in business spending.

Flow-of-funds modeling was applied to the household sector in 1973. A set of equations allocates personal savings among the various assets that are available to households, including the thrift accounts of various institutions, short-term securities, bonds and stocks. These allocation decisions are determined by relative yields on the various investment media and by the inherited portfolio position at the beginning of the period. Consumer borrowing, particularly of installment credit, is also estimated, principally from spending behavior. Mortgage indebtedness depends primarily on housing outlays and construction activity. Personal savings flows are simultaneously allocated among the various financial assets that are available to households, including the deposit accounts at financial intermediaries, short-term securities, bonds, stocks, and money.

The asset and debt position of households is an important element in the consumer spending equations. Real financial assets, along with income, serve to determine long-term spending growth. Variations in the consumer debt position have a strong influence on short-term variations in automobile and other spending categories. These financial elements in the household sector accentuate the cyclicality of the model by making consumer spending vulnerable to past household portfolio imbalances and to short-run variations in the cost and availability of credit.

Finally, the DRI model contains a highly disaggregated representation of mortgage market activity to represent the process which links monetary policy to the housing cycle through the financial system. The savings flows of households are the suppliers of funds for major categories of financial intermediaries, including commercial banks, savings and loan associations, savings banks, and life insurance companies. The equations represent the portfolio decisions of these institutions. Depending on relative yields and their inherited portfolio positions, these institutions make available varying amounts of funds to the mortgage market. The quantity and price of available mortgages are important determinants of residential construction activity. Housing policy is represented by various levers, including the mortgage purchases of the Federal National Mortgage Association and the Government National Mortgage Asssociation, the outstanding advances of the Federal Home Loan Bank Board, the new mortgage commitments from the Federal Home Loan Mortgage Corporation, and the required liquidity reserve ratio.

4.2 Stage-of-Processing Approach to Prices

Popkin and Earl[22] developed econometric models which trace inflationary impulses from the raw materials stage through semi-finished, finished wholesale and retail prices. At each stage of processing, the prices from the previous stage provide an estimate of material costs. Labor costs and demand measures are added to the equations for the price indexes of the successive stages.

This approach was built into the DRI model in 1974. It permits the model to reflect the impact of alternative OPEC pricing strategies or varying agricultural prices. Among the raw material prices in the sector are the price of world oil, lumber, and the composite wholesale price index for agricultural commodities. The prices of semi-finished goods include such processed materials as metals, paper, and the composite price of energy, as well as fabricated metals. Finished goods prices at wholesale include machinery, transportation equipment and processed foods. At the retail stage, the model includes the consumer price indexes for food, nonfood commodities, and services. GNP deflators are calculated principally from the particular wholesale prices for goods, following the technique employed by the Bureau of Economic Analysis. Deflators for services are based on energy costs, equations for rent, and labor costs.

4.3 More Elaborate Modeling of Supply Conditions and Their Impacts on Prices and Inventory Behavior

Econometric models represent market behavior rather than government controls of physical quantities or price ceilings. Thus, modeling of supply conditions has to be carried out in the context of market behavior of prices

[22]Joel Popkin, "Consumer and Wholesale Prices in a Model of Price Behavior by Stage of Processing," *Review of Economics and Statistics,* November 1974, pp. 486-501; and Paul H. Earl, *Inflation and the Structure of Industrial Prices,* (1973), D.C. Heath & Co., Lexington.

and quantities. The DRI model represents such behavior in several quite elaborate ways: first, the model calculates the utilization rates of manufacturing as a whole, the materials industries, primary processing industries, and advanced processing industries; capacities are estimated from investment outlays for 2-digit industries and technological trends. Production is estimated from the flexible coefficient input-output block in the model. These utilization rates are important inputs into the stage-of-processing equations for wholesale prices, and they also play a role in profit and productivity equations.

Utilization rates have long been criticized as imperfect measures, and it must be acknowledged that there is no theoretically airtight way to estimate capacity or utilization. Nonetheless, two decades of econometric modeling of prices, productivity, and profits have shown that even imperfect measures of utilization are essential variables to achieve adequate econometric results. Utilization affects both resource efficiency and strength of demand.

A second important measure was introduced in the DRI model of 1976 which increases the sensitivity of industrial prices to demand, particularly to excess demand. This is the measure "vendor performance," a widely reported response in the monthly Survey of Purchasing Executives. The executives are asked whether they are experiencing slower deliveries. Vendor performance has long been recognized as a leading business cycle indicator. Used in wholesale price equations, it greatly increases explanatory power.

Third, the model calculates aggregate supply (potential output), which affects the unemployment rate, wages and prices. Finally, when a particular commodity is in an extraordinary supply situation not created by market forces and therefore not reflected in price behavior—e.g., strike disruptions or OPEC embargoes—special model solutions can be developed with demands held back by the particular supply constraint.

4.4 Inventory Behavior and the Inventory-Production-Price Loop

The models have long used the standard econometric theory of inventory behavior, relying on the relationship between sales and the stock of inventories as the principal explanatory factor.[23] The adjustment of the actual inventory stock toward the optimal stock occurs gradually, of course. The earlier DRI model contained one innovation: the utilization rate of industry was shown to affect inventory behavior. When manufacturing utilization is

[23] Lloyd A. Metzler, "The Nature and Stability of Inventory Cycles," *Review of Economics and Statistics*, August 1941, pp. 113-129; and Michael C. Lovell, "Manufacturers Inventories, Sales Expectations, and the Accelerator Principle," *Econometrica*, July 1961, pp. 293-314.

high, delivery periods lengthen, and the optimal inventory stock is therefore larger for a given level of company sales.

However, the utilization rates are sluggish and imprecise measures for inventory policy. Consequently, it has proved necessary to develop an approach which corresponds more closely to the highly unstable behavior actually observed. This new approach is based on the use of the vendor performance measure that was found so powerful in price equations. When vendor performance deteriorates, the response of purchasing executives is to become more aggressive, to seek to hold larger inventories, and to place multiple orders.

The equations for vendor performance, production, utilization, inventory investment, and industrial wholesale prices constitute an interdependent loop which easily generates inventory and price cycles. Vendor performance is itself determined by such factors as preceding inventory-sales ratios and utilization rates. Consequently, if utilization exceeds a critical level, vendor performance deteriorates, triggering inventory hoarding. The attempt to build up inventory boosts production. Companies are typically unable to distinguish an increase of sales caused by customer inventory hoarding from an increase validated by final demand. Consequently, they respond to their better sales by expanding their own activities, reinforcing the inventory cycle. As inventory investment boosts production, utilization rates are driven higher still, worsening vendor performance and triggering further inventory hoarding. Industrial prices advance to reinforce these destabilizing tendencies. Sooner or later, usually within a few quarters, the inevitable correction sets in.

4.5 Modeling Expectations and Error

The experience of the last few years has shown that businesses do make mistakes on occasion by acting on false expectations about the future paths of their markets, prices, and costs. The econometric models of the 1960's and early 1970's emphasized adaptive expectations and sluggishly acting distributed lag formulations which typically understated the important role of error in the business cycle.

The 1977 DRI model marks the beginning of a major research effort to develop spending equations with sufficiently elaborate expectations mechanisms to make it possible to calculate the deviations between business expectations and actual results. In the initial round of research, it has been found that much progress can be made using simple expectations mechanisms. Thus, several of the current model's equations, including inventory investment, productivity, and business equipment, contain sales expectations variables in which the current quarter's sales are calculated to exceed the 4-quarter earlier results by the same percentage as experienced in the preceding quarter. This mechanism reflects the reality that business makes virtually all of its decisions on seasonally unadjusted data, on the basis of 4-quarter or 12-month comparisons. This expectational element allows the model to track previous episodes of business error more precisely. This includes particularly business spending in 1973 and 1974, as well as the minor inventory cycle of 1976.

Rational expectations, which are receiving much attention from macro-theorists, are not yet modeled explicitly. They pose considerable technical and conceptual problems to the model builder. They require knowledge of solution answers for future quarters in solving a current quarter. The Gauss-Seidel method of model solution, which moves iteratively through successive quarters, cannot deal with this case. Some limited aspects of the rational expectations theory can be simulated in the model, such as the point of view that price expectations are derived from the money growth target. But rationality on this definition relates to a simple monetarist model rather than a full forecasting system.[24]

4.6 Modeling Consumer Confidence and Uncertainty

It has long been recognized, in the DRI model and elsewhere, that inflation and unemployment raise the personal saving rate, presumably because consumers become more uncertain about their future incomes. In the 1977 model, the consumer sector represents this process more elaborately than before. The consumer sentiment index (University of Michigan) continues to play a role in some of the more volatile consumer spending categories, and the index itself is still easily modeled from observed inflation and unemployment. In addition, this year's model introduces the variance of consumer income into spending equations: following a period of high variance, consumers will save more, because they will project a greater risk for their future income expectation. This behavior is derived from conventional portfolio theory: the use of credit magnifies income risk into a larger consumption risk because of the leverage introduced by outstanding interest and repayment obligations.

This new variable reduces the multipliers on temporary tax reductions, at least to a small degree. Surcharges and rebates accentuate the variance of

[24]For an exploratory study, see Paul A. Anderson, "Rational Expectations and Policy Evaluation in Macroeconometric Models," paper presented to the Ottawa Meeting of the Econometric Society, June 22, 1977 (mimeo, Federal Reserve Bank of Minneapolis).

consumer income, thereby raising the consumer's expectation of future income variance, and increasing his saving rate.

4.7 A Disaggregated Foreign Trade Sector

The worldwide boom of 1971-73, the subsequent crisis and the changed world energy situation have shown that domestic progress is affected by developments abroad. Therefore, the DRI model now includes a detailed structure of U.S. foreign trade. The equations follow economic theory quite closely, relying on relative prices, relative activity levels, and a few commodity-specific variables. The activity levels of the foreign trading partners are modeled through their production indexes which are typically available more quickly and with less interpretation than their GNP accounts.

In actual forecasting, the DRI U.S. model uses the forecasts developed by the DRI International Group. Simultaneous solution of national macro models in the DRI family is limited to the European economies. The iteration of solutions among Europe, Canada, Japan and the United States is still conducted informally for each forecasting cycle.

However, to make the simulation properties of the U.S. model more realistic, reflection ratios are used for our trading partners. Thus, the DRI U.S. model does not assume that foreign economies and policies are left unaffected by our actions. The U.S. economy is so large that one must calculate its impact on its partners, and the reflection of their changed situation back on U.S. exports, imports, and activity.

4.8 Other Innovations in the Third Generation DRI Models

The annual reworkings of the model, with the benefit of new data, fresh ideas and another year of forecasting and simulation experience, have brought various additional innovations into the model.

(1) The industry production equations embody elements of the input-output structure within production. Previously, econometric models used "bridge" coefficients that derive production from final demands. The new structure explicitly shows how finished goods production determines materials output, thereby allowing inventory and other changes in a "downstream" industry to impart a greater sensitivity to materials industry activity.

(2) The investment equations, while still using the Jorgenson neoclassical approach as their point of departure, have reintroduced utilization rates as proxies of future business output expectations: current utilization is given

some weight in assessing future capacity needs. Also, a more precise measure for the cost of capital is now employed, reflecting the actual mix of financing and the cost of equity capital. This modification strengthens the balance sheet effects.

(3) Industry investment equations, which are necessary for the calculation of utilization rates, and which are applied to the 22 industries which comprise the BEA plant and equipment statistics, now use a uniform neoclassical approach. Of course, the dynamic structure of the equations differs among industries because of the great variations found in the structure of their physical capital.

(4) The housing sector explicitly models the supply of three types of housing, relying heavily on financial and profitability factors. Housing demand is modeled from demography, permanent income, wealth, confidence and relative cost vis-a-vis consumption. Market disequilibrium, including vacancy rates and the number of houses for sale, introduces important information into the model and heightens the sector's sensitivity to demand changes.

These innovations have substantially increased the size of the DRI models. In the years 1975-77, the various editions of the model had 700 to 900 equations. As the speed of computers increased, it became possible to make most of the equations simultaneous. Thus, the third generation of models is two to three times larger than the end of the second generation.

5. *Implications*

The third-generation DRI model simulates differently than its predecessors. The principal changes can be summarized as follows.

5.1 The model has become more cyclical.

As shown above, numerous elements have been developed to simulate actual business cycle behavior with suitable sensitivity. The impact of balance sheet behavior on spending and the impact of monetary conditions on balance sheets play a large role. The inventory-production-price loop makes the economy more vulnerable to "pauses" and subcycles, and can compound a major cycle as occurred in 1973-74. The inclusion of new demand measures in the wage-price sectors and the stage-of-processing modeling of such price shocks as world oil prices not only make the model more inflation prone, but also affect subsequent financial conditions, spending behavior, and help intensify the business cycle as a whole.

Figure 1 shows that the model can generally reproduce the violence of the recent business cycle experience. It contrasts a full dynamic eleven-year simulation of the model, over the years 1966-76, with the actual experience. The simulation is not perfect: the model still does not fully reflect the expectational errors which carried business spending forward during 1974 when the foundations for prosperity were already gone. Thus, the real GNP path turns down too early, but that is not the worst sin for a forecasting model. Further work will explore these expectational matters more deeply.

Figure 1
The U.S. model in dynamic simulation:
Real GNP
(billions of 1972 dollars)

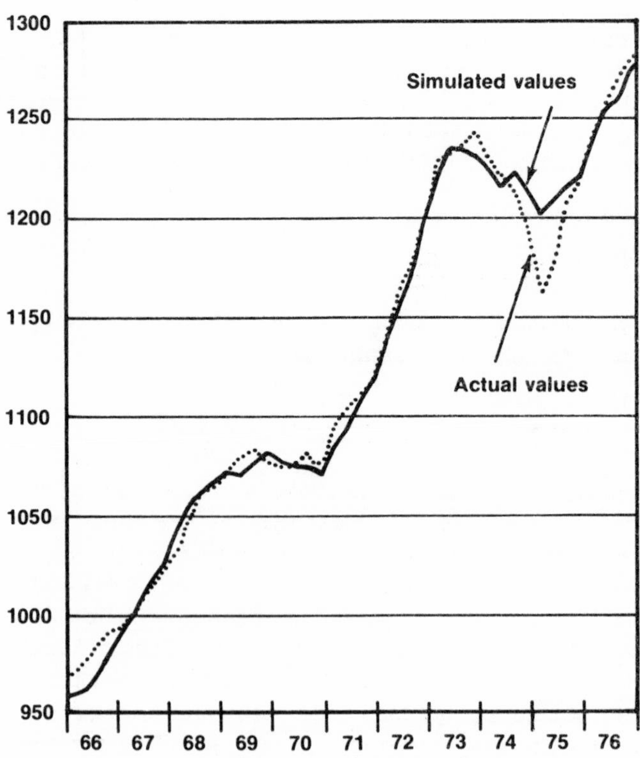

5.2 The fiscal multipliers are modest, temporary and cyclical.

Figure 2 shows the path for a basic fiscal multiplier, the result of a $5 billion increase in the real volume of Federal non-military spending. It can be seen that the multiplier peaks above 2 after two years, but then fades away and turns negative. A second, smaller cycle begins in year eight. The downturn is due to higher inflation, higher interest rates, some partial "crowding out" of private credit due to the government deficit, and reduced spending created by deteriorated balance sheets. There are also some accelerator-type, stock-flow adjustment processes in consumer durables, housing and business fixed investment which reinforce the cyclical character of the multiplier. It should be noted that this simulation, with its constant real increment in Federal spending, actually assumes a strongly expansionary policy; despite extra inflation, the real stimulus is maintained, i.e., fully escalated. If the multiplier were run on a nominal spending increase, it would show substantially smaller values. The specific multiplier values also depend on the base situation on

Figure 2
Impact of a $5 billion increase in
real non-military federal government spending
on real GNP
(billions of 1972 dollars)

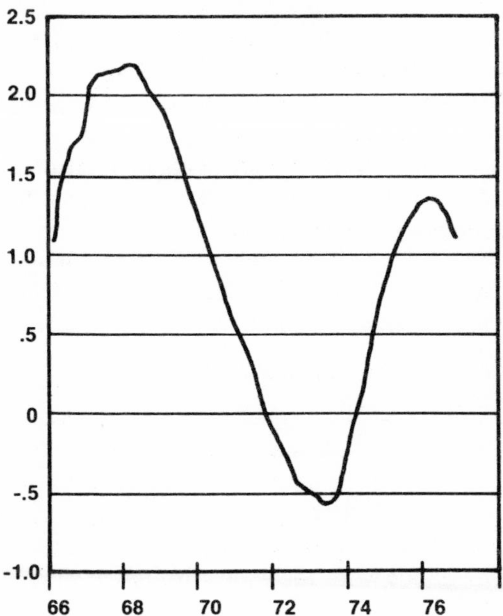

which the exercise is run. In this example, the eleven-year dynamic historical simulation was used. Its credit crunches, war, and recession limit multipliers at times.

5.3 The Phillips curve has become increasingly nonlinear.

In earlier DRI models, the Phillips curve was already heavily conditioned by the previous history of inflation. But the recent improvements in the model have greatly heightened the sensitivity of prices to demand conditions, and have allowed the DRI model to begin to escape what has been the biggest bugaboo of large-scale models: a short-run Phillips curve which is so insensitive that policy analysis always showed large near-term benefits of stimulus at little near-term cost. Figure 3 shows a variant of the Phillips curve for the current DRI model, the relationship between real growth over four years against the associated inflation rate. The conventional Phillips curve, plotting inflation against a steady unemployment rate, is difficult to identify from the current data because price expectations are so high in the initial conditions, and exogenous inflation elements, particularly world oil prices and domestic energy price policies, introduce further ambiguity.

5.4 Inflation hurts spending.

From its beginning in 1969, the DRI model has had the property that higher inflation reduces real activity. This effect was mainly caused by the impact of inflation on interest rates and on housing, and by the definition of some spending categories in nominal terms.

The third-generation DRI model contains additional relationships between inflation and spending, including the impact of inflation on consumer attitudes. When exogenous elements in inflation are increased, all categories of spending are hurt. Business spending is hurt by the higher real capital costs and increased uncertainty. For Federal outlays, the model contains a policy lever which allows a choice whether to use real or nominal measures for the exogenous purchases of goods and services. State and local government spending is hurt by the financial drain of higher prices and wages.

5.5 Still bigger effects for money and finance.

The trend toward more powerful monetary effects continues in the 1977 DRI model. The equations for the business balance sheet, the household flow-of-funds and balance sheet, and the mortgage market are becoming increasingly interrelated. The several subsectors of the short-term money market are simultaneously interrelated, showing more explicitly how monetary policy and private credit demands work their way through the financial system. As a

Figure 3
Inflation-growth tradeoff:
average annual rate of growth of
real GNP versus average annual price inflation,
1977 to 1980

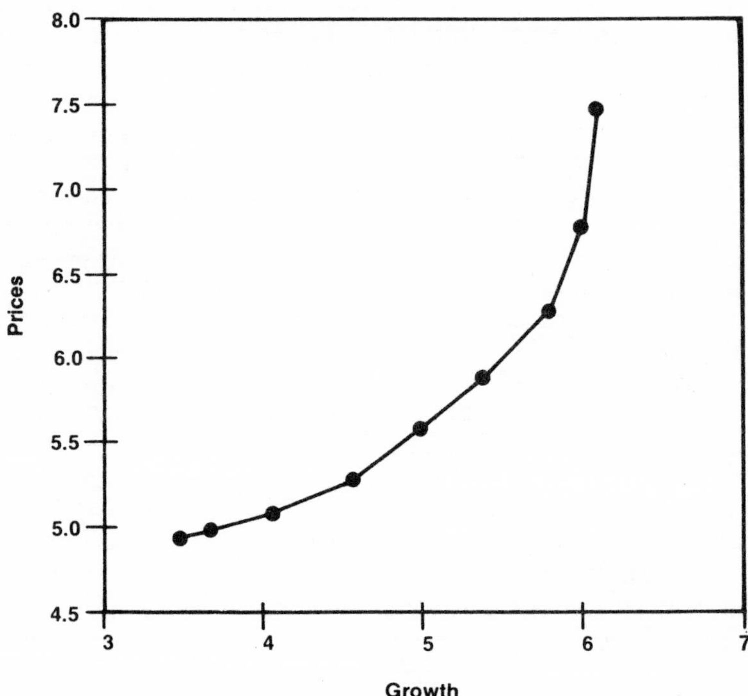

result, the model is able to provide more elaborate and accurate answers to the behavior of the financial system itself. Our 1977-78 research program calls for a complete presentation of the full flow-of-funds and balance sheets for every sector in the economy, including the various types of financial institutions, government, and the external world.

6. *Does It Work?*

The DRI Quarterly Model of the U.S. Economy is large and complicated, requiring 25 full-time professionals to develop and operate it on a continuing basis, as well as general purpose computers at the top of the available range. Thus, the project today probably represents the largest private (or public) undertaking in macro forecasting history. Is there a reward of more accurate forecasts for this sizable investment of technology and people?

DRI has always left the evaluation of forecasts to third party scholars.[25] We feel it is impossible for a forecasting organization to be utterly objective about its own work. But perhaps the following observations can be made.

First, in its brief history, the third-generation DRI model has produced very good forecasting results, substantially better than what could be found before. Forecasts prepared with second-generation models, including DRI's, failed to anticipate the full violence of the 1973-75 crisis, although strong warnings of the dangers in faulty policies and in the economy were issued by the second quarter of 1973. But since the adoption of the new generation model in early 1975, the forecasting record is good by any reasonable standard. Our forecast users see the full record in the quarterly track record exercises published in the *Data Resources Review* which show the forecasts made over the preceding several years for that quarter for two dozen strategic variables. The extent of the economy's recovery and the composition were anticipated reasonably well. Table 1 summarizes annual forecasts for a few key variables. The table compares various annual estimates with the forecasts without correcting for data restatements. This procedure is crude, but it illustrates that government data revisions are sometimes as large as forecast errors, and that early forecasts are sometimes closer to the ultimately reported figures than they are to the preliminary data. The forecasts are sometimes misled by the preliminary estimates.

The forecasts for business fixed investment, which had been a weak spot in DRI's pre-1974 work, have been quite accurate since financial factors, expectational factors and uncertainty have been given a heavy weight in the model structure. Forecasts of prices have been reasonably accurate, with the errors tending to be overestimates. The disaggregated stage-of-processing approach, combined with the emphasis on more sensitive demand variables such as vendor performance and an accelerationist wage equation, has improved inflation forecasting.

On the other hand, it must be recognized that much error remains, enough to preserve some modesty and to be a warning to user organizations against acting on univalued projections. Even in *ex-post* simulations, the model cannot calculate the timing of the minor inventory cycles. It just takes too little to set off the speculative bubbles in which purchasing executives hoard inventories against imagined shortages, driving up production and utilization rates, and deteriorating vendor performance in a self-inflaming way.

[25]The principal studies are by Stephen K. McNees in various issues of the *New England Economic Review*, most recently in the March/April 1977 issue.

The model also requires some major exogenous elements which are very difficult, if not impossible, to forecast. The OPEC price of oil and the patterns of Federal energy programs are one course of unpredictable cost changes. The Federal Reserve occasionally is a puzzle. Its monetarist behavior should make its behavior predictable, but there are moments when it acts on other principles. Truly exogenous factors, such as the weather or world political and military disturbances, remain as powerful as ever and act upon an economic system in which the cushions and margins are not what they were 15 years ago. Finally, research on the modeling of the psychological-cum-expectational element in private decision making is still in an early stage and will provide a continuing agenda for further work.

Table 1
Track Record, Monthly *Ex Ante* Forecasts of Annual Results
Using the DRI Model, 1975 to 1977

Forecast Date	Real GNP Growth Rate 1975	1976	1977	Implicit Deflator (% Change) 1975	1976	1977	Unemployment Rate (Percent) 1975	1976	1977
12/28/74	-2.3	5.7		9.5	6.0		7.8	7.6	
1/25/75	-3.1	5.4		10.8	6.4		8.2	8.2	
3/12/75	-3.9	6.7	6.5	9.6	5.3	4.8	9.3	8.9	7.3
4/2/75	-3.6	6.0	4.8	9.2	5.5	5.2	8.9	8.4	7.5
4/28/75	-3.4	6.7	5.5	8.8	5.2	4.9	8.9	8.2	7.1
5/27/75	-3.6	6.4	5.3	9.2	5.7	5.2	8.9	8.3	7.4
6/28/75	-4.0	6.5	5.5	9.0	5.5	5.1	9.0	8.3	7.3
7/29/75	-3.7	6.5	4.5	8.9	5.7	5.5	8.7	7.9	7.2
8/26/75	-3.5	6.3	3.9	9.4	7.6	6.2	8.5	7.8	7.2
9/26/75	-3.3	6.0	4.2	9.2	7.2	6.0	8.5	7.7	7.1
10/27/75	-3.1	5.8	4.3	8.9	7.0	6.0	8.5	7.7	7.1
11/24/75	-2.9	6.3	4.5	8.8	6.0	5.9	8.5	7.5	6.9
12/31/75	-2.9	6.2	5.3	8.8	6.2	6.0	8.5	7.5	6.6
2/3/76	-2.9[1]	5.9	5.3	8.8[1]	6.1	5.6	8.5[1]	7.6	6.8
3/15/76	-2.0[2]	5.9	5.3	8.7[2]	5.8	5.5		7.4	6.7
4/8/76		6.4	5.6		5.6	5.5		7.2	6.3
4/26/76		6.9	5.8		5.3	5.8		7.2	6.3
5/24/76		7.1	5.7		5.5	5.9		7.3	6.3
6/25/76		6.7	5.5		5.3	5.9		7.3	6.4
7/30/76	-1.8[3]	6.5	5.4	9.2[3]	5.1	5.4		7.3	6.5
8/24/76		6.3	5.3		5.3	5.6		7.5	6.8
9/27/76		6.2	5.7		5.2	5.2		7.6	6.9
10/28/76		6.2	5.1		5.1	5.2		7.7	7.2
11/22/76		6.1	4.8		5.1	5.2		7.7	7.3
12/29/76		6.2	4.8		5.1	5.3		7.7	7.1
1/31/77		6.2[1]	4.8		5.2[1]	5.5		7.7[1]	7.4
2/23/77		6.1[2]	4.8		5.1[2]	5.8			7.4
3/25/77			5.0			5.9			7.2
4/25/77			4.8			5.7			7.2
5/23/77			5.0			5.7			7.1
6/23/77			5.2			5.6			7.1
7/29/77	-1.3[3]	6.0[3]	5.0	9.6[3]	5.3[3]	5.5			7.1
8/25/77			4.8			5.6			7.1
9/25/77			4.8			5.5			7.1
10/26/77			4.8			5.6			7.1
11/25/77			4.9			5.6			7.1
12/21/77			4.9			5.6			7.1
1/25/78			4.9[1]			5.6[1]			7.0[1]
2/20/78			4.9[2]			5.6[2]			

Forecast Date	Real Consumption Growth Rate 1975	1976	1977	Housing Starts (Millions of Units) 1975	1976	1977	Real Business Fixed Investment Growth Rate 1975	1976	1977
12/28/74	-0.1	5.3		1.402	1.874		-5.0	3.4	
1/25/75	0.2	4.5		1.327	1.867		-7.6	3.3	
3/12/75	-0.8	6.3	5.9	1.364	1.886	2.061	-9.3	9.0	7.4
4/2/75	-1.0	4.9	4.4	1.368	1.930	2.052	-11.2	7.4	10.5
4/28/75	-0.2	5.2	4.9	1.293	1.919	2.042	-13.0	4.7	11.4
5/27/75	-0.2	4.9	4.8	1.250	1.808	1.955	-14.1	4.5	11.0
6/28/75	-0.3	4.9	4.8	1.246	1.833	1.911	-14.7	4.5	11.5
7/29/75	0.6	4.7	3.3	1.193	1.745	1.933	-14.0	3.5	8.7
8/26/75	0.7	4.5	2.6	1.187	1.693	1.781	-14.5	3.8	6.4
9/26/75	0.7	4.5	3.3	1.182	1.661	1.718	-14.2	2.4	5.9
10/27/75	0.7	4.4	3.6	1.170	1.641	1.702	-13.7	2.9	6.2
11/24/75	0.8	4.8	3.8	1.181	1.652	1.747	-13.7	2.4	5.9
12/31/75	0.7	4.8	4.9	1.182	1.675	1.871	-13.6	3.3	8.4
2/3/76	0.7[1]	4.6	4.5	1.173[1]	1.578	1.865	-13.2[1]	2.0	7.4
3/15/76	0.9[2]	5.2	4.6	1.164[2]	1.497	1.855	-12.0[2]	2.9	8.9
4/8/76		5.3	5.1		1.568	1.847		4.2	9.7
4/26/76		5.8	5.4		1.591	1.868		4.7	9.2
5/24/76		5.7	5.3		1.574	1.872		6.0	9.7
6/25/76		5.4	5.3		1.512	1.800		5.0	8.2
7/30/76	1.5[3]	5.8	5.2		1.483	1.681	-13.3[3]	4.8	8.8
8/24/76		5.6	5.3		1.466	1.685		4.3	7.9
9/27/76		5.6	5.5		1.481	1.694		4.4	8.4
10/28/76		5.5	4.7		1.524	1.739		4.1	7.4
11/22/76		5.4	4.7		1.543	1.803		4.1	6.7
12/29/76		5.6	5.0		1.545	1.828		4.1	6.2
1/31/77		5.5[1]	5.2		1.561[1]	1.824		3.9[1]	6.0
2/23/77		5.6[2]	5.0		1.541[2]	1.794		3.9[2]	5.9
3/25/77			4.9			1.842			5.8
4/25/77			4.9			1.900			6.8
5/23/77			5.6			1.910			7.6
6/23/77			5.9			1.911			8.3
7/29/77	1.9[3]	6.0[3]	4.9			1.892	-13.7[3]	3.6[3]	9.6
8/25/77			4.7			1.910			9.3
9/25/77			4.7			1.933			9.2
10/26/77			4.4			1.932			8.8
11/25/77			4.5			1.958			8.4
12/21/77			4.6			1.966			8.6
1/25/78			4.8[1]			1.982[1]			8.9[1]
2/20/78			4.9[2]			1.966[2]			8.7[2]

[1]First estimate by source agency
[2]Second estimate
[3]Later estimate
Source of forecasts: *Data Resources Review*, monthly, January 1975 to January 1978.
Source of "actual" data: Bureau of Economic Analysis, Department of Commerce.

INDEX